1992

IN
THE
WORKSHOP
OF
HISTORY

FRANÇOIS
FURET

Translated by Jonathan Mandelbaum

The University of Chicago Press · Chicago and London

FRANÇOIS FURET is president of the Ecole des Hautes Etudes en Sciences Sociales, Paris. His published books include *Livre et société dans la France du XVIIIe siècle* (1965) and *Penser la Révolution française* (1978).

This book was first published as *L'Atelier de l'histoire*, © 1982, Flammarion, Paris.

The University of Chicago Press, Chicago 60637
The University of Chicago Press, Ltd., London
© 1984 by The University of Chicago
All rights reserved. Published 1984
Printed in the United States of America

93 92 91 90 89 88 87 86 85 84   5 4 3 2 1

Library of Congress Cataloging in Publication Data
Furet, François, 1927–
  In the workshop of history.

    Translation of: L'atelier de l'histoire.
    Includes bibliographical references and index.
    1. Historiography—France—History. 2. Historiography
—History. I. Title.
D13.5.F8F8713 1984   907'.2   84-2638
ISBN 0-226-27336-9

CONTENTS

INTRODUCTION ■

French historians of my generation have led a happy existence. They have easily found positions; they have had time to read and write; their work has been well received both in France and abroad; and they constitute a relatively homogeneous group, in which relations are more often friendly than not. Above all, they are the heirs to a historiographical tradition that is itself a success story. Renewed between the wars by the *Annales* under the aegis of Marc Bloch and Lucien Febvre, the old discipline arrived at virtual unanimity during the 1950s and 1960s among historians of my age. This consensus expressed itself in a collective agreement to extend the traditional boundaries of history, as "historical" projects were launched in areas previously staked out by other disciplines, such as the social sciences. As the historians' guild has little taste either for epistemology or for the history of its own history, it has usually satisfied itself with this conquering spirit of unanimity, which does continue to stimulate very active, and sometimes brilliant, research. But such unanimity also encompasses, by definition, an almost infinite variety of scientific practices: the sociological unanimity of the discipline masks its epistemological fragmentation. It is this contrast that I have sought to investigate in depth in the course of my professional experience and that informs this book.

Compared to the social sciences, history can claim greater seniority and legitimacy, and its recent renewal has not invalidated its credentials in these respects. History remains a discipline inseparable from the nation, essential to the meaning of nationhood. Hence, history still has its rules, usages, university chairs, and learned societies, all of which provide

Pages 1–19 of this Introduction first appeared as "En marge des *Annales*: histoire et sciences sociales," *Le Débat*, no. 17 (December 1981), 112–26. A slightly different form of the English version was published in the *Journal of Modern History*.

1

it with a common language and a professional consensus. Its prestige has not been impaired by the fact that, in the course of the fifty years that have elapsed since the first issue of the *Annales*, it has gradually ceased to see itself as the interpreter of the national phenomenon. Having espoused "modern" concerns, history now explores the secrets of societies rather than those of nations; it has become that much harder to teach, but also more rewarding to construct and write. Moreover, history has still kept an eye on the nation, even if it reconstructs the nation's past from new standpoints, using society to shed light on nationhood. In France, history has never been so solidly entrenched institutionally and never enjoyed so great an audience among the educated public, whatever the temporary problems raised in secondary education by the increasing indeterminacy of the field.

There is, moreover, a certain logic to the fact that the only major research and teaching institution founded in France since the war in the field of social and human sciences owes its existence precisely to the *Annales* historians: the Sixth Section of the Ecole Pratique des Hautes Etudes, founded by Lucien Febvre in 1948, which in 1975 became the Ecole des Hautes Etudes en Sciences Sociales. The transformation of a journal into an institution expresses and codifies history's sponsorship of the social sciences—one of the functions that history has taken on by way of rewarding itself for its renewal. This new institution has certainly played an important part in perpetuating history's guiding role.

But the academic crystallization of what was more than a journal—and less than a doctrine—has above all accredited the mistaken notion that the *Annales* historians as a group share a common and unified concept of the discipline, a concept in conflict with the traditional approach. Institutions have their own logic; there is nothing like their rivalries to confer an imaginary degree of intellectual coherence to political, collective, professional, or personal differences. In this respect, the petty institutional war and the great symbolic clash that from the very outset have characterized the relations between the former Sixth Section of the Ecole Pratique des Hautes Etudes and the former Facultés des Lettres in the universities—chiefly the Sorbonne—have concealed a twofold intellectual phenomenon, one that would have helped to moderate the conflict had it not become more institutional than intellectual. First, during the 1950s and 1960s, the topics and research methods advocated by the founders of the *Annales* gradually spread well beyond their initial home. They became the common property of historians, regardless of their institutional allegiances. Second, historians of the Ecole *stricto sensu* were working in directions that were too diverse for those historians to be easily assembled under a single intellectual banner.

By their diversity, they were at least being faithful to the undogmatic approach of the *Annales* since its inception. They were taking the utmost advantage of the journal's specific feature, which was a simple and powerful idea: history was to be freed to wander in every field. Ultimately, that is the intellectual heritage that historians such as Alain Besançon, Emmanuel Le Roy Ladurie, Jacques Ozouf, Denis Richet (just to mention those who were closest to me in my generation), and myself received from Lucien Febvre and Marc Bloch via Fernand Braudel. It is a crucial heritage, since it gave us, from both the intellectual and the professional points of view, exceptional opportunities and freedom. But this, simply, was our only legacy. We settled into a historiography that was already dominant when we were taking the *agrégation* examination and whose very success, embodied by the existence of the Sixth Section, gave it an even greater receptive capacity. Thus, the *Annales* fulfilled its role more than ever, since that role is synonymous with hospitality and openness. From our point of view, the *Annales* offered an almost boundless range of topics and methods—a heaven-sent oasis on the path away from Stalino-Marxist historicism, whose power to mystify we had only recently come to recognize.

Indeed, when I try to define, twenty-five years later, what we still have in common, apart from reminiscences and feelings, I wonder whether our prolonged adolescence in the ranks of the Communist party did not play a greater role than our career as historians in the Ecole des Hautes Etudes. From the former, we acquired not only a treasure trove of rather embarrassing memories but a set of intellectual and political references that mark and date our common inoculation. In the course of the latter, we received the blessing of a providentially welcome and open institution, but we did not reach a new historiographical consensus. When abroad, I am often asked what constitutes the *Annales* School. It is a difficult question for me, because it evokes the somewhat ritual aspect involved in simply managing cultural capital; I am tempted to answer that the question is practically meaningless. Lucien Febvre and Marc Bloch would have provided—and did provide—brilliant answers, as Fernand Braudel did later. But the point is, they did reply. All the battles won against professional narrow-mindedness and self-satisfaction—battles that eventually led to the founding of an institution—have gradually eliminated their own raison d'être. The *Annales* School is at the apogee of its reputation in France and abroad; for lack of specific adversaries, it meets with nothing but widespread praise. It is lauded for being both conceptual and narrative, interested in individuals and searching for laws, open to Marxism and well disposed toward Marxism's opponents, and so on. There is some truth to these statements, since they can all be supported by good examples; but by now they describe only a hegemony of influence and reputation, not a school of thought nor even, any longer, a collective spirit.

There was, in fact, no school of thought to begin with. It would be vain to search for the traces of a doctrine or a favorite mode of explanation in the prewar *Annales*. History, a polymorphous discipline whose object cannot be defined, let alone circumscribed, remains faithful to its fundamental indeterminacy down to the very intellectual revolution that is supposed to have transformed its methods and subject matter. Nor is this revolution itself easy to define, and it emerges more sharply by contrast to its adversaries' profile than by virtue of its founders' concepts. That is perhaps one of the reasons for the frequency of polemical arguments in the prewar and postwar *Annales*, especially when Lucien Febvre was involved. The martial vocabulary, the call to battle in defense of worthy causes, the sense of adventure intellectually heightened by the breathless prose—all these are telling signs of the extent to which the opening of the discipline to new objects was a reaction against traditional historiography. Indeed, now that these new objects have become the common property of our profession, it is hard for us to imagine how eccentric they once appeared. What, then, is the *Annales* School if the territory it claimed for history has become a public domain?

It seems to me that the simplest way of describing the ambition and development of the school is to consider jointly two objectives—two ideas: first, that history should add to its subjects and methods by borrowing from neighboring disciplines and even by the temporary abolition of divisions between disciplines; and, second, that it should nevertheless remain an all-embracing and ecumenical discipline, bringing together the conditions required for the fullest understanding of social phenomena. Neither of these two ideas is simple or clear; nor is their compatibility self-evident, unless one regards it as a wish, a program, or an ultimate ambition. Instead of paving the way for its intellectual unity, history's borrowings from the social sciences only add to the diversity of the discipline by expanding its field of inquiry almost to infinity. But, while these borrowings provide history with greater methodological eclecticism, they do not necessarily guarantee additional knowledge—unless, of course, history would precisely exploit this greater conceptual indeterminacy in order to assert its superiority over the social sciences. By borrowing right and left, history does not tie itself to any one of its creditors; on the contrary, it claims to bestow its own preeminent dignity on all of them. Thus, in its comprehensive embrace, history absorbs the social sciences instead of simply representing their temporal dimension.

In order to examine the situation of history today, a half century after the founding of the *Annales*, one can therefore begin by examining its relation to the social sciences. This is probably the least unreliable instrument for a methodical assessment.

The social sciences aim, like Marxism, to explain social facts. But they do not constitute a unified body of doctrines, nor even a corpus of partial interpretations that could be unanimously accepted. The social sciences delimit specialties, or objects of study, or approaches to a problem, without ever securing the consensus of specialists. Consequently, they have renounced the ambition of providing comprehensive explanations and scientific forecasts of contemporary phenomena. Indeed, the social sciences define their positivity by their distrust of the philosophy of history; to this extent, they cannot escape—any more than any other intellectual examination of our world—the fact of being rooted in their time. They express this rootedness by recognizing their limitations and no longer by voicing vast ambitions.

However, the social sciences have not easily accepted this renunciation of their capacity, or of their claim, to provide a total explanation. All they need is to adopt the singular form—social science—in order to regain the prestige of the scientist prophecy: from Auguste Comte to Durkheim, the sociologist propounded and embodied the notion that not only is it possible to study man in society, but the analysis of his social determinants can alone provide the key to the celebrated "essence" of man. More recently, the same hopes have been pinned on structural anthropology, in circumstances that one of the essays in this book attempts to elucidate: the search for constants within the diversity of social manifestations in space (rather than time) can or must lead to a unitary theory of man.

In its renewed form, history remains actively engaged in that rivalry among the social sciences in which each aims, by claiming a higher objectivity and an all-embracing knowledge, to subsume the others. Its claims are no longer "historicist." It no longer regards the time scale as the yardstick for stages in human progress, stages punctuated by the creation of nation-states and the spread of "civilization," that is, of the European model. On the contrary, history today is no longer endowed with the primal, implicit significance attributed to time; it has abandoned the linear vision that made it a royal discipline whose task was to weigh the merits of the various "periods" of the past. At the same time, history has turned to a broader range of topics. It confers its dignity less selectively: everything has become historical, from an apparently "nonhistorical" gesture to the bill of fare in an inn to the division of a plot of land. Thus, history has constantly encountered the social sciences. Indeed, it is hard to say whether it is the discovery of new research areas that has led history to an apprenticeship in more specialized disciplines or whether, on the contrary, it has borrowed from social sciences such as economics or demography certain objects of research that have already been defined outside history. The two phenomena have been concurrent and have influenced each other.

This process, which corresponds very roughly to the establishment and growth of what is known as the *Annales* School of history, has been accompanied by a claim on the part of history to exercise hegemony over the social sciences, as if history alone, armed with the partial forms of knowledge developed by neighboring disciplines, were destined to present a unified vision of man under the name of "total history." Such a claim is, in a sense, a way of making up for the fragmentation and specialization of the objects of historical analysis. Even as it ceases to act as an organized representation of time, providing mankind with the vision of its progress, history still maintains the notion of its superiority on the grounds that it alone can study certain objects exhaustively, from every angle—whereas in actual fact, like other disciplines, it deals with limited objects. Thus, in the midst of a crisis in historicist history, the historian has fallen back on a less charismatic notion of his learning without suffering any epistemological loss.

Yet the idea of total history is elusive. Naturally, it no longer denotes the nineteenth-century view of history as a privileged discipline, designed to encompass all the significant manifestations of man in society and to interpret the development of these manifestations as so many necessary stages in a history of mankind. Total history merely expresses the ambition of providing a fuller perspective, a more exhaustive description, a more comprehensive explanation of a given object or problem than can be provided by the social sciences whose conceptual and methodological innovations it has borrowed. But if the secret of the flow of time is no longer vested by definition in history, how can history still be regarded as a superior discipline? Is this privilege justified by the temporal dimension that history is thought to bring to the study of social phenomena? All the social sciences—no less than history—deal of necessity with problems whose past constitutes the only available laboratory in which they can be studied. Admittedly, history's central purpose is to analyze the development of any number of those problems, sometimes over very long periods; but this temporal dimension, however far back it may reach, does not in itself justify a peculiar privilege of "totality." It enables historians to describe and analyze the series of changes and transformations of the phenomenon in question and thus to introduce, with the aid of time, an implicitly comparative perspective that is essential, since it enables one to enrich the concept or concepts used in the analysis—but no more: temporality cannot lead us to what does not exist, that is, to a concept capable of explaining every aspect of the object under study.

Social science *tout court* remains the goal of all the social sciences, but it cannot constitute the "true" essence of any of them. If history, after sociology and along with anthropology, has staked a claim to such intellectual authority, that claim must not be taken for granted; such presumption stems both from the pathological tendency to generalize that contaminates every important study of society undertaken in France and from the rivalry among university disciplines for supreme legitimacy. Having been enticed out of its position as the soothsayer of national destiny and prophet of human progress, history has studied the social sciences only the better to appropriate for its own advantage the ambition of Durkheimian sociology.

But the important feature of history's recent development is not this illusory ambition; it is, on the contrary, what that ambition masks and perhaps serves to make up for: the fact that the historian, like the demographer or the anthropologist, constructs the object of his research. Having abandoned the naïve notion that facts speak for themselves—a naïve notion because it assumes without ever saying so that time has a predetermined meaning—the historian has by the same token abandoned the superstition of chronological divisions and periodization. If phenomena of every sort are no longer primarily interpreted in a temporal framework, one must first define objects of research and then determine, by trial and error, the relevant time span for describing and analyzing them. Hence, specialization in a given period, for so long a basic feature of the profession, has become a lesser imperative compared to familiarity with a particular issue or problem. The historian of what used to "constitute" the reign of Louis XIV is less a historian of the seventeenth century than, let us say, a specialist on absolutism or on the court phenomenon.

In other words, history is no longer wholly contained in a genealogical construct in which earlier events explain later ones and must consequently be reconstituted with painstaking attention down to their remotest origins. Indeed, history used to be a form of learning obsessed with origins, seeking through erudition to assign an ever-earlier date to the great secret of beginnings. Moreover, the entire process that it ennobled was, by definition, a genealogy of the nation or of mankind: in its bibliographical classifications, seventeenth- and eighteenth-century European culture distinguished between the inventory of time—the object of history—reserved for European peoples and states, and the inventory of space, the realm of travelers, an immense repository of immobile societies. In the non-European portion of the inhabited globe, these societies also testified, in a certain sense, to the origin of man, since the savage was the ancestor of civilized man. Thus, in the order of knowledge, space was subordinated to time, and travel to history. This was a way of depicting human progress. Somewhat later, when ethnology and anthropology emerged as disciplines, they dealt only with societies whose culture was unwritten, leaving outside their purview, for instance, the great oriental civilizations. Here again, the division was based on the same principle: China and India share with European nations the privilege of historicity; their time, too, has meaning.

If all societies today have regained a history, it is not only in the sense that universal history, through the world market, colonization, and decolonization, has integrated them into its vast currents; it is also because history, as a form of knowledge rather than an actual process, is no longer the preserve of a small number of societies or nations but a discipline that can apply to any one of them. While totally distinct, these two phenomena are not in fact unconnected, for the spread of nationalism to the entire planet has led to a resurgence of the genealogical history of nations, on the old European model. But, in order to assess the present situation of history, it is better not to focus on this contamination of the present by the past but to concentrate on what is truly new: the fact that everything has been historicized.

Such an assertion seems obvious, but in fact it is not. For example, immobility was for centuries regarded as nonhistorical. Only change was historical; history was considered to be the movement that carried human communities toward progress through the development of nation-states. And "ancient" history, too, which dealt with remoter periods, was meant to study and bring to life the civilizations that had been the ancestors and guides of Europe's nation-states. Even as the guiding thread of history snapped, history at last opened itself up to all the languages that European societies have been constructing for several centuries in order to interpret, understand, or govern themselves; by the same token, history opened itself up to a wide variety of phenomena and a truly infinite number of events. The size of an age cohort, the rules of marriage, the structure of a rural estate—these have become historical facts. What has remained motionless for centuries deserves examination no less than what has not lasted.

This seems to me to be the fundamental change that has taken place in historiography over the last few decades. The change, linked, as always, to phenomena outside the realm of scholarship, cannot be understood without reference to the decline of Europe in the twentieth century and the crisis of its dominant nations, the traditional agents of the progress of "civilization." But the historiographical change has drawn on crisis and decline: a thorough reorganization of history's inner realm has been carried out, both by an extension of the range of its objects of study and by an at least partial transformation of its language.

The two shifts were inseparable from the outset. They both reflect the fact that history, taking advantage of the immense flexibility of its boundaries, has fallen back on, and reconquered, the social sciences. While everything has become "historical," the need has arisen to define, within the historical field, a certain number of objects—or, less accurately, research themes—whose historical development had not already given them a predetermined meaning. As history's inventory was being renewed, the greatest number of suggestions came from the specialized social sciences, such as economics, demography, and ethnology. But, because these sciences deal with their objects not only in terms of specific concepts but, more broadly, in a language alien to the historian's familiar mode of explanation, it is the intellectual landscape of historiography that has gradually been transformed.

Traditional historical explanation obeys the logic of narrative. What comes first explains what follows. Since history thus defined has a meaning that predates, so to speak, the set of phenomena that it encompasses, historical facts need only be arranged on the time scale to become meaningful within a process known in advance. The very selection of those facts is predicated upon the same, implicit logic: the period takes precedence over the object being analyzed; events are chosen according to their place in a narrative defined by a beginning and an end. Little does it matter, therefore, if the events are unique, not comparable, or even lacking in homogeneity with one another, since their significance derives from an external source. But, as that significance tends to turn events into markers of change, signaling the dips and breaks along the imaginary route of time, they are chosen for their capacity to embody change and the phases of change. The model of this type of history is political history, both because nation-states are held to be the major agents of change and because politics, in a wide sense, constitutes the prime repertoire of change: it is the main mode in which modern societies experience and interpret their transformations.

Thus, too, political history is primarily a narrative of human freedom as seen through change and progress. Although political history does describe the framework, that is, the constraints within which men act, its major function is to describe the thoughts, choices, and actions of men—primarily great men. Politics is the quintessential realm of chance, and so of freedom. It gives history the structure of a novel, except that its plot must be composed of authentic facts verified according to the rules; and this history is indeed the true novel of nations.

In contrast, the language of the social sciences is founded on the search for the determinants and limits of action. Since it borrows from natural science the aim of isolating constants, if not laws, this language seeks by definition to describe and study objective behavior, regardless of the deliberate intentions of the actors. That is why it prefers to select, among the traces of human activity, sets of internally homogeneous data that are repetitive and comparable, allowing it to measure the value or simply the relevance of a question. The social sciences cannot attain the purity of hypothetical-deductive reasoning, but they strive to do so. By building their hypotheses and data explicitly and moving constantly from one to the other in order to experiment and correct, the social sciences do not assign to the materials on which they work a prior significance determined by time. They remain inside an intellectual circuit defined by this experimentation through reconstruction, without attributing to it, *a priori*, a third dimension containing its secret.

This temporal dimension, far from dominating research, is subservient to it, for the period chosen for the study of a question depends on the nature of that question; in other words, time is no longer homogeneous and no longer has an all-embracing significance. Birthrates do not change at the same pace as systems of international relations, and a "great" period of history, defined for example by the temporary hegemony of a given nation, can be devoid of significance in the chronology of an economic cycle. The historian's celebrated "dates" depend on the problem that interests him. And the conditions of his analysis are all the more productive when the object studied "moves" less: in order to identify with the greatest possible accuracy the variables that explain it or are linked to it, the object must be considered over a long and stable time span before the reasons for its transformations can be understood. This is why the language of the social sciences is partly in contradiction with that of "historicist" history. The social sciences focus primarily on unchanging phenomena so as to simplify—that is, to make possible—the mode of reasoning that underlies their language. And it is no accident if historians, thanks to the social sciences, have rediscovered the long term—the *longue durée*—and even "immobile" history. For historians, this is a way of saying in their own language that there exists a category of historical objects on which time has only very gradual effects. Concentrating on these categories of objects, historians harmonize their practice with the concepts they borrow from the social sciences.

In so doing, historians have been led to give up not only the major form of their discipline—narrative—but also its favorite subject matter—politics. Just as narrative was the logical way of presenting an interpretation based on temporal significance, so the analysis of a problem in the light of data developed for that particular purpose obeys the logic of demonstration. The only common element in the two genres is the apparatus of scholarly notes that establishes or discusses the nature of the data or their veracity. But the internal structure of the two discourses is radically different, even when they happen to mingle and when the old one lives on by force of habit after the appearance of the new. Finally, their respective contents have also, by force of circumstance, been dissociated. As we have seen, the historical narrative genre is chiefly concerned with the realm of political facts, the uppermost ridge of the past, the memory of human action, the patrimony of nations, but is also a laboratory for change and progress. It is in the study of politics, of human choice, that history best expresses its capacity to create and to constitute the arena for the study of man. However, the price paid by history for remodeling itself on the pattern of the social sciences is that it focuses primarily on what underlies those choices, on what determines them and makes them inevitable despite the appearance of freedom. It prefers to analyze deeper trends rather than superficial changes, to study collective behavior rather than individual choices, to examine economic and social determinants rather than institutions or government decisions. Thus, demography, economics, and sociology have taken over a field increasingly deserted by its traditional inhabitants—kings, notables, nations, and the theater of power around which they never ceased to gravitate.

If one wants to understand the fundamental difference between history in its traditional form and history reshaped on the pattern of the social sciences—a distinction that must not be confused with what the two types of history have to say about themselves—the best approach is to take "pure" examples borrowed from traditional history and use them in order to analyze its mechanisms.

My first example is taken from one of the most classic areas of historiography, the French Revolution. This is a blessed event for historicist history, almost custom-made, punctuated by unavoidable dates, and admirably suited to narrative, for it combines change and progress like inseparable twins, establishing politics as the fountainhead and instrument of freedom. The Revolution is not so much a topic in modern history as one of its chief manifestations, in that it embodies a mode of change and human action that is fundamental to its significance. While it is true that, from its very outbreak, the Revolution has occupied a central position in the historical imagination, all the histories of the Revolution deal with a topic far vaster than the history of the Revolution: they are actually constructing a meaning for time itself. That is probably why history-as-a-social-science has dealt so cautiously with this historical object. It does not know how to tackle such a short period, how to grapple with a succession of events so difficult to simplify, and how to avoid a practically spontaneous chronological—that is, narrative—approach. One need only consult a set of the prewar and postwar *Annales*: the French Revolution is virtually absent, as if this *locus classicus* of national history were the special preserve of the "other" history. Even the partial transfer of the theme to social history, carried out in Georges Lefebvre's early work, does not invalidate this apparent rule.

The social dimension of the event has been absorbed, whittled down, smothered by its political dimension. The social history of the Revolution does not consist in describing or analyzing the changes that took place in late eighteenth-century French society in order to measure the relation between the political and institutional upheaval and the actual fabric of society. That relation is taken for granted as being wholly deducible from political history, evidenced by the fact that the social history of the Revolution deals either with the analysis of contradictions and conflicts within prerevolutionary society or with the study of revolutionary personnel in the broad sense—crowds, militants, and leaders. In the first case, the aim is to assemble or expand the collection of "causes" within a chronological framework whose turning point is 1789; in the second case, the aim is instead to examine, after 1789 and within brief time spans, *who* made the French Revolution. But the common element in these two approaches is that both implicitly subscribe to a vision of the Revolution as a political event that cuts French national history in two. If the second approach extols more often than not the newfound sense of initiative of the popular classes, the first has conferred on the people's freedom the additional blessing of historical necessity. In the historian's trade, the French Revolution is the professional specialty in which the period chosen strictly determines the content of possible "subjects" by virtue of an implicit notion of the event that filled that period. However varied, these subjects are designed to describe or explain the revolutionary break, since that is the prior meaning ascribed to the period.

Hence, the outstanding feature of the type of history that I call traditional—to distinguish it from the so-called *Annales* history—is not that it is a "history of events" or even a strictly political history; for every study of the past reconstructs events, and there is no logical criterion enabling certain categories of facts rather than others to be enshrined as "events." The most general characteristic of this mode of historical writing is the notion that the period is more important than the problem studied and that, since the study of a "period" establishes such a priority, the task of historians is to add new facts or to correct the interpretation of historical change within the period. The historian becomes a genre painter: the frame (that is, the period) and the subject (that is, what he will choose within the period) are supplied to him more by chance than by intellectual effort. But the frame and subject tell us nothing about his art, which is the real secret of his craft and does not consist in imagining connections between various sets of facts hitherto thought to be independent or in asking new questions about known facts; what the historian must do above all is to bring back to life, by the magic of his narrative, all the lives, thoughts, and passions lost in old manuscripts that no one, until he did so, had ever read again.

Perhaps I shall be accused of exaggerating. Here, then, is a second example, taken not from a historiographical field but from the work of a contemporary historian, Richard Cobb. Admittedly, he is British, but the field of historical studies common to British and French historians is sufficiently homogeneous for them to be included in the same analysis; moreover, Richard Cobb has devoted his life to French history; and, finally, his loathing for the *Annales* School makes him all the more interesting to me. Straddling both countries, he remains just enough of an Englishman to hate what he might well have been had he been born a Frenchman. Indeed, every time I read him I am reminded of the chapter in the second volume of *Democracy in America* in which Tocqueville explains why the English hate abstraction: as products of an aristocratic civilization, they are interested only in the particular, in the concrete and unique individual, whereas democratic equality leads men to generalize and to formulate abstract judgments or laws that apply to classes of individuals, if not to all of mankind. Cobb would have been a perfect Englishman for Tocqueville, for he is interested only in individuals and abhors general ideas. And since, for lack of a theory—an absence based on principle—he displays a jealous passion in making an example of the type of history that he produces and loves, he provides me with the best example of what I am trying to define.[1]

At the core of this concept of the historian's craft and discipline lies the archive, preferably a local one, a holy of holies that the historian must gradually occupy if his activity is to have any meaning. The archive is an unpredictable depository, its only reason for existence being the fact that it is there; the patient examination of its contents gently guides the researcher toward his subject. The archive cannot provide answers to a question or questions raised externally, since its contents are the fruit of chance and, by definition, cannot be compared to those of a neighboring depository despite the uniform system of classification. And the historian's activity par excellence is the researcher's colloquy with his archives, provided he accepts beforehand that they are to have the "last word" (p. 15). This does not simply mean that, where he hesitates about a fact or an interpretation, the document itself will decide; it means, more profoundly, that the archives mined by the researcher are ultimately responsible for determining the content and horizon of his research. Hence the sort of professional priority assigned not to the object of research but to the geographical boundaries within which it is to take place and to the site, that is, the depository, that is to be its center stage.

This concept of history and of the historian conceals a number of elements that are worth bringing to light. First, at the most invisible level, there is the existential choice of a way of life and a culture. The manuscript document and the archive are the images and instruments of cultural differentiation; they allow the historian to embark on the same imaginary voyage that physical travel offers to the anthropologist. The traveler is taken to an apparently exotic field, which he can master by learning the ways of otherness. Indeed, in Richard Cobb's mind, the two varieties of exoticism—temporal and spatial—are combined, since the British historian must become familiar with the "savage" territory called France, and the sign of his success is his being told by the local archivist that he has become an *"excellent joueur de boules"* (p. 24). France is a museum, both in its past and in its present, and one can "learn" it by studying not only its archives but also its present customs, provided they have not changed too much. The passion for history is rooted here in a choice at once aesthetic and moral: Oxonians do not like all the fuss being made over change and modernity.

At the same time, the subjects and even the spirit of this history are determined and bounded by that choice: it is a history that aims at reconstituting the past, not at interpreting it. For that matter, the term *reconstituting* itself contains an ambiguity: if it means that the historian's work must bring the past "back to life," it is stating an ambition that is either absurd or solely dependent on the techniques of the art—in which case, the existence or nonexistence of documents and the historian's faithfulness to them are not crucial. *Reconstitution* makes sense only if it means that history reconstructs not only what actually happened but the way in which what happened was perceived by contemporaries. The first part of the program is intellectually the simpler; the second, having an ill-defined object, contains an irreducible element of uncertainty. But it is true that the modes of reaction to (and, thus, of perception of) an event are essential historical phenomena; it remains to be determined where and how to find them.

This type of history-as-reconstitution, which I am distinguishing here

from history-as-interpretation, involves no special methodological innocence. The dialogue between the historian and his archive, which enables
"the stranger in a strange land" to become "a friend in a familiar one"
(p. 25), can never in itself provide him with a subject. If the aim of the
dialogue is not the publication of manuscript material (a goal and an
activity indispensable to history but insufficient to constitute history), this
dialogue or, rather, this apprenticeship must necessarily be determined
by earlier intellectual choices, whether explicit or not; otherwise, it can
lead only to a collection of unpublished anecdotes that struck our Martian
as memorable. That is not what happens, however. The Martian is not a
faux naïf, and he has come to the archives equipped with questions and
his chosen period. Granted, the questions may be vague and the period ill
defined, but the tyranny of vagueness and imprecision is worse than that
of clarity, for it conceals its own existence from itself. It never ceases to
control the apparently unprejudiced dialogue between the historian and
his documents and to impose its constraints on him. This type of archival
research seems to dispense with the need for genuine conceptual plan-
ning. It provides mental indolence not only with the alibi of period flavor
but with the semblance of intellectual work. It is the paradise of
documentary platitude. That such research, as in the case of Richard
Cobb, can be rescued from its demons by literary talent in no way alters
the nature of the intellectual activity it implies. Literary talent gives life to
what is a rewriting of archives; it does not add a single idea.

What rewriting does, however, is to reveal the traces, not of hypotheses or concepts, but of what must necessarily substitute for them in order
to permit a minimum of selection in the ocean of documents. That
substitute consists primarily of a period, as well as a particular form of
curiosity, a set of questions, or all these ingredients combined more or
less explicitly. What is interesting about Richard Cobb and his books is
the sort of rigor with which the British historian constructs and applies the
doctrine of his preferences. Carrying his hatred of ideas and of intellec-
tualism to the extreme, he turns history into a laboratory for a purely
existential preference, combing the archives for material of literary value
and transforming the quest for knowledge into a passion for novelistic
narrative. Cobb is a historian of society for whom only individuals exist—
pure empirical entities independent of all intellectual constructs.

Consequently, there is only one way of organizing these empirical
entities into historical material. The controlling assumption becomes the
randomness of human existence, the flow of time, or the life story. The
interesting feature is that our historian makes narrative a necessity for his
brand of history, for he clearly sees the link between the fact—conceived
as a "pure" fact, uncontaminated by any idea (whether prior or subsequent to it) and speaking, as it were, about and for itself—and history as
narrative. The two professions of faith (to deal only with the facts and to
tell a story) are presented as distinct yet inseparable. They are the sole

constituent elements of the *profession* and of the secret of the profession, handed down as such and thus learned or repeated more than thought about. In truth, the specific feature of these tenets is that they are both mistaken if stated separately. Each holds true only in the presence of the other. As historians are periodically told—without their really heeding the warning—there is no such thing as a "pure" fact. A historical fact is an intellectual choice—and this choice is what distinguishes history from the wholesale publication of manuscript material. Moreover, narrative is not a sufficiently distinctive feature of the historian's art, since the novel, too, adopts the narrative form in most cases. But here comes the miracle. The most general and most superficial definition of the historical fact—that "it happened," that it actually took place—provided it is combined with narrative, constitutes history. Under the guise of a mere form, narrative is in reality assigned the task of making a fact understandable. For want of its being integrated into an analytical framework of questions (since it derives its falsely objective character—supposedly imparted to it by reality itself—from the absence of such integration), the criteria for selecting and explaining the fact are derived from chronology alone, which is the fabric of narrative.

In this game, the historian wins on every count. He dresses up the professional respect for facts and dates in a form that resorts only to the "logic" of before and after in order to explain them. Narrative endows scholarship and archival research with the charm and even the pleasure of a novel. Because it is built on a succession of concrete and unique facts, it calls on the historian's evocative powers more than on his specifically intellectual ability, on his art more than on his mind, on his sensitivity more than on his intelligence. The ease with which historical material can fit into the narrative mold explains why a learned discipline can also be a popular genre—and why it is sometimes difficult to distinguish between the various levels of historical output.

Indeed, acquaintance with historical writings reveals that nothing blends so well as erudition and an affective commitment. The narrative of the past, if well produced—that is, not only "true" (as regards the facts recounted), but put together with even a modicum of depth—is inseparable from the historian's sympathy with the "life" of the period whose events he is describing, that is, with the way in which contemporaries perceived and experienced the events that constitute the substance of the historian's narrative. But this sympathy, which makes possible, if not *the* reconstruction, at least *a* reconstruction of what has disappeared, belongs to the realm of affection, of ideology, or of the two combined. It replaces the explicitly formulated question as a link between past and present; it creates the vacuum that the historian's craft, in this case, is supposed to fill.

Much of what has been somewhat loosely called *histoire des mentalités* is informed by this dialectic between the experience of strangeness and the act of familiarization. It is no accident if this type of history has enjoyed its greatest popularity in the past decade or two, in a French society violently torn from its past by economic growth and feeding in compensation on a world of nostalgia. My generation has seen a transfer of the values of rootedness, tradition, and the soil away from a residual right-wing mythology to a vast left-wing consensus. The *histoire des mentalités* thrives on this feeling as the history of nations does on patriotism. It is linked to the past less by a series of specific questions than by a passionate desire to convey to us, as if they could come alive again, the emotions, beliefs, and mental universe of our ancestors. The secret of this history is, above all, a secret of sensitivity. It views the past as a mirror image of our present, but this mirror image, too, *is* our present.

At the same time, this history, owing to the vagueness of the word that gives it a label if not a content, presents an almost infinite range of methodological possibilities. The study of *mentalités* in a society or group can, for example, be based on the contrast between conscious and unconscious manifestations, on the distribution of psychic and intellectual activity according to cultural levels, on the Freudian notion of repression, or on a number of other similar investigative tools. In another intellectual context, and because it embraces both the history of objective behavior and the perceptions of such behavior, the *histoire des mentalités* can create the illusion that it enables us to grasp a sort of comprehensive social entity—a fusion of infrastructure and superstructure. Thus, in the random pattern of its various applications, the *histoire des mentalités* blurs the classic distinctions observed in the study of individuals and societies all the more effectively as it gives the impression of transcending those distinctions. All too often it is merely a Gallic substitute for Marxism and psychoanalysis. This semantic prestidigitation—a good illustration of the casual manner with which historians have traditionally treated their conceptual tools—adds no real explanatory power. However, it presents French historiography with the danger of self-satisfaction in a vacuum, since the word that it holds up like an emblem—*mentalités*—has no equivalent in other languages.

Finally, the uncontrollable expansion of what is regarded as the "historical" field threatens to increase the quotient of insignificance. The lack of definition of this vast field—an area that is supposed to signal the emergence of a "new" history—leads to the unending pursuit of new research topics, turned up by the accidents of life and having no other basis than a passing intuition or an ephemeral fashion. In reality, such topics are found, not built; they pave the way for a proliferation of histories that study the psychological realities of the past on the basis of arbitrary curiosity, without a prior theory, using ambiguous sources and yielding endlessly debatable results. As one of the essays in this book shows, the use of past demographic behavior to reconstruct underlying attitudes is fraught with uncertainty.

That is why there is no longer an automatic link between a history of the "new" variety, however misused the adjective, and the broadening of the historiographic field. That this broadening is related to curiosity or to feelings rooted in the present does not suffice to make it a novelty; the study of the past has always been inseparable from the historian's relation to the present. And the example of history à la Cobb shows that, to the extent that this relation remains purely emotional and devoid of questions and concepts, the wholesale conferral of historical dignity on the lower classes and marginal individuals in no way alters the nature of this variety of history, which still remains a narrative of bygone times.

For the most part, the so-called *histoire des mentalités*, even when it styles itself "ethnological," still belongs to such a breed of history. The reference to ethnology, when it simply indicates that the historian is dealing with subjects that used to be considered outside his province and were invented by that neighboring discipline (marriage, kinship, the constraints of sociability, for example), is only a token homage to the interdisciplinary approach. Far from establishing or even maintaining the cultural distance between the observer and the observed—a distance that lies at the very heart of ethnological analysis—it reflects precisely the opposite: a return to Peter Laslett's "world we have lost," the search for an anchorage in the deepest stratum of the familiar, below the sediments modernity has deposited in us. The reference to ethnology extends the scope of genealogical research, adapting it to our feelings toward the present, but it does not alter the nature of that research; history has moved from the genealogy of nations to the genealogy of societies. To be convinced of this, one need only consider the fact that ethnohistory as practiced in France does not represent a comparative form of knowledge but remains confined to French rural society. Furthermore, as it seeks less to explain the unfamiliar than to discover the familiar behind the illusion of the unfamiliar, it is subjected to the temptation of the picturesque, which constitutes its link with the general public.

Thus, for history to proclaim its indebtedness to another discipline is not enough to turn it into a form of knowledge different from what it was fifty or a hundred years ago. This claim or assertion can mean only that history has broadened its scope, not that it has transformed its intellectual approach to the past. In this respect, one can understand the irritation of an aggressively traditionalist historian such as Richard Cobb when confronted with the "interdisciplinary" inflation that characterizes the present-day vocabulary of historical studies in France. This almost compulsory terminology can sometimes apply, in fact, to a type of research or exposition entirely similar to those practiced and cherished by the British historian: old events, found in unpublished documents, used in a narrative to reconstruct the particular atmosphere of a period through the life of one or more individuals. Like all forms of extremism, Cobb's reactionary radicalism—in addition to its literary charm—has the advantage of exposing the duplicity of words.

Actually, the distinction I am trying to draw between two types of history—the sort of history recommended by Cobb at one extreme, the type represented, for example, by historical demography at the other,—is an imaginary boundary, in that it is constantly being crossed by mixed genres. But it is always useful, for clarity of argument, to visualize extremes: on the one hand, periodized history, chronological narrative, reconstruction of human experience, the empiricism of "facts" as opposed to preconceived ideas; on the other, problem-oriented history, the analytical examination of a single question over reputedly heterogeneous periods, the interpretation of human experience with the aid of a theory or idea. This theoretical opposition defines the space within which our discipline floats today, in the context of a general transformation represented by the broadening of its curiosity and fields of research.

It is fairly easy to reconstruct the phases of this transformation. At times the expansion of the field was accompanied by a marriage between history and another previously constituted discipline—such as demography—already occupying a given portion of the wider field. History brought to demography a precious store of additional data even as it borrowed demographic methods and concepts. That is how historical demography—or demographic history—was born. Because of its simplicity, it offers the purest example of the renewal of the study of the past with the help of a particular social science. But, in the course of its expansion, history at times also overlapped with disciplines that were far less clearly defined, such as sociology, or even certain research topics—such as *mentalités*—that had yet been honored by any social science in particular. In these instances, the historian had to tinker, borrowing a concept here, a method there, a technique elsewhere. There is no "sociological history" or "ethnological history" in the same sense as there is a "demographic history." In the latter specialty, history cast itself entirely into the mold of another discipline, without modifying its objects, concepts, or research methods. The renewal of demography stimulated by history stems from the deepening of the chronological range and from the possibilities for comparison, and thus for new hypotheses, offered by such an expansion. The study of shifts in demographic equilibriums in particular has been enriched by crucial insights. In the case of sociological or ethnological history, the historian who practices it generally borrows not so much a rigid set of research topics and concepts as a sort of general guideline for his curiosity. In other words, he will stress, for example, problems of social stratification or attitudes toward death in a specific society at a given period. But this type of curiosity may imply no other commitment than a particularly strong belief in the determination of the individual by society or a particularly keen desire to discover the elementary and the identical underneath the diversity of social phenomena, even under the mask of modernity.

Thus, between good old narrative history, which reconstructs true facts according to the chronological framework of a novel, and the history that calls itself new because it borrows part of its equipment from nearby disciplines, the opposition is neither as sharp nor as genuine as the second type of history would have us believe. The confusion stems from the fact that the renewal and extension of history's subject matter—phenomena on which all historians now agree—do not necessarily entail a change in the way of treating that subject matter. Richard Cobb, too, is a "new" historian, in his fashion—even though he loathes the *Annales*—since he devotes himself with such ardent solicitude to beggars and vagrants, the forgotten individuals of traditional historiography. He has swapped dukes for tramps, respectable folk for the destitute, great men for small fry, deeds for daily life. Although staged on another scene, the show he produces nonetheless observes conventions that Georges Lenôtre would not repudiate. To open the noble realm of history to other heroes and other actions—a gesture that all historians applaud—does not necessarily imply that one looks at them differently or that one bestows on them an original intellectual treatment.

As for the history I like, now defined not negatively but positively, the studies that follow aim precisely at delineating its contours. I am deliberately using this vague expression, for these texts do not pretend to be normative. History, even scholarly history, is not and never will be an exact discipline, as one speaks of the exact sciences. There will never be a consensus among those who write history as to the criteria that distinguish scientific from nonscientific history. The only rules of the trade are the procedural rules developed by European scholars between the sixteenth and nineteenth centuries. These rules remain essential, indeed indispensable, but all they define is a profession not a science. To establish a "true" fact in its complexity is one thing; to find the law that governs its emergence or existence is another. And if historians attach an almost fetishistic importance to mastering professional "skills," which concern only the documentary aspect of their work, it is because they have no other criteria for defining their guild.

Scholarship must serve as the basis for all imaginable types of history, from the most narrative to the most conceptual. In other words, scholarship makes it possible to distinguish between good and bad history but not to establish a hierarchy of historical genres. It constitutes a minimum requirement, beyond which the range of intellectual preferences remains open almost to infinity. I believe that one must remain firmly attached both to that obligation and to that freedom—to that obligation because the damage caused by amateurism and shoddiness has perhaps never been so visible as today; to that freedom because it is periodically being called into question by conflicting but equally superficial dogmatic approaches, one of which clings to the intransigent cult of narrative, the other to the pretense of a "scientific" form of knowledge.

In the relatively vast area within which the discipline is fluctuating today, my preferences, as the essays that follow indicate, go toward an intellectualist history that builds its data explicitly on the basis of conceptually developed questions. History, it seems to me, can advance only by paying far closer attention to the formulation and reformulation of problems and by making a clearer distinction in historical writing between documentary evidence and interpretation. To that extent, it is indeed true that narrative is to my mind a somewhat lazy mode of writing history, since it avoids questions and mingles facts and ideas in the magic flow of time. But there are two illusions of "truth" in the historical field. First, there is the illusion stemming from almost spontaneous adherence to the temporal logic of a series of events that appears as an objective datum, existing since all eternity and simply revealed by the historian. Second, there is the illusion that consists in the rational consent given to the *ex post facto* reconstruction of a necessity: nothing was possible except what took place. As for problem-oriented history, it unmasks both scholarly rationalization and the pitfalls of spontaneous understanding. By constructing its own hypotheses and data, it endows them with an autonomous existence that restores freedom to the actors it studies and open-endedness to historical situations; thus, conceptual history protects its analytical power against the scientistic illusion.

History represents a particularly valuable form of knowledge in that the social sciences are just emerging from a period in which anthropology and sociology were dominated by the notion that society speaks and acts autonomously. According to this view, social agents simply enact their society's rules of operation and reproduction without knowing that they do so, and enjoy no other freedom than the possibility of entertaining the illusion of freedom. Whether Marxist or Freudian, the notion that the intentions and actions of historical agents are intelligible only in relation to an external source of meaning has played an indispensable role in a French intellectual milieu long hostile to, and protected against, the theoretical spirit. But history, because it deals with human action at the level closest to the freedom of invention, is the best antidote against the misleading simplifications and illusory rigor inherent in the notion of a science of society. It is all the more effective an antidote for having dropped its traditional qualms about hypotheses and ideas. Indeed, as history has borrowed hypotheses and ideas from the social sciences, it can test their explanatory power.

At the same time, history has never lost sight of the fact that part of its curiosity is rooted in the present. Contrary to what the positivists believed, history's relation to the present is one of the ingredients of its relation to truth—an ingredient of greater or less importance, depending on the problems and periods examined, but an ever-present one. A searching formulation of a question allows the historian to avoid being trapped inside a period and enables him to use the past as a repository of experiments that are in some ways comparable, even if not concomitant.

In the same way, the explicit discussion of his relation to the present is an intellectual exercise that enables him to understand his own "objectivity." The celebrated point "from which" he speaks is constantly being explored in the shuttling comparison between past and present. However, the present must not be reconstructed as the only possible outcome of that past but analyzed as what turned out to be the most probable outcome, independent of the intentions or predictions of historical agents. Thus, the historian can rediscover the gap between intention and real process, a gap that characterizes his type of inquiry since it defines the two poles of historical investigation.

There are no concepts for explaining the past that do not bear the stamp of the present and do not therefore date the historian. Conversely, however, without an analysis of the present there can be no concepts at all. The first proposition is not enough to define a good conceptual history, for it does not guarantee a choice of sound analytical tools; but it does lay down a minimum requirement. It accepts the limits of historical objectivity the better to abandon the fallacy of "bringing the past back to life" or the temptation to tell a mere story.

From this point of view, the distinction of sorts sometimes drawn between contemporary history and plain "history," reputedly more reliable, seems to me to have no other justification than the vantage point involved: the closer one gets to the present, the less "distance" one has. For example, the consequences of the Reformation for the history of mankind are easier to understand than those of the Bolshevik revolution, since there are four and a half centuries of temporal distance in which to study them. But this perceptual advantage, which, moreover, varies according to the subject treated, does not in itself confer intellectual merit: depending on the historian or the work, one can encounter superficial histories of Protestantism and insightful histories of Bolshevism. And the contemporary world can offer the attentive observer a host of considerations that will help him understand the past, if only the historian displays an interest in the present.

Indeed, the contemporary world, in its natural state, provides him with the central problem of historical analysis: the problem of change and of interpreting change. As regards "what happens" every day—the events rehashed by endless comment in the media—the historian's familiarity with the past enables him to come up with additional questions or to establish new connections between events. The raw form of change that constitutes what we call "news" must immediately be made as intelligible as circumstances permit. But the historian is best equipped to restore these developments to their unfamiliar dimension, precisely by focusing on the features that make them comparable to past events. Thus, he can isolate the repetitive element and the totally new aspects of current events. Admittedly, as an actor in his own epoch the historian is not immune to the temptation to adopt any one of the explanations of "what is happening" that belong to the conventional wisdom of his time. But, although the privilege of immunity is not granted to the historian when he takes up his trade, it becomes more readily accessible to him in that the nature of his knowledge teaches him both the constraints of action and an awareness of its ambiguities.

In addition to a series of essays on history yesterday and today, I have included some pieces that do not concern the intellectual analysis of time but deal with two communities, two histories that are constituent elements of my cultural environment—America and Judaism. My aim here is to demonstrate that for me the work of learning about the past is inseparable from the effort to understand the world in which we live. The two enterprises are identical in nature; the first draws on the second for some of its inspiration and even some of its techniques.

As we have seen, the central change in historical studies over the past fifty years has come from the spread of this type of knowledge to the whole of mankind and has thus involved the relativization of European history, western European history in particular. The recourse to the language of the social sciences—a process that has overlapped with the quest for another universality—is easily explained by the crisis in the evolutionary approach to time developed in the nineteenth century. As one can see in the works of Claude Lévi-Strauss and Louis Dumont, which are comparable from this angle, the relativization of European history required comparisons with other civilizations and societies. But I have never had much ethnographical curiosity. I know very little about the great non-European civilizations, and I have worked only on what was familiar to me. However, as I have at the same time measured the value of "unfamiliarity" in the construction of the objects of our studies, particularly of the topics that seem the most readily intelligible, it seems to me that I have never ceased to be interested in the Jewish and the American experiences as instruments for historical comparisons. Beyond the accidents of life, it was the European features of these phenomena that allowed me to find anchorage in them. Yet they also provided me with reference points located outside my mental habits, since the core of these experiences had been built outside of Europe and even in opposition to it.

European reflections on the United States have, over the past two centuries, been inseparable from a comparative analysis, implicit or explicit, whose second term of comparison is the history of Europe; Tocqueville is the classic illustration. Having become the world's most powerful nation, America has lost none of its power to evoke a universal future. Despite its brutal and almost involuntary appearance in global power politics, it remains the society that comes closest to eighteenth-century credos: it is the most pristine laboratory for our modern beliefs. As for "the Jewish question," as it used to be called, it is for all members of my generation the very crux of the European tragedy of the twentieth century. Nazi anti-Semitism, the complicity it fostered or encountered, and the massive extermination it performed give a pathological measure of what our secular and democratic societies are capable of producing—following the intolerance of the Catholic church and contrary to the beliefs of the enlightened nineteenth century. As for the other aspect of contemporary Jewish history—the events leading up to the state of Israel—it offers exceptional material for historical analysis, not least because so few of its developments conform to predictions. Jewish history as a whole is endlessly surprising, in the tragic as in the happy sense. The state of Israel provides an example of an unlikely nation of latecoming immigrants, fleeing the European scourge—two or three centuries after the English dissenters—in order to people a Promised Land blessed by God. In this respect, Israel presents the French historian with a problem similar to that posed by the United States: a model of nation building and a type of society radically different from those with which he is familiar, since they are founded on the recent choice of their makers and engendered by a religion, by an ideology, or simply by misfortune—causes that, moreover, are not incompatible. But the creation of Israel is even more astonishing and thought-provoking than that of America, for it combines an infinitely older belief with a far more recent historical scheme. The founding of the Israeli nation is predicated on both the socialist notion of a new society and an ancient belief in a "return"; in almost every Israeli citizen there is a mixture of extreme modernity and extreme archaism, and Israeli society illustrates the extraordinary diversity of the chemistry of nationhood. Its existence confronts the observer with all the problems of the world in which we live. These problems are present in Israel in a condensed form but at a level deep enough for the historian to feel that he is on familiar ground: the extraordinary survival of a religion and a people scattered throughout the Christian and Arab worlds, the relations between democracy and pathological anti-Semitism in the twentieth century, the historical and modern elements of a national consensus, the clash between religion and secularization on the natural battleground of the state, and, finally, the watertight confrontation between civilizations, in which the Israelis, involuntary heirs to European colonialism, represent in the Arab mind the world that persecuted the Jews and from which they fled.

By adding to some general considerations on history in French intellectual life today a number of studies devoted to the American world and the Jewish world, my aim has been not only to establish cultural bearings in relation to problems that interest me; I have also wanted to express my belief that history is inseparable from an understanding of the contemporary world—a world that supplies history with its questions and its raison d'être.

1

French Intellectuals:
From Marxism to Structuralism

The "end of ideologies," as diagnosed by Raymond Aron, for instance, in one of his books,[1] refers generally to the developed societies of America and western Europe. It connects prosperity, economic growth, and social integration on the one hand with the progressive decline of political extremisms on the other; the car, the refrigerator, and television are said to have killed revolution. This type of analysis has already inspired endless comment on neocapitalism, the Gaullist regime, and the kind of political torpor that has characterized France since the end of the Algerian war, as if one of the functions of Gaullist nationalism were now to counterbalance an objective process of French "Americanization."

But does the end of ideologies mean the end of ideologues? If it is true that present-day France tends in its social depths to be dozing off into a society of abundance and social integration, is the diagnosis also true of the groups and the individuals whose profession is thinking and writing? It may be objected that this question implies a certain modification of our initial proposition, for the relations of intellectuals to ideologies differ in nature from those of the general public; at any rate, they are more complicated (even if they are apparently simple or deliberately simplified). But French intellectuals, because of the authority they have enjoyed since the Enlightenment, have often been indicative of the problems and choices of society as a whole. There can be no greater historical oversimplification than deifying the intelligentsia's purely protesting role; claiming a long line of great but damned ancestors is a cheap way of entering into an exceptional heritage. But Voltaire was the most

First published in *Preuves*, no. 92 (February 1967). An English translation entitled "The French Left: From Marxism to Structuralism" appeared in *Survey*, no. 62 (January 1967), 72–83. The present text is a slightly revised and expanded reprint of that translation.

acclaimed hero of the eighteenth century, the Revolution put Rousseau in the Pantheon, and Victor Hugo's coffin was followed by an enormous crowd. The intellectual Left has rarely governed the France of its time, but it has supplied its universal values. Neither the Dreyfus affair nor the Popular Front nor the postwar spread of communism is intelligible if the part played by the intellectuals and their ideological elaboration is left out of account.

That is why ideology is far from consisting exclusively of a theory of history, though in the France of yesterday Marxism-Leninism was the most widespread and extreme form it took. Ideology is born of the feeling that a great historical problem can and must be solved by individual commitment. Hence the passion inseparable from it, the proselytism, the condemnation of the enemy and even of the indifferent, the identification of personal morality with historical necessity. The class struggle has different aims according to Guizot or Marx. The former hails the triumph of the bourgeoisie, and the second the advent of the proletariat; but both, even if this is denied, as it is by Marx, imply a moral view of politics, distinction between good and evil, and commitment to the side of the good.

Thus, the French Left has no monopoly of ideology; on the contrary, for nearly two hundred years the conflict between Right and Left has been the warp on which ideologies have been woven. The Frenchman of the Right, armed with Barrès versus Zola, Maurras versus Romain Rolland, and Drieu La Rochelle versus Aragon, also has his cultural pedigree, whose assumptions and political hypocrisy the Left has frequently denounced. The national masochism of the Pétainist bourgeoisie or, fifteen years later, the nationalist enthusiasm for l'Algérie française refers back to the same system of intellectual and moral arguments, only the terms of which vary with the event. Why, then, the privileged position enjoyed today by the ideology of the Left and by the left-wing intellectual? The answer is that the last great battle of right-wing ideology was fought by fascism—and lost. Since the end of the war, ideological elaboration has consequently been a quasi monopoly of the Left.

How the celebrated Hegelian tribunal, which had become the "opium of the intellectuals," was wildly misused by the victorious Left after it had been "proved right" by history was described by Raymond Aron even before the politico-moral tribunal of Stalinism broke down with the death of Stalin. Up to that moment, historical certainty and moral judgment had combined and reinforced each other; now both factors in the apogee of the ideological age were simultaneously punctured by developments in the contemporary world.

Destalinization raised the issue of justice and truth in the Communist world; there turned out to be other enemies besides the bourgeoisie, and it came to be seen that the Soviet Union was not always, necessarily, and inherently in the advance guard of human history. This led to a new diaspora of Communist and progressive intellectuals; a whole world

PART ONE

HISTORY TODAY

collapsed, as I well remember, because I was a part of it. Warsaw, Budapest, the Chinese schism have only accentuated the process, providing the last rites for a Marxism-Leninism that had been both incarnate and universal. But during those very years a new universalist mirage, an ersatz messianism, presented itself to the revolutionary intellectuals, namely, the struggle for independence of the Third World or, in the French context, support for the FLN in the Algerian war. This additional experiment in ideological extremism was the more characteristic of left-wing intellectual circles in that it was experienced in social isolation, disclaimed by the Communist party, and not understood by the working class. The Western intellectual looked overseas for his (mythical) tie with the oppressed and the agents of world revolution, in the ranks of an enemy who was assumed by definition to be socialist and internationalist. The Muslim fellah celebrated by Fanon had become the latest ally of revolutionary defeatism of the Leninist type. The outcome is familiar. The left-wing intellectual had invested his liquid revolutionary capital in religious nationalism; in seeking the Bolshevik party of 1917, it found Islam; and, instead of Lenin, it found Boumediene.

The disconcerting outcome in Algeria and the very victories of the colonial peoples have slowed down left-wing intellectual investment in the Third World, for the difficulties in the way of economic "takeoff" are often too technical in nature to nourish passion, and the love affair between the FLN's French wartime friends and the Algeria of Colonel Boumediene has ended in disappointment. Nevertheless, the economic setbacks that have taken place in most of the recently decolonized countries have in a way restored to honor the idea of a Leninist—or Maoist—dictatorship. For lack of suitable soil for experimentation of this type at home, some Western intellectuals proclaim its necessity in the underdeveloped countries as the only way of demolishing the many obstacles in the path of mobilization of labor and national saving for capital formation. A few years ago it was chiefly the romantic and antibureaucratic character of the Cuban revolution (which contrasted so sharply with socialism of the Soviet type) that roused enthusiasm, but the Chinese model now seems to be restoring priority to economic rationality, and this classic slant may again enable it to be used in defense of totalitarianism. But it is too obviously inapplicable to European conditions, its culture being too "exotic" and its antecedents too well known, and so it is unlikely to rally a great deal of support; and, finally, the hostility of the French Communist party deprives it of a great deal of influence.

The irruption into history of the nations of the Third World, instead of promoting a "Chinese" version of Marxism, has in fact contributed to hastening the end of the ideologies in contemporary French culture. Superficially and for a brief moment, it seemed to revive great universal visions of social transformation, but in reality it served to discredit lastingly and in depth the philosophies of history of the nineteenth century. This phenomenon could be crudely summed up by saying that, in the context of French intellectual life—so sensitive to fashion and so prompt to generalize—the prestige of structural ethnology has been partly due to the fact that it offered an "antihistory."

A disappointed intellectual Left, demoralized by history, turned to primitive man, not to decipher mankind's infancy—which would have led back to history—but to find man's "true" situation. The approval of the "savage" by a society that considers itself to be saturated with wealth and "civilization," to use the term already current in Rousseau's time, is not a new phenomenon. But the interesting feature of the present vogue is that the savage has become, for a time, the model for the human sciences. It is probably not by chance, nor is it the mere result of an incidentally only too obvious cultural chauvinism, that structuralism, which has dominated European linguistic research since the first postwar period, was popularized in France not by linguistics but by ethnology. Nor is its success solely attributable to the work of Lévi-Strauss, whose *Structures élémentaires de la parenté* dates from 1948—nearly ten years before he achieved notoriety. It took the dislocation of Marxist dogmatism between 1955 and 1960 for ethnology to fulfill a social expectation and meet a historical situation. Decolonization revealed to all the secrets of the ethnologists, those pioneers of anticolonialism: namely, that cultures are multiple, are equally worthy of respect, and manifest themselves in terms of permanence rather than of change. French colonization (which, it must not be forgotten, was often Left in origin) claimed to place them in Western "time," putting them through European stages of progress whether they liked it or not. Now, however, there is perhaps a trace of expiatory masochism in the revaluation of these extra-European worlds.

Furthermore, these exotic and impoverished worlds have the virtue of focusing all the distaste for, and rejection of, the "affluent society": even if they are no longer centers of revolution and are gradually sinking below the survival line, they are at least pure and innocent in the eyes of a Left that is at heart moralistic and more Christian than it thinks. They remain a geographical refuge for the frustration with the historical immobility of a nonrevolutionary West. Provided the flame of revolution keeps smoldering in the Third World (as in South America) or flares up there (as in China), the students of prosperous Europe will someday be able to transmute their despair into hope. Above all, a profound change has taken place in the French intellectual's idea of the world and the part played in it by his country. The transference of his revolutionary hopes to the Soviet Union and then to the Third World was in itself an implicit confession of impotence concerning the possibilities in his own country. But it also betrayed the survival of the Jacobin tradition, nostalgia for the France of 1793, a patriotism temporarily frustrated but nevertheless optimistic: France would one day again pick up the torch of revolutionary history. Now even this dream is fading. Not only has the Soviet flame gone out and the Third World disconcerted or disappointed its friends of the heroic age, but France itself is no longer France. The French intellectual, heir to a prestige less fragile than power and unconsciously used to a universal radiation of his culture, is not yet reduced to the sad state of the Belgian, but he is increasingly aware of being a citizen of a country that, in spite of Gaullist rhetoric, senses it is no longer making human history. Having been expelled from history, the France in which he lives consents the more willingly to expel history. It can look at the world with eyes no longer veiled by its own example and civilizing obsession, with eyes now sceptical about the "lessons" and "meaning" of history. Valéry admirably foresaw this phenomenon after the First World War in his *Regards sur le monde actuel.*

Thus, the recent disappointments of the French intellectuals and the general political situation combine to cast doubt on history—for so long a tyrannical mistress before she became an unfaithful one.

It is without doubt this situation that explains the great impact of the thinking of which Lévi-Strauss is generally regarded as both a model and a representative. It is, however, uncertain—even unlikely—that Lévi-Strauss, who has a passion for accuracy, would accept this vague and general attribution of paternity affixed to him under the label of "structuralism." But, from the point of view of the social character of his audience, that matters little. On the other hand, it is significant that a work as specific and as technical as his should have had so widespread an impact on men of letters, art critics, and philosophers. To enumerate its great themes and aspirations is not to evade the significance of the intellectual movement that reflects the scope of its influence, since that is precisely what has to be understood.

In the first place, however abstract and high-powered it may be, the effect of his work is to revive something like the great Rousseauist paradox that split the eighteenth century. One feels it to be suffused by love of nature, the countryside and flowers, a fondness for "primitive" man that inevitably stimulates nostalgia for a happiness lost by industrial societies. Lévi-Strauss writes of a world in which the eagle, the bear, and meadow sage still exist, but he believes no more than Rousseau, who is one of his favorite authors, in a return to a primitive happiness that has disappeared forever. The heir to Boas and Mauss knows that there is no such thing as a state of nature but, rather, myriad communities and cultures, each representing a different form of man's confrontation with nature; and he also realizes that there is no objective way of establishing any hierarchy among them. Thus, the industrial society of Europe or America loses the privileged position to which it believes itself entitled in relation to tribes buried in the forests of the Amazon. "A great deal of egocentricity and naïveté is required if one is to believe that the whole of man has taken refuge in a single one of his historical or geographical modes of being, while the truth about man lies in the system of their differences and common properties" (*La Pensée sauvage*, p. 329). Thus, the savage does not provide us with an image of man's childhood, as was believed in the eighteenth and nineteenth centuries in accordance with a naïvely European model of human history; he does not even provide us with one adequate image among others. As soon as it is granted that he has conceived quite varied societies and uses a logic as profound—or simple—as that of modern science, he no longer exists as a "savage" or as a "primitive." He merely offers us, as the so-called developed societies do, a multiplicity of cultural solutions of the eternal conflict between man and nature.

The role of the ethnologist is thus to classify cultural systems, to undertake for each of them an objective analysis of their systems of symbols and their articulation. The objectives of the psychoanalyst are implicitly transferred from the individual to the collective, from clinical analysis to the "decoding" of a social language such as myth. In his last years, Freud was greatly attracted by the interpretation of ethnological data (which he had not completely mastered). Lévi-Strauss rejects the methodological confusion implied in this illicit ethnology-psychoanalysis relationship; he never extrapolates into his own field the procedures of psychoanalysis. But his ideas about myths extend to the collective sphere the objectives of individual psychoanalytic treatment; they are intended to bring to the surface the subconscious structure of social beliefs, the code that underlies man's thinking and ultimately determines what he does think of himself and of others. On this, Lévi-Strauss agrees with Marx and Freud. Like that of myth, the realm of ideologies is the realm of false consciousness of reality, which must be explained at another level. But, unlike Marx, he sees no historical remedy for this false consciousness, no reconciliation of man and his true history.

Moreover, structural ethnology at long last promises an advance of the human sciences to a methodology as rigorous as that of the exact sciences, for in one sense the work of ethnological analysis resembles a laboratory experiment. In both cases the object under observation is treated as a natural object, is laid out in space, is amenable to any amount of experimentation, and there is a great awareness of the distance between the observer and the observed. In another sense, however, the methodological quarrels of the ethnologists threaten the assimilation of ethnology to the exact sciences. Lévi-Strauss is constantly aware both of the kinship and of the gap still to be filled, hence the originality of his work and no doubt also its wide range, which contrasts with the deliberately restricted nature of ethnological description. Working with a few societies into which history has not introduced its chaos and in which reduction to a few variables is relatively easy, he has been able to satisfy his concern for scientific rigor and his obsession with the linguistic "model" in the best possible conditions.

It is true, as he often repeats, that he has never ventured beyond, though, as always happens whenever a book becomes fashionable, imprudent or overzealous disciples tend to extend his method toward building up a general theory of societies. Frivolous or perhaps illusory though this anticipation may be, it underlines the methodological influence of his work. Is not this entomologist of human behavior, capable of the feat of emerging from his own cultural world, the reverse of Sartrian man, on whom engulfment in history and the emergence of a revolutionary practice impose his celebrated commitment? The fact that he belongs to the same generation as Sartre and has lived through practically the same history and is also considered to belong to the Left is thus immaterial; to him these things belong to the domain of opinion and not to that of science. And in what way does he belong to the Left? The term hardly has meaning to a man who believes that, in their state of babbling infancy, the human sciences to which he has devoted his life and outside which he wishes to say nothing have for the time being nothing serious, still less useful, to offer to the polis and its struggles—except a relapse into ideology. In fact, their chance of one day deserving their name specifically depends on their keeping silent. "One may legitimately ask the exact and natural sciences what they are, but the social and human sciences are not yet in a state to render accounts. If these are required of them, or if on political grounds it is considered clever to pretend to do so, it will not be surprising if all one gets is phony balance sheets" (*Revue internationale des sciences sociales*, 1964).

Is this scruple to be regarded as a real break with history? It would be highly significant for our argument if it were so. But Lévi-Strauss continually denies it and pays explicit tribute to history, allowing it even to "reserve its rights" (*Leçon inaugurale* at the Collège de France, 1960). But until when? And what is the history to which he refers? Is it the meaning of history created by Sartre's dialectical reason? Evidently not, for, except at the price of unscrupulous falsification, looking back cannot demonstrate in the present the necessary outcome of the past. To Sartre a man can always draw logical conclusions; to Lévi-Strauss he can only think that he does so. A stubborn illusion grants the present a rather foolish privilege without seeing that the present itself introduces into successive events a connecting link drawn from its own depths. Thus, the assurance of a retrogressive movement of truth vanishes under the ethnologist's eye, and the philosophy of history becomes a myth, the necessity of which only emphasizes its lack of substance. Lévi-Strauss, criticizing the fabrication of historical meaning by Sartre's dialectical reason, wrote this significant passage on the history of the French Revolution: "Those described as men of the Left still cling to a period of contemporary history that granted them the privilege of consistency between practical imperatives and patterns of interpretation. Perhaps that golden age of the historical conscience has already passed; and the fact that one can at least imagine the possibility shows that this was merely a fortuitous situation, resembling the chance 'focusing' on a heavenly body of an optical instrument with which it happened to be in a state of relative motion. We are still 'focused' on the French Revolution; but, if we had lived earlier, we might have been focused on the Fronde" (*La Pensée sauvage*).

Once this pseudoscience has been exposed, however, the fact remains that societies change and there are histories—if not a single history—that are entitled to their observers. History, like Le Verrier's planet, thus becomes a perpetual "disturbing factor" introducing structural disequilibriums. Now, it is impossible to grasp everything at once; synchronism and diachronism cannot be taken in at the same glance. Increasing one's knowledge in one field proportionally diminishes one's chances of acquiring it in another. Thus, structural ethnologists are needed to study order, and historians to study disorder. This division of labor is equal only in appearance, however. The study of structures has a double advantage, chronological and logical: chronological because the description of structures provides it with a starting point, and this gives complete autonomy to the work of the structuralists, while the opposite is not true (the work of the historian is dependent, ornamental, or, at all events, relegated to a distant future); and logical because, contrary to structural analysis, historical analysis pulverizes norms when it deals with events. Moreover, history is very difficult—perhaps impossible—to rationalize.

From this point of view, which is perhaps the most significant for our argument, Marx and Sartre are on the same side of the barricade, that of history, while Lévi-Strauss is on the other, that of structure. Like Hegel and Marx, Sartre still describes an advent, a history of human fulfillment, while Lévi-Strauss reduces multiple man to common mechanisms, dissolves him in a universal determinism, in the last resort displays him like a natural object. His books, written with a rather precious rigor, are a pitiless commentary on man's nothingness, marking a probably fundamental epistemological breach with the "ideological era." This is systematized by Foucault in *Les Mots et les choses*.

I do not wish to lapse into overly facile identifications, unduly confusing books and authors, but from the point of view of this analysis it is permissible to compare the work of Barthes and Foucault with that of Lévi-Strauss, particularly considering the connection that intellectual opinion has spontaneously established among the three. Their fields of work are very different, but the methodological inspiration is the same: it is to try to obtain an ethnological view of contemporary societies and cultures. Foucault, imitating the use of the ethnologist's cultural telescope and reversing it, tries to gain more light from it that way. Lévi-Strauss mingles the Jivaro world with his European outlook, while Foucault sets out to consider European culture from a Jivaro angle in order to conjure away its presence at last and turn it into a scientific object. He tries to describe not individual patterns, which pertain to the study of opinions, but the conceptual structures that in each period make those opinions possible; the present intellectual revolution consists in his view in the breach with historicism and the end of humanist anthropocentrism. This makes Sartre the last "nineteenth-century philosopher"— which cannot be pleasing to him. Foucault's methodological aggressiveness, probably one of the clues to the success of his book, is of interest in that it tries to systematize the general significance of structuralism in present-day European culture; the analysts of man's "dissolution" have succeeded the prophets of his advent.

If what Foucault says is indeed true and if structuralism confines Marx to a nineteenth century intellectually dominated by history, it is very curious and sociologically extremely interesting that structuralism should have developed in France so systematically and so late and in the same left-wing intellectual circles that (in the broad sense of the term) had been Marxist since the liberation. This leaves us with the task of trying to describe and understand this paradoxical phenomenon as well as the curious and, I think, specifically French mutual contamination that has taken place between Marxism and structuralism.

At the first level of analysis, it is evident that if Marxism continues to lie at the heart of the French intellectual debate, it is less as a theory than as an ideal, less as an intellectual tool than as a political heritage. Twenty years have now passed since Sartre tried to reconcile the existentialist self with Marxist determinism, that is, his theory of personal liberty with his progressive opinions. It is this that forced him in his last philosophical book to substitute his dialectics of individual liberty for Marxist dialectical materialism while quoting as "self-evident" and approving without the slightest critical analysis the sum total of the propositions put forward in *Das Kapital*, that is to say, the essentials of the Marxist philosophy of history.[2] By this subterfuge, he reconciles his philosophic conscience with his political progressiveness but at the same time illustrates the profound duality of his work and the uneven quality of his intellectual rigor. What interests him is the establishment of new existential foundations for human history and the revision of what he considers the mark of "scientism" in Marx. The respectful and distant doffing of his hat to *Das Kapital* does not derive from the same level of analysis; it signifies merely his allegiance to the left-wing intelligentsia, the resistance of yesterday, and the present-day struggles against imperialism. It is the historical symbol of an age that is the ideological age. Sartre speaks and will always speak as an elder brother to all those who lived profoundly through the times of fascism and communism. The genius of this professional philosopher resides, paradoxically perhaps, in the secret of his sensibility and art rather than in the clarity of his thought. In vain he refuses to be what he has become, for he is caught up in the pitiless history of literature. He has turned into a patriarchal figure, a revered elder aging in glory, a Nobel Prize winner in spite of himself, but a Nobel Prize winner all the same. That is the last trick played on him by "words."

It is true that Lévi-Strauss has also emphasized his debt to Marxism, but his debt is of a different kind. Having deliberately abstained from postwar political struggles, shut in his academic ivory tower, he has felt no need to state his position in relation to communism or anticommunism; the few interviews that—obviously without pleasure—he has given the press betray more than prudence: a professional desire to keep his distance from his own cultural world and the chaotic history that introduces its disorders into it. Nevertheless, he can perhaps be considered more faithful than Sartre to Marx's philosophic premises and materialist determinism. He has inherited from Marx the scientific ambition of interpreting in intelligible terms the ideas that men form about the natural and social worlds by another system underlying them; he accepts the idea of a homogeneous society in which the determining factors will in the last resort be the relations between man and nature. But he transforms it profoundly by drawing up a veritable theory of superstructures. One of the plainest symptoms of the end of the ideological age among French intellectuals is, incidentally, this passion for the study of superstructures, as if they desire to track down, unveil, and understand the intellectual products of men and groups from their most hidden motivations. This is also the weakest point in Marx's analysis. To Lévi-Strauss, who made himself plain on the subject in *La Pensée sauvage*, the primacy of infrastructures is like a hand dealt at cards; what societies do with the hand imposed upon them depends on man's cultural inventiveness. But this inventiveness does not suggest an unlimited number of variables. On the contrary, it is governed by structures and logical systems whose appearance and mutations, far from being necessary and inevitable as so many stages in an identical human evolution, depend on a calculation of probabilities; this accounts for the concomitant multiplicity of societies and cultures.

Admittedly, from other passages in his books, less materialist and less Marxist interpretations can be drawn, for one can never be sure whether the logical structure brought to light by the analysis is the same nature as the material produced by it or whether it informs reality. In fact, the problem of whether it is materialist or Kantian (a Kantianism without transcendental subject, Paul Ricoeur has said)[3] is of little interest to Lévi-Strauss, who seems to accept both hypotheses; that is to say, he takes little interest in his philosophical relations with Marxism.

Moreover, he has always refused all extrapolation of his analytic procedures to mythologies, beliefs, or "historical" societies; he did so explicitly in reply to Edmund Leach, the British anthropologist, who suggested a Lévi-Straussian "decoding" of the Book of Genesis—and the contrast between the theoretical ambition implicit in his ideas and the narrowness of their field of application rouses the mistrust of many of his colleagues in the English-speaking world, who remain attached to the empirical accumulation of facts.[4] In France, however, it is this ambition, or rather its special contribution to South American ethnology, that has roused the enthusiasm of intellectuals and led rapidly to discussions at the most general level—existentialism, Marxism, and structuralism. The left-wing periodicals bear witness to this; the ethnologist has been consecrated a philosopher rather in spite of himself. Perhaps this should be regarded, as do certain English-speaking anthropologists, as a special feature of the French national tradition. But in this instance the fascination exercised by Lévi-Strauss over many Marxist or formerly Marxist intellectuals seems to me to have a more specific explanation. It is born neither of fraternity of political opinion (for Lévi-Strauss is the opposite of a "committed" man) nor of philosophical kinship (which is highly problematical, if it exists at all, and is in any case a matter of indifference to Lévi-Strauss) but from an inverse relationship in which nostalgia for Marx has been able to insert itself. Stated simply, the structural description of man as object has, in every respect, taken the place of the historical advent of the man-god.

There is yet another and still more surprising aspect of the relationship between the Marxists and the structuralists. It is significant that a whole trend of Communist thought implicitly relies on structuralism, not to break with Marxism but to renovate it. That is the meaning of the work of Althusser and his friends, who are trying to restore the theoretical value of the work of Marx and Lenin by rigorous analysis of their operative concepts in order to free it of the banally humanist ideology with which Garaudy diluted it. Instead of being concerned, like Sartre, with reconciling an epistemology with progressive ideas, they aim to marry structuralist method and Marxist theory. From this there emerges a Marxism purged of its Hegelian paternity and of all contamination by bourgeois humanism and differing from Marx's ideas about his own doctrine, since the latter is redefined by the bringing to light of its fundamental conceptual structures. It is on this condition alone, in Althusser's view, that Marxism can again become what it really is (which was masked by the huge amount of social and historical sedimentation that has taken place): that is to say, *the* theory, *the* science par excellence, as opposed to the ideologies. This explains the curious path taken by Althusser. Trying as he is to "deideologize" Marxism, he nevertheless uses it both as an object of study and as his sole point of scientific reference. Structural analysis, an attempt to extend the methods of natural science to the "human sciences," is thus subtly diverted in the direction of Marxist dogmatism, which is assumed as a self-evident premise—for the Marxist model is assimilated from the outset to the scientific model. Hence the epistemological contradiction and political ambiguity of the works of Althusser and his friends, which are devoted to restoring life to Marx by rigorous analysis but are blocked by bigoted adherence to a conceptual apparatus that, brilliant though it may have been, dates from another age and another world.

Perhaps on another plane this ambiguity is significant of the development of some Communist intellectuals who have remained in the party since the destalinization crisis and of younger ones who have since joined it in a climate that has become much more tolerant and much more critical than that of the fifties. Althusser simultaneously offers structuralism and Marxism, critical study and doctrinaire intransigence, loyalty to the French Communist party and reservations about it. There are many reasons to suppose that a sociological study of his present audience would disclose these factors, which are so characteristic of the present and recent past of Communist intellectuals. No matter that they are contradictory; it is precisely because they are contradictory that a structuralist interpretation of Marx is able to offer them a temporary home. Intellectual and sociological contradictions mutually explain and reinforce each other; the structuralist "deideologizing" of Marxism undoubtedly offers a way of living through the end of the ideologies inside the Communist world.

If this analysis is as a whole correct, if there is indeed a link between a general phenomenon like the end of ideologies and the attractiveness of structuralism in the special environment of the French intellectuals, it will strike one as surprising that the disintegration of ideological certainties and of the "meaning" of history has not led to a return to favor of empirical research and the gathering of factual information in the manner of the English-speaking world. Not that such research and the accumulation of factual information is not growing in France; on the contrary, there as elsewhere sociological surveys, public-opinion polls, and large-scale investigations of archives are multiplying. But everything is more than ever subordinated, even more than it was yesterday, to the search for a general theory. Everything is happening as if the crisis of Marxism had cleared the way for a methodology of another kind but at the same level, heir to the same ambition for total, systematic understanding. What for lack of a better term is called the Parisian "passion" for structuralism—that is, its social success and its timing—would thus be explained by its deep relationship, both contradictory and homogeneous, to Marxism. The natural-sciences model has displaced the history model, man as object has taken the place of man as subject, structure has taken the place of determinist ambition and derives from the same desire to decipher what underlies the apparent or merely conscious meaning of human behavior.

It is probable that the end of the ideological age among the French intellectuals embraces two distinct phenomena differing in nature. Destalinization, the Sino-Soviet schism, the crisis of the Third World—and French and European prosperity—have punctured the progressivism of the fifties that was so characteristic of the ideological age. Hence, there was a receptiveness of intellectual opinion, a kind of expectation—rather as a century ago the inglorious failure of the romantics of 1848 preceded and facilitated the formation of the realist and positivist generation. But it helped this generation to emerge; it did not create it: this intellectual change does not itself call for sociological explanation. At the present time, the political disappointments suffered by progressivism have profoundly weakened the influence of Marxism among the left-wing intellectuals, but it is Lévi-Strauss and not Raymond Aron who reigns in the void thus created. What prevails is not a liberal and empirical criticism of Marxism but a hyperintellectual and systematic way of thinking that aims at a general theory of man. Not only have Marxists or former Marxists been able to invest their past in this without repudiating it; they have also rediscovered in it their ambition for a comprehensive science of man and their old all-embracing dream, "deideologized" and freed from the naïvetés of commitment and of the meaning of history. To that extent perhaps the case of the French intellectuals deserves to become a classic; the end of the ideological age has found its doctrinaires.

2

Quantitative History

Quantitative history is fashionable just now both in Europe and in the United States. Since the 1930s, historical research has been making rapidly increasing use of quantitative sources and of calculation and quantification procedures. But, like all fashionable phrases, *quantitative history* has come to be used so sweepingly that it covers almost everything, from critical use of the simple enumerations of seventeenth-century political arithmeticians to systematic application of mathematical models in the reconstruction of the past. Sometimes quantitative history refers to a type of source, sometimes to a type of procedure; always, in some way or other, explicit or not, to a type of conceptualization of the past. It seems to me that if one goes from the general to the particular and tries to pinpoint the specific nature of historical knowledge in relation to the other social sciences, one can distinguish three groups of problems relating to quantitative history.

1. The first group concerns the methods of treating the data: problems having to do with the formation of different families of data, the geographical unity of each family, and its internal subdivisions; with correlations between different series; with the values, in relation to the data, of different models of statistical analysis; with the interpretation of statistical relationships; and so on.

First published in an English translation by Barbara Bray as "Quantitative History," *Daedalus*, Winter 1971, 151–67. Reproduced by permission of *Daedalus*, Journal of the American Academy of Arts and Sciences, Boston, Mass. A revised version in French was published as "L'Histoire quantitative et la construction du fait historique," *Annales: économies, sociétés, civilisations*, January–February 1971, 63–75, reprinted as "Le Quantitatif en histoire" in Jacques Le Goff and Pierre Nora, eds., *Faire de l'histoire* (Paris: Gallimard, 1974), vol. 1, *Nouveaux problèmes*, 42–61. The present text is a slightly revised and expanded reprint of the earlier English translation.

These problems belong to the *technology* of research in the social sciences. It is true, they may also include questions of methodology, not only because no technique is "neutral," but because, more specifically, all statistical procedures are bound to raise the problem of whether, and to what extent, historical or sociological knowledge is compatible with, or can be dealt with exhaustively by, mathematical conceptualization of a probabilistic kind. But neither the technical nor the theoretical debate is specific to history: both arise in connection with all the social sciences. In this respect, quantitative history is no different from, for example, what is now called "empirical sociology," which in this context is simply contemporary quantitative history.

2. Quantitative history also refers, at least in France, to the aims and researches of certain economic historians,[1] who attempt to turn history into a kind of retrospective econometrics,[2] or, in other words, on the basis of modern national accounting, to fill in all the columns of an imaginary input-output table for past centuries. The champions of this econometric history advocate total and systematic quantification, in their view indispensable both for the elimination of arbitrariness in selecting data and for the use of mathematical models in their processing. This processing is based on the concept of general equilibrium as imported into economic history from political economy.

According to this argument, genuine quantitative history would be the result of a twofold reduction of history: first, at least provisionally, the reduction of its field to economics; and, second, the reduction of its descriptive and interpretative system to the one worked out by the most rigorously constituted of the social sciences today, political economy. The same analysis could be applied to demography and demographic history: here again, a conceptually constituted science indicates the data and supplies the methods for a particular historical discipline, the latter thus becoming a sort of by-product of the other discipline, whose questions and concepts it merely transposes into the past.

Of course, there have to be data for the past just as for the present; or at least it has to be possible to work them out with a sufficient degree of accuracy or to reconstruct or extrapolate them. This necessity sets the first limit to the complete quantification of historical data. Complete quantification, even if possible at all before the nineteenth century, could not go back beyond the introduction of the statistical or protostatistical recording of data, which coincides with the centralization of the great European monarchies. But history did not begin with William Petty or Sébastien Vauban.

Moreover, there is no reason why the historian should agree, even provisionally, to have his field of research reduced to economics or demography. There are two alternatives. Either history is only the study of a previously determined, limited sector of the past, into which mathematical models established by certain social sciences are imported in order to be tested. In which case, we come back again to contemporary political economy, which seems to me the only one of the social sciences with such models at its disposal. History then becomes nothing more than an additional field of data. Or—the second alternative—one takes history in the widest sense, that is, as a discipline not strictly reducible to a set of concepts and with countless different levels of analysis, and then addresses oneself to describing these levels and establishing simple statistical connections between them on the basis of hypotheses that, whether original or borrowed, depend on the intuition of the researcher.

3. This is why, even if one qualifies history as "quantitative," one cannot escape what is the specific object of historical research: the study of time, of the diachronic dimension of phenomena. But, looked at from this point of view, quantitative history's most general and elementary object is to form historical fact into temporal series of homogeneous and comparable units, so that their evolution can be measured in terms of fixed intervals, usually years. This fundamental and logical operation constitutes what Pierre Chaunu has called "serial history,"[3] a necessary though not sufficient condition of strictly quantitative history as defined above. For serial history offers the conclusive advantage, from the scientific point of view, of substituting for the elusive "event" of positivist history the regular repetition of data selected or constructed by reason of their comparability. It does not, however, claim to give an exhaustive account of the whole body of evidence nor to be a comprehensive system of interpretation nor to be a mathematical formulation. On the contrary, the division of historical reality into series leaves the historian confronted with his material broken down into different levels and subsystems, among which he is at liberty to suggest internal relationships if he chooses.

Defined in this way, quantitative and serial history emerge as at once connected with and distinct from each other. But they share an elementary basis in that both substitute the series for the event, both make a construction from historical data in terms of probabilistic analysis. To the classic question What is a historical fact? they both give a new answer that transforms the historian's raw material—time. It is about this internal transformation that I should like to put forward a few ideas.

To avoid any misunderstanding, let me say at once that this essay does not set out to prescribe quantitative history as the only kind permissible. During the last ten or twenty years, serial history has turned out to be one of the most fertile approaches in the advancement of historical knowledge. It has also the immense advantage of introducing into the ancient discipline of history a rigor and efficiency superior to those of qualitative methodology. But it is nevertheless true that there are important sectors of historical reality that it is by nature unable to treat or even to approach, either for circumstantial reasons such as irremediable lack of data or for fundamental reasons such as the irreducibly qualitative nature of the phenomenon concerned. This explains why, for example, historians of antiquity, who work with data very discontinuous in time, or specialists in intellectual biography, concentrating particularly on what is unique and incomparable in creativeness, are usually less attracted by serial history than, say, historians of the agrarian structures of modern Europe.

From this point of view, another, and perhaps more basic, problem should be raised. Serial history undoubtedly provides accurate methods for measuring change, but to what extent does it enable the historian to interpret change? By definition, data series are composed of identically constructed units, in order to make comparisons possible. The long-term variation of these units in time, when it takes the form of cycles, brings us back to what one could call change within stability and thus to an analysis in terms of equilibria. But sometimes the temporal variation of one or more series takes the shape of an open-ended growth trend, that is, a cumulative process. If one breaks down this trend into relatively small units (annual or ten-year periods, for example), it becomes harder to define the threshold beyond which the time structure and the rates of change are transformed. This raises tremendous problems of dating and periodization. Moreover, the decisive historical change cannot be inserted into any series endogenous to a given system; instead, it must be the product either of an innovation unrecorded in any previous quantification or of an exogenous factor that upsets the centuries-old equilibrium of the system. These methodological problems lie at the heart of the present debate over the question of industrial takeoff.[4] In other words, if it is true that no methodology is innocent, serial history, by concentrating on the long term and on the equilibrium of systems, seems to me to put a premium on conservation. It is a good antidote to the identification of history with change—a nineteenth-century inheritance—and thus a crucial phase in the development of history as a discipline. Nevertheless, the premises and limits of serial history must also be realized.

But the fact that serial history has limits—a subject that might be discussed on another occasion—does not excuse intellectual indolence or uncritical observance of tradition. If a number of historians today are breaking away from narrative in order to concentrate on problems, this is largely due to changes in the pieces of the puzzle used by historians to reconstruct the picture of the past. Because of serial history, they are now confronted with a new panorama of data and a new awareness of the premises of their profession. It is probable that we have not yet exhausted the possibilities offered by quantitative methods.

The Historian and His Sources

Quantitative history presupposes the existence and elaboration of long series of homogeneous and comparable data, and the first problem that presents itself in new terms is that of sources. In general, European archives were formed and classified in the nineteenth century, in accordance with procedures and criteria reflecting the ideological and methodological preoccupations of the period. This meant that national values predominated and that priority was given to politico-administrative sources. It also meant that documents were preserved and classified in accordance with the special and limited purpose of a particular inquiry: archives were built up to witness to events rather than to time. They were constituted and criticized in themselves and not as factors in a series; the point of reference was external. What was in question was the historical "fact" of the positivists, the naïve mind's illusory sheet anchor in what is supposed to be real, as distinct from mere testimony—a particular, discontinuous, elusive sequence within either an indefinite flux or a chronology preestablished in terms of centuries, reigns, and ministers. In short, archives are the memoirs of nations, just as the letters a person keeps show what an individual has chosen to remember.

But the data of quantitative history refer not to some external, vaguely outlined "fact" but to internal criteria of consistency. A fact is no longer an event selected because it marks a high spot in a history whose meaning has been predetermined, but a phenomenon chosen and sometimes constructed by reason of the recurrence that makes it comparable with others in terms of some unit of time. The whole conception of history based on archives is radically transformed at the very time when its technical possibilities are multiplied by the electronic processing of information. This simultaneous and interconnected revolution in methodology and technique enables us to think in terms of a new kind of archive preserved on perforated tapes. Such archives would not only be built up according to a deliberately planned system; their criteria would also be quite different from those of the nineteenth century. Documents and data exist no longer for themselves but in relation to the series that in each case precedes or follows: it is their comparative value that becomes objective, rather than their relation to some elusive "real" substance. Thus, incidentally, the old problem of the *critique* of historical documents moves on to different ground. "External" criticism is no longer based on credibility as derived from contemporaneous texts of another kind, but on consistency with a text of the same kind occurring elsewhere in the temporal series. "Internal" criticism is simplified inasmuch as many of the necessary cleaning-up operations can be entrusted to the memory of the computer.

Consistency is introduced at the outset, when the data are first sorted out, by a minimal formalization of each document that makes it possible to retrieve, over a long period and for each unit of time, the same data in the same logical order. From this point of view, the historian's use of computers is not only an enormous practical advance in the time it saves (especially when the sorting is done verbally by tape-recording, as in the Couturier method);[5] it is also a very useful theoretical discipline, in that the formalization of a documentary series that is to be programmed forces the historian from the very beginning to abandon epistemological naïveté, to construct the actual object of his research, to scrutinize his hypotheses, and to make the transition from implicit to explicit. The second critical process, this time an internal one, consists in testing the consistency of the data themselves in relation to those that come before and after—in other words, in eliminating errors. It thus emerges as a sort of consequence of the first process and can in fact be done largely by automation through programmed methods of verification.

Naturally enough, serial history in its manual form began by using those historical series that were easiest to handle, that is, economic, fiscal, and demographic documentation. The revolution introduced by the computer into the collection and processing of data has steadily multiplied the extent to which such numerical series can be explored. The technique can now be applied to any kind of historical data reducible to a language that can be programmed—not only tax rolls and market price lists, but also series of relatively homogeneous literary collections such as medieval chartularies or the cahiers of the states general of monarchical France.

Thus emerges the first task of serial history, the imperative of its development: the constitution of its subject matter. Classical historiography was constructed from archives worked on and processed according to the critical rules bequeathed to us by the Bendictines of the age of Enlightenment and the German historians of the nineteenth century. The serial history of today has to reconstruct its archives in terms of the dual methodological and technical revolution that has transformed the rules and procedures of history.

This being so, the question arises of the problematical nature of history's subject matter, the hazards of its survival, its partial destruction and sometimes total disappearance. I am not sure this question distinguishes history as much as is sometimes alleged from the other human sciences whose objects are more specifically defined. The characteristic feature of history is the extraordinary and almost unlimited elasticity of its sources. As the researcher's curiosity roves further and further, huge dormant areas of documentation are revealed. What nineteenth-century historian bothered with the parish registers that have now become, especially in England and France, one of the surest sources of our knowledge of preindustrial society?

Moreover, if the researcher invests them with a new significance, sources already exploited once can be used again for other purposes. Descriptions of price movements can lead to sociological or political analyses; Georges d'Avenel is followed by Ernest Labrousse. Demographic series studied from the point of view of, for example, the use of contraception by married couples can also throw light on problems of mental attitude or religious practice.[6] Signatures to legal documents can give statistics about the spread of literacy. Biographies systematically grouped in terms of common criteria, on the basis of a given working hypothesis, can build up documentary series imparting an entirely new life to one of the oldest kinds of historical narrative.

Hitherto, history has been almost exclusively based on the written traces of men's existence. No doubt live interrogation, which provides empirical sociology with so much of its data, will always be beyond the reach of the historian except for the period in which he lives. But how much unwritten evidence there is still to be cataloged and systematically described. The physical conditions of rural life, the divisions of the land, iconography sacred and profane, the layout of early towns, what the houses were like inside—one could go on forever listing the elements of civilization that, once cataloged and classified in detail, would make it possible to establish new chronological series and put at the historian's disposal the new subject matter that the conceptual enlargement of history demands. For it is not the sources that determine the approach, but the approach that determines the sources.

Of course, this type of argument must not be pressed too far. To the documentary demands of certain contemporary social sciences, history can answer only with irreparable gaps. It is difficult to see what substitutions or extrapolations could ever fill in the columns of an input-output table of the French economy in the time of Henry IV, not to mention periods even more distant. But all this means, really, is that, conceptually, history is not reducible to political economy. The problem of sources, for the historian, lies not so much in absolute lacunae as in series that are incomplete, and this not only because of the difficulties of inter- and extrapolation, but because of the chronological illusions they may lead to.

Take the classic example of popular revolts in France at the beginning of the seventeenth century. Because of the great abundance of administrative documents relating to the subject at that time, this period has become the best-known chronological sector in the history of peasant risings between the end of the Middle Ages and the French Revolution. The hazards of survival have even seen to it that a large part of these archives, the Fonds Séguier, ended up in Leningrad, enabling Soviet historians to advance a Marxist interpretation of France's *ancien régime*. The subsequent controversy has enhanced the interest of the documents still further. But another problem arises before that of interpretation, and this concerns the presupposition common to both interpretations here: that is, that there really was, during the period when the absolutist state was coming into being and there was probably a rapid increase in taxation, a special chronological concentration of that classic phenomenon in French history, the *jacquerie*. The existence of such a concentration could be definitely established only by the study of a long homogeneous series and comparison between this section of it and those before and after. But for several reasons such a series cannot be constructed. In the first place, there is no unique and homogeneous source for such revolts over a long period. Moreover, there is every reason to believe that the survival of such a collection as the Fonds Séguier in Leningrad, a collection especially rich in this respect but limited to the papers of one family and thus subject to the hazards and possible distortions of individuals' careers, falsifies our chronological perception of the subject. In any case, a *jacquerie* is a story without direct sources, a rising of illiterates. We can glimpse it today through the medium of administrative or legal archives, but by this very fact, as Charles Tilly has remarked, every revolt that escapes repression escapes history. The relative richness of our sources during a given period may be a sign of changes that are institutional (reinforcement of the apparatus of repression) or purely individual (special vigilance on the part of a particular official), rather than of any unusual frequency in the phenomenon itself. The difference between the number of peasant risings under Henry II and under Louis XIII may reflect first and foremost the progress of monarchical centralization.

Therefore, in handling serial sources the historian is forced to think carefully about the influence that the way they were constituted may have on their quantitative application. I think we may distinguish between such sources as follows, in order of increasing complexity in their conversion into series.

1. Structurally numerical sources, grouped together as such and used by the historian to answer questions directly connected with their original field of investigation; for example, French parish registers for the demographic historian, prefectoral inquiries into industrial or agricultural statistics in the nineteenth century for the economic historian, the data on American presidential elections for the specialist in sociopolitical history. These sources sometimes need standardizing (as when there is a variation in local units or a modification of the classifying criterion); also, when there are gaps in the documentary sequence, one may have to extrapolate certain elements. But in such cases both operations are carried out with the minimum of uncertainty.

2. Sources that are structurally numerical but used by the historian substitutively, to find the answers to questions completely outside their original field of investigation; for example, the analysis of sexual behavior on the basis of parish registers, the study of economic growth through price series, the socioprofessional evolution of a population through a series relating to taxes. Here the historian encounters a double difficulty. He has to define his questions all the more meticulously because the documentary material was not assembled with them in mind, and the question is constantly before him of the relevance of such material to such questions. He usually has to reorganize the material completely in order to make it usable and in so doing makes it more arbitrary and so more open to objection.

3. Sources that are not structually numerical but that the historian wants to use quantitatively, by a process involving two substitutions. In such cases he has to find in his sources a univocal significance in relation to the question he is asking. He also has to be able to reorganize them in series, that is, in comparable chronological units, and this demands an even more complex process of standardization than in the preceding paragraph. Data of this third type, which become more and more frequent the further one goes back into the past, can be subdivided into two classes: first, nonnumerical sources that are nevertheless serial and thus easily quantifiable, such as modern European marriage contracts drawn up by notaries, which, according to the historian's choice, can give evidence about endogamy, social mobility, income, literacy, and so on; second, the sources that are strictly qualitative, and therefore not serial, or at least particularly difficult to standardize and arrange in series, such as the administrative and legal series referred to above or iconographical survivals of forgotten faiths.

Whichever kind of source he is dealing with, the historian of today has to rid himself of any methodological naïveté and devote a good deal of thought to the way in which his knowledge is to be established. The computer gives him the leisure to do so by freeing him from what used to take up most of his time—the recording and card-indexing of data—but at the same time it demands from him rigorous preliminary work on the organization of series and their meaning in relation to the inquiry. Like all the social sciences, but perhaps with a slight time lag, history is passing from the implicit to the explicit. The encoding of data presupposes their definition; their definition implies a certain number of choices and hypotheses, made all the more consciously because they have to conform to the logic of a program. And so the mask finally falls away of that historical objectivity that was supposed to lie concealed in the facts and to reveal itself at the same time as them. Henceforward the historian is bound to be aware that he has constructed his own "facts" and that the objectivity of his research resides in the use of correct methods for elaborating and processing them and in their relevance to his hypotheses.

So serial history is not only, or even primarily, a transformation of the raw material of history; it is a revolution in the historiographical consciousness.

The Historian and His "Facts"

The historian, working systematically on chronological series of homogeneous data, is really transforming the specific object of his knowledge—time, or rather his conception and representation of it.

1. The so-called *histoire événementielle* is not to be defined by the preponderance it gives to political facts. Nor is it made up of a mere

narrative of certain selected "events" along the time axis. First and foremost, it is based on the idea that these events are unique and cannot be set out statistically and that the unique is the material par excellence of history. That is why this kind of history paradoxically deals at one and the same time in the short term and in a finalistic ideology. Since the event, a sudden irruption of the unique and the new into the concatenation of time, cannot be compared to any antecedent, the only way of integrating it into history is to give it a teleological meaning. And as history, especially since the nineteenth century, has developed primarily as a mode of interiorizing and conceptualizing the sense of progress, the "event" usually marks some stage in the advent of a political or philosophical ideal—republic, liberty, democracy, reason, and so forth. The historian's ideological consciousness can assume very subtle forms. It may group knowledge relating to a certain period around unifying schemas not directly linked to political options or values; for example, the spirit of an age, its Weltanschauung. But basically the same compensating mechanism is at work: in order to be intelligible, the event needs a general history apart from itself and independently determined. Hence the classic conception of historical time as a series of discontinuities described in the mode of continuity—that is, as narrative.

Serial history, on the other hand, describes continuities in the mode of discontinuity: it is a problem-oriented history instead of a narrative one. Because it has to distinguish between the levels of historical reality, it breaks down all previous conceptions of general history, calling in question the old postulate that all the elements of a society follow a homogeneous and identical evolution. The analysis of series has meaning only if it is done on a long-term basis, so as to show short or periodic variations within trends. The series reveals a time that is no longer the mysterious occasional spurt of the event but an evolutionary rhythm that is measurable, comparable, and doubly differential in that it can be examined within one series or as between two or more.

A wedge has thus been driven into the old carefully enclosed empire of classical historiography, and this by means of two distinct but connected operations. First, by the analytical breakdown of reality into different levels of description, serial history has opened history in general to concepts and methods imported from the more specifically constituted social sciences, such as political economy. This opening has probably been the operative factor in the recent historical revival. Second, by quantitatively analyzing the different evolutionary rhythms of the different levels of reality, it has at last turned into a scientifically measurable object the dimension of human activity that is history's raison d'être—time.

2. Now that the historian's hypothesis has shifted from the level of the philosophy of history to that of a series of data both particular and homogeneous, it usually reaps the advantage of becoming explicit and

formulable; but, at the same time, historical reality is broken down into fragments so distinct that history's classic claim to give a universal view of things is endangered. Must the claim be abandoned?

I would say it may probably be kept as a goal on the horizon but that, if history wants to go forward, it should abandon this ambition as a point of departure. Otherwise, it might fall once more into the teleological illusion described above. Present-day historiography can progress only insofar as it delimits its object, defines its hypotheses, and constitutes and describes its sources as carefully as possible. This does not mean it has to restrict itself to microscopic analysis of one chronological series. It can group several series together and put forward an interpretation of a system or subsystem. But today a comprehensive analysis of the "system of systems" is probably beyond its power.

We may take as examples demographic and economic history, the most advanced sectors now in France and probably elsewhere. It so happens that for the past twenty years or so the period that in France is called "modern"—that is, the period between the end of the Middle Ages and 1789—has been the subject of the largest number of studies in serial history, both demographic and economic. So it is the one we are least ignorant about from this point of view. French historiography,[7] starting out from reconstructed commodity price series, has compared these with the evolution in the number of people as shown in demographic series. Thus, there has gradually been built up the concept of an "economic ancien régime," based on the preponderance of a cereal production exposed to the vagaries of meteorology and on the periodic purging of the system by recurrent crises. These crises are indicated by sudden steep rises in price curves and the collapse of those indicating size of population.

But the price series, the meanings of which can be quite varied and ambiguous, have been supplemented by more specific indications concerning volume of production and by the use of series relating to the evolution of supply and demand, itself a factor in the evolution of prices. On the subject of production, though the tithe records concern the same percentage of the harvest every year and so tell us nothing absolute, they are valuable because of their relative comparability. For production we also have the protostatistical sources brought together by the administration of the ancien régime and possibly reorganized on a national scale. On the subject of demand, in addition to general demographic records, we can also turn to the reconstruction of the great masses of liquid money: the treasuries of communes and seigneuries, tithes, rents, profits, wages.

The combination of many demographic and economic series has recently enabled Emmanuel Le Roy Ladurie to make a wider analysis of the old agrarian economy.[8] His book gives a sampling of data covering the whole of the Languedoc, a long-term chronology (from the fifteenth to the eighteenth century), and a rich and varied quantitative documentation. Thanks to the cadastral surveys, the latter makes possible a study of rural property owning. The fifteenth to the eighteenth centuries tell the story of a very long agrarian cycle characterized at the same time by a general equilibrium and by a series of states of disequilibrium. The general equilibrium roughly corresponds to the Malthusian model—the model that Malthus discovered and made immortal at the very moment it ceased to be true, at the time of England's takeoff. The economy of early rural Languedoc was dominated in the long term by the relation between agricultural production and the number of men. Society's inability to raise agrarian productivity and the absence of an unlimited reserve of cultivable land, together with the famous "monetary famine" beloved of the price historians, presented structural obstacles to decisive growth. Though the monetary explanation loses its central role, it is integrated into an interpretation both more complex and more unified.

The structure of the old economy acted in the long term as an internal regulator. Nevertheless, within the system, the different variables—number of men, evolution of property, distribution of income from rents, fluctuations in productivity and prices, and so on—make it possible to distinguish separate periods in accordance with the position each variable occupies in relation to the whole, in terms of the annual rhythms and cycles of each particular curve. The complete structure thus chronologically comprises several types of combinations of series, that is, several different situations. And, in fact, it is through the careful examination of these successive situations, and the features they have in common or in which they differ, that the structure itself emerges. This, incidentally, may shed some light on the dispute over synchronic and diachronic, which often divides anthropologists and historians and which at present is at the heart of the evolution of the social sciences. The short- or medium-term periodic movement that constitutes an "event" on the economic plane does not necessarily clash with the theory of general equilibrium. On the contrary, an empirical description of such movements may make it possible to define the theoretical conditions of the equilibrium, whose elasticity indicates the limits within which it operates.

3. The Languedoc example quoted above is a special case in that the correlation there between the different demographic and economic series is made within a comparatively homogeneous region and a limited sphere of human activity (agrarian economy). The sectional application of serial history to different areas usually leads to the analysis of regional or national disequilibriums. And general, or would-be general, serial history, even when restricted to a limited geographical area, tends to lead to the analysis of temporal disequilibriums between the different evolutionary rhythms of each level of human activity.

The first point is now well known, thanks to the increasing number of studies on regional economic history. The specialist is used to the idea of there being measurable differences between different countries and between areas influenced in different degrees by the same situation or reacting in different ways to similar situations occurring at different times. There are countless examples, some of which raise problems that have become classic in European history. Such, for instance, are the recently revived question of the comparative growth of France and England in the eighteenth century;[9] the antithesis between the rise of agriculture in Catalonia in the eighteenth century and its decline in Castile, which has been shown by Pierre Vilar,[10] and the contrast in seventeenth-century France between the Beauvaisis revealed by Pierre Goubert,[11] poor and seriously stricken by the middle of the century by economic and demographic recession, and the Provence described by René Baehrel,[12] comparatively fortunate, or at least not affected by the downturn of expansion until much later. More generally, the date of this reversal, this plunge into the "tragedy" of the seventeenth century, varies considerably according to region and to the nature of the local economy. It becomes increasingly unlikely that there was only one economic *conjoncture* for both urban and rural economies.[13]

Thus, serial history opens out at once into the analysis of situations either differential or simply separated from one another in time (in other words, into what might be called the geography of serial history's chronology) and into the study of structural differences that may be indicated by chronological discrepancies. Cycles occurring at different times in the same or different regions, but fundamentally comparable internally, exhibit only geographical variations of the same theme. Contradictory developments, on the other hand, whether within the same geographical area (for example, between town and country) or between two different areas, may present the historian with differences in economic structure.

But history cannot be reduced just to the description and interpretation of economic activity. If it has a specific character distinguishing it from the other social sciences, this consists precisely in having no specific character and in claiming the right to explore time in all its dimensions. It is easy to see why economics has been the primary sphere of quantitative history—because of the necessarily measurable character of its indicators; by the preciseness of the concepts it makes available; and by its theoretical approach in terms of growth, the favorite image for historical change in Western thought today. But man is not merely an economic agent. The contemporary world offers too many examples of cultural resistance to the general adoption of growth on the Western model for the historian not to mistrust the Manchester-school approach to progress (or its Marxist inversion). He is bound to want to analyze the societies of the past in terms of politics and ideology as well as economics.

Even so, he does not and cannot revert to the old teleological history of progress, which extrapolates into cultural life the rhythms of economic development, whether this is supposed to occur by a kind of peaceful, natural adaptation or through the necessary medium of revolution. These ideological postulates of another age are useless now; it is not by clinging to them that the historian can preserve the universality of history. The only way to do so is by setting out to list and describe by the methods of serial history the other levels of human activity besides the objective processes of economics; by starting from the hypothesis that chronological rhythms, and the researcher's attitude to time, may vary according to the different levels of reality or to the particular part of the system being analyzed.

On the practical plane, almost everything still remains to be done. The historian must look for the possible indicators, quantifiable or not, of what may be called a "politico-ideological" society; he must establish its documentation and what constitutes representativity and comparability from one period to another. For all this, there are sources as abundant and series as homogeneous as in the field of economics or demography: they exist for popular literacy,[14] the sociology of education and religious sentiment,[15] the absorption of ideas by elites, the manifest or latent contents of political ideologies, and so on. On the theoretical plane, the main task, of course, is to build up gradually the components of a comprehensive history but first and above all to analyze the different rhythms of development at various levels of a historical complex. This is the only way to achieve two of the priorities of historiography today. These are:

1. To revise the traditional general periodizations, which are mainly an ideological inheritance from the nineteenth century and which presuppose precisely what is still to be demonstrated, that is, the roughly concomitant development of the most diverse components of a historical complex within a given period. Instead of beginning from a set of periodizations, it is probably more useful to start by examining the components concerned. It is probable, for example, that while the concept of the Renaissance is relevant to many of the indicators of cultural history, it is devoid of meaning in relation to the data for agricultural productivity.

2. Then to define, within a complex of data of different kinds, which levels are developing rapidly or changing decisely and which in the medium or long term are in a state of inertia. It is not clear, for example, that the dynamism of French history from, say, the great expansion of the eleventh and twelfth centuries is economic in character; it may be that education, culture (in the broad sense), and the state (the latter through the various public offices) played a more fundamental role here than the increase in the national product. Perhaps I shall be allowed to conclude on this bold hypothesis if I add that it will remain unverifiable until general history has sat at the feet of serial history.

3

From Narrative History to Problem-oriented History

History is the child of narrative. It is not defined by an object of study but by a type of discourse. To say that history studies time is just another way of saying that it arranges all of its objects of study in a temporal framework: to produce history is to tell a story.

A narrative, then, is an account of "what happened": to someone or something, to an individual, to a country, to an institution, to the people who lived before the moment of the narrative, and to the products of their activity. Narrative history brings to life the tangle of events that make up the fabric of an existence, the thread of a lifetime. Its model is naturally biography, because the latter describes something that man can view as the quintessential image of time: the clean-cut duration of a lifetime from birth to death and the identifiable dates of the major events that took place between its beginning and end. The choice of a chronological segment is inseparable here from the empirical nature of the "subject" of the story.

A history of France or of any other country basically follows the same logic: it can begin only with the country's origins, followed by an account of the stages of its growth and the adventure of the nation, illustrated by chronological divisions. The only difference is that such a history leaves the future open; however, the narration of the past—the description of the nation's patrimony—is also intended to give some indication of this future and thus to freeze time.

First published as "De l'histoire-récit à l'histoire-problème," *Diogène*, no. 89 (January–March 1975), 113–31. The present text is a substantially revised version of the translation by Susanna Contini, "From Narrative History to History as a Problem," *Diogenes* (English-language edition of the same journal), no. 89, 106–23. Reproduced by permission of the International Council for Philosophy and Humanistic Studies.

Historical narrative, therefore, must follow a division of time inherent in the raw datum of experience. Essentially, it records the recollections of individuals and communities. It keeps alive what they have chosen of their past, or of the past in general, without taking apart or reconstructing the objects within that past. In other words, it deals with moments, not objects. Even when it discusses or tries to discuss, "civilizations," this kind of history cannot avoid the rule. When Voltaire compares the age of Pericles or of Augustus to that of Louis XIV, the concrete incarnations of these successive periods of greatness are proof enough that he is comparing periods, not concepts.

No doubt that is one of the reasons why narrative history has been primarily, although not exclusively, biographical or political. Within the collective experience of humanity, what witnesses have found most fascinating and what lends itself best to narrative is the saga of great men and of states. Little wonder, then, that history, first in Greek and Roman antiquity, then in modern Europe, developed into chronicles of power and war. The divisions of the narrative tended to underline the misfortunes and victories of mankind—the great moments of history.

The events in such a history consist precisely of moments. Their ephemeral nature is what characterizes them above all else. Events are the unique points in time in which something happens that cannot be assimilated to what has come before it or what will come after it. That "something"—the historical fact promoted to the rank of event—can never be compared, strictly speaking, to a preceding or subsequent fact, since it is its empirically unique nature that determines its importance. The battle of Waterloo and Stalin's death occurred only once; they cannot be likened to any other battle or any other death, and they have transformed world history.

And yet an event, if considered in isolation, is unintelligible. It is like a pebble picked up on a beach—meaningless. For it to acquire significance, it must be integrated into a pattern of other events, in relation to which it will become meaningful. That is the function of narrative. Waterloo can acquire significance in the context of a history of Napoleon's life, the First Empire, or nineteenth-century Franco-British rivalry. Stalin's death becomes important in the context of the history of twentieth-century Russia, international communism, or any other imaginable chronological constellation of facts. Thus, in narrative history, an event, even though it is by definition unique and not comparable, derives its significance from its position on the axis of the narrative, that is, on the axis of time.

Since an event is not an object intellectually created to be studied, it cannot acquire significance by means of an analysis of its relationship to other comparable or identical objects within a system. As it belongs to the realm of experience, of what has happened, it cannot be organized or even simply named except in relation to the external and general significance of the historical period of which it is one of the features. All narrative history is a succession of origin events, or, if one prefers, a history of events. And all history of events is teleological history: only the "ending" of the history makes it possible to choose and understand the events that compose it.

That ending can differ considerably from one historian to another and according to their chosen topics. For a long time endings were enveloped in religious apologetics or moral edification, which is no longer fashionable. The same cannot be said for the glorification of national power or national consciousness, which is still one of narrative history's most important functions, after having been, no doubt, its initial mainspring. All peoples need an account of their origins and a memorial to their times of greatness that can serve at the same time as guarantees of their future. Just as the ability to write brings power, so our archives are the memories or symbols of power. Not even transnational history, generally referred to as history of civilizations, can escape the inevitable obligation to assign a prior meaning to time. In our secular world, narrative history, apart from emphasizing national consciousness, more often than not embodies the other great collective experience of mankind since the eighteenth century: the feeling of progress. Progress assumes different names and aspects; it sometimes refers to the development of material goods, but more often to the problematic advent of reason, democracy, freedom, or equality. Confronted with the uncertainties that such a list brings to mind, we must recognize at the same time the full ambiguity of the deeds and values that characterize the contemporary world and the impossibility of not summoning them up as implicit foundations of a particular history. The narrator must, after all, place his own world at the end of the period he is describing.

In short, narrative history reconstructs an experience along a temporal axis. This reconstruction requires some conceptualization, but the latter is never made explicit. It is concealed within the temporal finality that structures and gives meaning to all narrative.

Yet the recent evolution of historiography seems to me to be characterized by the possibly definitive decline of narrative history. While it still flourishes in productions destined for mass consumption, it is being increasingly abandoned by professionals in the field. In my view, there has been a sometimes unconscious shift from narrative history to problem-oriented history, at the cost of the following changes:

1. The historian has surrendered before the immense indeterminacy of the object of his knowledge: time. He no longer claims to describe past events, not even important events, whether in the history of mankind or in that of a part of mankind. He is aware that he is choosing what to examine of the past and that in the process he is raising certain problems relative to a particular period. In other words, he constructs his own object of study by defining not only the period—the complex of events—but also the problems that are raised by that period and by those events

and need to be solved. He therefore cannot avoid a minimal amount of explicit conceptual elaboration: a good question or a well-formulated problem is becoming more important—and is still less common!—than the skill or patience needed to bring to light an unknown but marginal fact.

2. As he breaks away from narrative, the historian also breaks away from his traditional source material: the unique event. If, instead of describing a unique, fleeting, incomparable experience, he seeks to explain a problem, he needs historical facts less vague than those to be found in human memory. He must conceptualize the objects of his inquiry, integrating them into a network of meanings and thus making them nearly identical, or at least comparable within a given period of time. Quantitative history provides the easiest—though not the only—means for this kind of intellectual task.

3. In defining his object of study, the historian must also "invent" his sources, for, in their original form, historical sources are usually unsuited to his inquiry. Naturally, he may come across a set of records that not only will be usable in themselves but will lead him to new or more valuable ideas and theories. History does provide such blessings, but the opposite is more often the case. Yet the historian who is trying to formulate and solve a problem must find pertinent sources and organize them into comparable and interchangeable units in order to be able to describe and interpret the phenomenon he is studying on the basis of a certain number of conceptual hypotheses.

4. The fourth change in the historian's profession derives from the above. The conclusions of a study are becoming ever more closely bound up with the verification procedures upon which they are based and with the intellectual constraints imposed by those procedures. Narration's particular kind of logic—*post hoc, ergo propter hoc*—is no better suited to the new type of history than the equally traditional method of generalizing from the singular. Here the phantom of mathematics takes form. Quantitative analysis and statistical procedures, provided they are suited to the problem and sensibly applied, are among the most rigorous methods for "testing" data.

Before proceeding further, one ought to look at the possible reasons for these changes in historiography. They are probably related to factors external to the discipline itself, such as the general crisis affecting the idea of progress—a crisis that is challenging not only the concept of an evolution dominated by the nineteenth- and twentieth-century European model but the very notion of an all-embracing and linear history. However, the changes in historiography are also related to internal, intellectual factors such as the widespread influence of Marxist theory on the social sciences; the brilliant development of the social sciences dealing with limited and defined objects (economics, demography, anthropology); or the impact of computer technology, which makes it possible to carry out hitherto unimaginable calculations, provided the problems to be solved and the hypotheses to be tested have been rigorously formulated beforehand. Instead of discussing this vast problem at length, I should like to confine myself here to examining a few of the consequences of these changes on our profession and our historical knowledge.

The archives that serve as the basis for historiography are no longer collections of documents but data constructed in series. If historians are to work on conceptually clear objects of inquiry while remaining faithful to the specific character of their discipline—the study of the evolution of phenomena over time—they will need pertinent data (seldom available ready-made) that can be compared over a relatively long period. Historical facts no longer consist of the explosion of important events that shatter the silence of time but of chosen and constructed phenomena whose regularity makes them easier to identify and examine by means of a chronological sequence of identical data comparable within given time intervals. Such data no longer exist independently but as parts of a system that also includes earlier and later data. An examination of their internal consistency (by establishing their comparability within the system to which they belong) is a better test of their validity than an external assessment of their probability (by comparing them to other sources for the same period).

The intellectual process for defining the data is thus twofold. First, one must determine their significance in order to apply them correctly. For example, the major pre-nineteenth-century sources available to the historian interested in literacy are signature counts. But what significance does the ability to sign one's name have in relation to the usual criteria for measuring literacy: the ability to read and write? To take another example, the historian who studies crises—particularly the different kinds of economic crises of modern times—makes considerable use of price series. However, he must first answer the question, What does a price mean? For what movements or levels of economic life does it serve as an indicator? Once the significance of the data has been established, the historian must arrange them in serial form, make them comparable to one another, decide what time unit they concern, what statistical methods are appropriate to use, and so on. All these procedures are more than mere techniques; they require methodological choices at each step of the process.

One can raise a preliminary objection to this view of historical research, namely, that the historian's sources often contain gaps, are fragmentary, or simply do not exist, depending on the hazards of survival. In any case, the difference between history and other social sciences is not one of principle but of situation. There are undoubtedly problems, particularly relating to the more remote periods of the past, for which source material has disappeared. However, it must be stressed that such material was not developed once and for all in the public archives in the

bstract, define, and measure than most products of human activity.
'urthermore, most European states have been creating and preserving
lata in these fields for many centuries.

Nevertheless, even within these "advanced" sectors of history, the
ituation is not as simple as one might deduce from the ranking above,
vhich is based on the academic classification of our disciplines. History,
>y virtue of its open-endedness, always tends to overflow the boundaries
>f the sectional advances in these specialized fields. The question that
irises is whether, and to what extent, by borrowing some of those
idvances and integrating them into its own practices, history has estab-
ished a knowledge of the past that could qualify as scientific.

The best way to tackle this very old problem is to study some examples, in
ncreasing order of complexity and uncertainty. I shall borrow them from
the field of historical demography, one of the most studied areas of
French historiography in the past twenty years. It is also one of the fields
that provide the greatest opportunities for formulating problems mathe-
matically. This special position is due to the particular nature of the
discipline and to the sacrifices it has made for the sake of defining its
object clearly. Demography is entirely predicated on the principle of
abstract equality, according to which Napoleon's birth has exactly the
same importance as that of any one of his future soldiers. Having adopted
a hypothesis that sacrifices all the particular aspects in the life of individuals—in other words, the essence of their history—it transforms historical individuals into interchangeable and measurable units, by means
of unvarying and comparable events: birth, marriage, and death.
Stripped of the layers of meaning that each civilization has in its own way
given them, these events are reduced to their most fundamental characteristic: the stark fact that they took place.

I am deliberately describing them all as "events," since I do not see, *a
priori*, what distinguishes one particular historical fact from another—for
example, a birth, however anonymous, from a battle, however famous.
In this respect, the current distinction between structural and narrative
history is irrelevant to historical data themselves: there is no such thing as
a difference between facts that are events and facts that are not events.
History is a permanent event. However, some classes of events can be
more easily conceptualized than others, that is, integrated into an intelligible system—as in the case of demographic events.

The raw and particularly simple data on births, marriages, and deaths
have become the object of a specific discipline: demography. They can
thus form the basis for a certain number of calculations and analyses,
which themselves are prefabricated objects of historical research. In
other words, they are objects or concepts elaborated by a discipline other
than history—in this case, demography, for which history, however, also
supplied primary material in the form of birth, marriage, and death

nineteenth century. On the contrary, the range of poter
almost infinite, and quite often their existence is revealed b
the historian's curiosity or by the problem he sets himse
example in this field is parish registers, which lay dormant f
French towns until the advent of historical demography in t
the discovery of their immense value. Moreover, a his
unable to find immediately pertinent data to answer the q
set himself can, in most cases, get around the obstacle by
ever data are available in such a way as to be able to use th

From this point of view, there is always the possibility (
tional" use of historical data. In a recent article,[1] I distin
kinds of serial data. The first kind is the simplest and
manipulate. It consists of the available quantitative data (
way that provides a direct answer to the question at hand
riages, and deaths listed in parish registers can be used in tl
demographic historian. The classic demographic rates can
from such data by means of minimal and standardized tr
technique used to reconstruct families). The historian of
tudes can use the same technique with election results. The
of source also includes quantitative data. These, however,
substitutional way to answer questions quite different fr
which the data had been originally assembled. An example
rian's use of the calculation of time intervals between births
spread of contraception and the patterns of sexual behavio
The specialist of economic growth also uses this method whe
price series. In these cases the main problem involved in
data is their relevance and the possibility of reorganizing the
to the problem examined. Finally, there is a third type of sc
requires even more careful handling: nonnumerical data th
rian nevertheless wants to treat quantitatively. In order to dc
not only establish the relevance and value of the data, as in tl
case, but also rearrange them systematically into conceptual
nologically comparable units. Two examples are the use (
marriage contracts to study endogamy, social mobility, fortu
acy; and the use of wills to analyze attitudes toward death.

Thus, if one wanted to classify the most recent advances ir
rary historiography according to their mathematical rigor,
have to take into account both the type of conceptualizatior
the problems studied and the quality of the sources used to
problems. For example, it is clear that historical demograpl
nomic history are, on those two counts and at least for th
modern period, the best-equipped fields. First, they can draw (
developed in specific disciplines, such as demography and p(
nomics—concepts that can be readily imported into history at
only minor adaptations; second, the objects of those studies a

records. To the limited degree that it works with reliable or verified data—though that "limited" degree is actually a considerable one, since the verification of numerical sources is no easy task—historical demography produces results comparable to those of demography itself: the set of relationships that allow one to measure the elements of a given population and the way in which they are evolving.

These elements, measured year by year, provide results that are unambiguous and certain—unlike their interpretation. Let us examine a century-long decline in the general mortality rate, for example in eighteenth-century France. In order to determine when the definitive drop in the mortality rate occurred, the rate must be calculated by age cohort, particularly to obtain the infant or juvenile mortality rate. Let us assume that there was a spectacular increase in the survival of newborns (from birth to one year). Such a phenomenon could be explained by any number of hypotheses, from an increase in the number of midwives throughout the countryside to a transformation of the nursing system, not to mention a sudden victory of medicine over a children's disease. How can one choose without testing each of these theories as well as several others?

Admittedly, one can proceed otherwise, starting not from a single variable but from the set of variables of a demographic system. Such an approach is more properly demographic than historical. It uses or constructs a reproduction model for a population that is considered stable, with the time factor provisionally set aside. Let us suppose that all the "blanks" in the model have been filled; one is left with the question that the historian must examine: How did the system evolve? Admittedly, by studying what happened or even simulating what might have happened if a given variable of the system had been missing or had been quite different, one can diagnose at what point the system changed—for example, how it expanded or regressed. However, the analysis of these strategic variables refers back, as in the previous case, to elements that are exogenous to the system and at the same time influence it: in other words, to hypotheses that lie outside the demographic field. These hypotheses involve not only concepts that have not yet been organized into a scientific discipline, but also indicators most of which remain to be invented.

Let us examine the problem of age at marriage, the main variable of demographic control in preindustrial Europe between the twelfth and nineteenth centuries. Although I cannot go into the question in detail here, the postponement of marriages seems to have been the basic endogenous factor that contributed to stabilizing the size of populations. External agents (such as famine, epidemics, and wars) also took their toll. However, their impact diminished during the period. The regulatory mechanism worked in two ways. In the long term, the gradual rise in the age at marriage, up to its classic "plateau" of twenty-five or twenty-six (for women), eliminated ten years of potential fertility and, independently of any recourse to contraception, reduced the number of children per "complete" family. In the short term, the considerable variation in mortality rates conditioned by particular historical situations was made up for by variations in the age at marriage. When a population experienced a demographic crisis (whatever the cause), marriages were put off and the age at marriage increased; but, once the crisis was over, marriages in younger age cohorts were added to delayed marriages. Thus, the temporary lowering of the age at marriage brought the population back to its precrisis size. It is therefore easy to devise and apply a demographic model enabling one, on the basis of variations in the age at marriage (all other factors being equal), to study population changes: in what conditions a population grows, and in what conditions it diminishes.

With this type of simulation one can isolate the role of a variable within a system, and even in the evolution of that system, but one cannot identify the causes at work. In other words, simulation allows one to describe, not to interpret, and still less to explain. As soon as one goes beyond it to ask which factors are capable of influencing a cultural behavior pattern such as age at marriage, one is confronted with any number of possible interpretations. In the long run, the rise in the age at marriage in seventeenth- and eighteenth-century Europe, up to twenty-five or twenty-six years, can be interpreted as an optimal adjustment of population density to available resources: witness Chaunu and Le Roy Ladurie rediscovering Malthus! In the rich, "developed" Europe of the period—a belt of high agricultural productivity extending from the London basin to northern Italy, passing through the Low Countries, open-field France, and the Rhine valley—the population density apparently stabilized at about forty inhabitants per square kilometer. But this statement, even if approximately true—which is not certain, since data on productivity and agrarian output for that period are difficult to handle—tells us nothing about the modes in which the adjustment of the age at marriage was experienced. To the extent that it was not accompanied by an increase in births of illegitimate children, did it mean a greater acceptance, during a longer adolescence, of the rules of sexual austerity? Or should one speak primarily of a socioeconomic adaptation—children waiting to get married and settle down until the preceding generation had turned over the family landholding to them?

It might be argued that one should begin by the easiest phenomena to interpret and that short-term variations in the age at marriage involve fewer uncertainties. Why, in a period of crisis, does a population postpone marriages? The answer is relatively clear: because of doubts about the future, which stem from the sight of the present. Historical awareness is determined by events in the short term; optimism or pessimism about the future is conditioned by the immediate situation. When a historian encounters reactions of this kind, which are conscious responses to specific events, it is fairly easy for him to reconstruct their progression by means of the traces they left behind; he is, after all, merely exposing the motives expressed by the historical agents themselves. Unfortunately, such redundancy does not lead very far. A crisis will delay marriages, prosperity will increase marriages, and the next crisis will cause a new drop—that much is clear. But one is left with the basic problem of understanding how, over a period of successive upward or downward adjustments, the age at marriage increased to such an extent that it slowed "natural" demographic growth in preindustrial Europe.

At this point a descriptive discovery such as the one above necessarily leads the historian to venture explanatory hypotheses that are fragile in two ways: first, because they were by nature out of reach of the people whose behavior he is studying, so that there are no directly usable written traces; second, because he will have to abandon a purely demographic analysis, and with it the factual and conceptual precision it requires. He will have to understand the mechanism by which the probability of collective behavior indicated in the analysis of data concerning age at marriage is embodied in the multiplicity of individual behavior.

Let us return to the two hypotheses mentioned earlier. As they are of a different nature, they are not incompatible. Their common feature is that the behavior patterns they describe would have made it easier for the people who lived in that period to harmonize their expectations with their actual opportunities. This process is one of the conditions of social life; it is the somewhat melancholy mechanism by which men predict and construct the most probable future for themselves. But the first hypothesis is of a psychological nature, the second of an economic nature. The first indicates a morality, the second a strategy. The first cannot be measured; the second can be, for the historian can establish a relationship between the demand represented by younger generations and the supply of farm estates or job vacancies generated by deaths in the ranks of older generations. If he does not have enough data at hand to work on a macroeconomic scale, he can at least tackle the problem through a series of monographs on family estates, which will enable him to see how generations succeeded one another on a single estate. This is an objective process that can lead, at least theoretically, to a clear conclusion. In contrast, the notion of the spread of a puritanical superego (on a sexual level) throughout seventeenth- and eighteenth-century Europe is a hypothesis that can lead only to ambiguous answers. It is easy enough to identify the factors that make it plausible: the Protestant ethic, the Counter-Reformation, or Norbert Elias's "civilization."[2] However, it cannot actually be verified or invalidated.

Why is that so? To begin with, the superego is an indemonstrable psychological concept. It is used to interpret behavior that could be interpreted in any number of other ways. For example, Weber's notion of individual self-control can be replaced by that of a reinforcement of external constraints imposed, in this case, by church and clergy. But there are no appropriate data—nor will there ever be—that can provide answers to hypotheses concerning the psychology of historical agents. The agents are dead, and very few of them, even among the fraction who wrote about themselves, bothered with the part of their being that, before Freud, they had neither the means nor even the curiosity to explore. Thus the historian of what is now referred to by the very vague term of *mentalités* must either base his investigation on scattered or ambiguous texts or find an indicator not of his subjects' psychology but of their behavior in order to deduce the psychological roots of this behavior.

In the first approach, the historian encounters the difficulty of assessing the significance of a both subjective and exceptional piece of evidence. Admittedly, all historical data (except the vestiges of men's material existence) are to a certain extent subjective. Even the registration of a birth or the accounts of an estate were, at a certain moment in time, put down on paper by an individual. But the constraints that govern the recording of an event differ considerably according to the phenomenon observed, the nature of the observation, and that of the observer; according to whether the event is normal and repetitive—that is, comparable to an earlier one—or extraordinary and therefore recorded precisely because it lies outside the norm of habit; according to whether one is dealing with a systematic observation governed by certain rules or with a chance testimony, a census, or an impression; finally, according to whether the relationship linking the observer to the object observed is or is not in the nature of knowledge.

With regard to my example, the historical evidence that can tell us about the psychological roots of behavior dating back several centuries is naturally of a literary nature. I use *literary* in the broad sense to include certain texts that posterity has not elevated to that rank: the handful of unpublished private diaries and of old manuscripts that can cast some light on the subject. But such evidence is scarce, impossible to use in systematic temporal series, and limited to a very narrow social environment. In order to bypass its random character, one will have to consult a different kind of documentation, this time of a normative type: manuals of good manners or specialized treatises on religious morality, such as penitentials. However, texts of this kind present the same ambiguity as government legislation. They prescribe an optimal conduct, but one can never determine to what extent it was accepted, obeyed, or internalized. Is the reiteration of rules of conduct over a long period a sign of their having penetrated into society or, rather, of the resistance they have provoked? The second hypothesis is as probable as, if not more probable than, the first. In this case, the normative text is more interesting for its "preamble" and whatever observations of actual behavior it may contain than for what it forbids or orders. But it serves primarily as evidence about the institutional environment in which it was produced, the state or the church.

That is why the historian of *mentalités*, who is trying to investigate the more common forms of behavior, cannot be content with the traditional literature of historical testimony, which is inevitably subjective, untypical, and ambiguous. He must examine behavior itself, that is, the objective indications of behavior. The hypothesis discussed above concerning a "Weberian" superego extending its control over the souls of seventeenth- and eighteenth-century Europe can be tested for many of the signs of a given behavior; for instance, the number of illegitimate births, the number of premarital conceptions, or the use of contraception. A decrease in, or a low incidence of, illegitimate births or premarital conceptions in a society characterized by a delayed age at marriage is indeed a sign of a long period of accepted chastity. However, for these indications to be meaningful, one would have to prove that the use of contraceptives in Europe during that period was not widespread. How can that be proved? Not by means of literary evidence—which is very rare in this realm par excellence of the unexpressed—but by measuring the spacing of children's births during the married life of couples. The statistical technique for measuring the behavior of this variable is well known. For a population of married women old enough to give birth, a ratio is established between the number of births and mothers' ages. If the fertility of couples decreases very rapidly after the first children and in relation to the mothers' ages, then the use of contraception can be deduced. Otherwise, one finds a succession of births, slowed down only by the nursing period for the latest-born child and the biological decrease in fertility as the potential mother grows older.

The conditions for this kind of experiment seem clear and simple. For example, graphs unambiguously prove that eighteenth-century Canadians were ignorant of contraception, while French dukes and peers of the same period practiced it. However, between these two extremes, the conclusions remain ambiguous. Precisely because the spacing of births during the life of a couple is also influenced by factors other than contraception, it is impossible to assess the specific role of contraception. An increased interval between births, if it is not abrupt, could be due to a change in nursing methods and a later weaning of the latest-born child. That is why categorical conclusions are difficult to reach, as witnessed by the discussions concerning this problem that have been going on since the mid-1960s.

To summarize the methodological aspects of the discussion, it seems to me that we are faced with insuperable difficulties on three levels. First, the concept of the superego as a sort of austere collective moral conscience governing individual behavior cannot be actually proven. Second, the subjective historical data and firsthand accounts are scarce, unrepresentative, and ambiguous. Third, the objective indicators are equally ambiguous. The hypothesis put forward is more in the realm of plausibility than in the realm of truth.

It would therefore be incorrect to believe that the passage from narrative history to problem-oriented history (or, if one prefers, to conceptualized history) suffices to enter *ipso facto* into the scientific domain of the demonstrable. From the epistemological point of view, conceptualized history is probably superior to narrative history because it replaces an understanding of the past based on the future by explicitly formulated explanatory factors. It also unearths and constructs historical facts intended to support the proposed explanation; thus, while carving out specific entities within the realm of history, conceptual historiography expands it considerably. Perhaps Max Weber chose the wrong path with his *Protestant Ethic*, but what a landmark it was! A conceptual discovery can be judged by the areas of research it opens up and by the traces it leaves behind.

Nevertheless, we still have not arrived at a scientific history. First, there are some questions and concepts that do not lead to clear, unambiguous answers. Second, there are some questions that in principle lead to clear-cut answers yet cannot be solved, either because of a lack of data or because of the nature of the data: the indicators may be ambiguous or impossible to subject to rigorous analytical techniques.

As we have seen—and one could give many more examples—these techniques are suitable to handling data that are clear (or have been made clear), available in chronological series, and capable of answering unambiguous questions generally formulated by the most advanced contemporary social sciences, such as demography and economics. To that extent, even history can lead to definite conclusions. For example, one can calculate the major variables in demographic behavior in western Europe since the seventeenth century. One can measure the increase in prices in eighteenth-century France or the takeoff of agrarian productivity in the nineteenth century. In other words, this kind of history, with its potential for extrapolating into the past a number of very specific questions usually formulated in other disciplines, is both highly profitable and very limited. It enables one to arrive at clear-cut conclusions and to obtain a good description of the particular phenomenon chosen for study.

However, the interpretation of these findings does not offer the same degree of certainty as the findings themselves. In problem-oriented history, interpretation is basically the analysis of the objective and subjective mechanisms by which a probable pattern of collective behavior—the very one revealed by data analysis—is embodied in individual behavior in a given period; interpretation also studies the transformation of these mechanisms. Thus, it goes beyond the level of described data in order to relate it to other levels of historical reality. It generally requires additional data that belong to another field and are neither necessarily available nor necessarily clear. Interpretation more often than not involves hypotheses that are not proven or not provable.

The problem posed by recent historiographical developments, particularly by the use of strict demonstration procedures, is not to determine whether history itself can become a science. Considering the indeterminacy of history's object of study, the answer to that question is undoubtedly negative. The problem is to determine the limits within which those procedures can be of use in a basically unscientific discipline. Although these limits are obvious, one should not deduce that history should revert to its former function as fortune-teller. Instead, the unreasonable ambitions of "total history" should be lowered and, in our exploration of the past, we should make the utmost use of the sectorial discoveries and methods of certain disciplines and of the conceptual hypotheses emerging from the great contemporary potpourri called the human sciences. The cost of this change is the breakup of history into many histories and the renunciation by historians of their role as social authorities. However, the epistemological gains may be worth such sacrifices. History will probably always oscillate between the art of narrative, conceptual understanding, and the rigor of proofs; but, if its proofs are more solid and its concepts more explicit, knowledge will stand to gain and narrative will have nothing to lose.

4

History and Ethnology

History and ethnology developed during the eighteenth century as both related and contradictory disciplines, whose relationship to each other was determined by two primal categories: time and space. Both disciplines were the instruments for describing the human universe; but history drew up an inventory of time, and ethnology an inventory of space. Thus, in the old bibliographical classifications of Baconian Europe, accounts of travels to faraway places come under the heading of "history" books; they represent a subcategory devoted to the description of foreign, and especially of exotic, countries. By providing the reader with an account of the mores of remote peoples, travelers were not only trying to popularize the picturesque aspect of otherness; they were also bringing back an image of the past situated in contemporary space. The savage state represented the infancy of civilized man. Thus, two readings of the same vision of man were brought together.

No doubt *brought together* is somewhat of an exaggeration, for the advent of the nation-state already stood between ethnology and history and played a decisive role in the emergence of history as a distinct form of knowledge. This process began in the seventeenth century with the secularization of time. The old apocalyptic chronology of the four monarchies was gradually abandoned. According to Daniel's prophecy, the four monarchies were supposed to succeed one another in an order of increasing degeneracy: the Roman Empire constituted an interminable ending

Originally delivered as a paper at an international seminar, "The Historian: Between Ethnology and Futurology," sponsored by the International Association for Cultural Freedom, the Giovanni Agnelli Foundation, and the Giorgio Cini Foundation (Venice, 2–8 April 1971). First published, in a revised form, as "L'Histoire et 'l'homme sauvage,'" in *Méthodologie de l'Histoire et des sciences humaines*; *Mélanges en l'honneur de Fernand Braudel* (Toulouse: Privat, 1973), 2:227–33.

to human history—a final phase that would perpetuate itself through the Holy Empire of medieval Christendom. The Old Testament legend succumbed first to humanist pressure, then to Protestant pressure, and finally to the rise of the nation-state. Humanist philosophers were too fascinated by antiquity to develop a historicist vision of the past. But humanism provided at least the intellectual groundwork for such a vision be inventing scholarship and distinguishing between "fables" and "true" history. In any event, the religious schism clouded the meaning of Scripture; it shifted the locus of the narrative of origins at the same time as it transformed eschatology. But the Protestant rejection of the Apocalypse and the church was a sign that the activity of deciphering the past could now focus on other objects—on the state, the notion of irreversibility, and the obsession with origins. History became secularized even as it turned to the study of nations. This phenomenon is clear in the French case, with Jean Bodin, La Popelinière, and the Chancelier Pasquier. Gallican history emerged as a reaction by French jurists against "Italian" humanism, which they suspected of embodying a double form of Roman imperialism: the imperialism of antiquity and that of the papacy. The French jurists were concerned with justifying royal power, particularly in the struggle against the extremism of the Ligues.[1]

Thus, between the sixteenth century and the Enlightenment, history—at least profane history, which was carefully distinguished from sacred history—was above all the history of nations, that is, of the states and peoples of Europe. Even Voltaire, who tried to adopt a broader perspective, used Louis XIV's state—the apogee of civilization—as the implicit point of reference for his universal history. The history of human progress is signposted by the nation-state. Fledgling anthropology was reserved for undeveloped peoples.

Accordingly, by the eighteenth century, when the description of "primitive" peoples was becoming a fairly systematic discipline, a single hierarchy of values ranked the study of time above travel literature. The national societies explored by the historian became the ideal model for the future of the groups described by the traveler.

The nineteenth century probably deepened the rift between the two disciplines by abolishing their complementary character. The imaginary temporal and spatial link between two universal phases—infant man and adult man, primitive society and civilized society—was destroyed by the notion that these were elusive and distinctive phenomena. The nation-state ceased to embody the collective progress of mankind and became the locus par excellence of antagonism and differentiation. Moreover, history was no longer dependent on a frame of reference that charted the stages of human development. It was now torn by an endlessly shifting balance of power and by conflicting justifications. The ideology of progress, which somewhat hastily extrapolated the extraordinary rhythms of economic change into the whole scope of human activity, transformed time into a sort of unending current, urged on by nationalistic rivalries. Progress was both an instrument and a stake of power politics, a breeding ground for confrontation between national histories. History dealt henceforth only with a handful of nations: those that produced, those that changed—in a word, those that mattered. The remainder of the inhabited world was thus abandoned as a historical nonentity, and travel lost its bibliographical and scientific status. Ethnology became a form of residual knowledge, defined negatively in relation to the history of western Europe and North America. Not only the attitudes of the great liberal economists and historians but also the extraordinary Europocentrism of Marx point to the fact that ethnology had turned into a subordinate and secondary discipline, an ill-defined by-product of European expansion, a combination of blindness and guilty conscience. Since the historian had turned an exception into a model, ethnology was left to reign over a mirror image of history, over a marginal yet vast realm: the henceforth distinct realm of the the unwritten as against the written, of immobility as against change, of the primitive as against progress.

Although this dichotomy is still with us, it is becoming increasingly difficult to live with, because it has been severly undermined by two series of contemporary events. The first series is external to the two disciplines, while the second relates to changes in the social sciences.

1. Many major events in contemporary history have called in question the idea of progress. Neither the Hitlerian apocalypse nor the transformation of the Russian revolution into a bureaucratic and ideological terror is easy to fit into a march of mankind toward the advent of rationality or freedom. The modern world, while increasing at an unprecedented rate man's mastery over nature, presents an ever-greater number of insoluble problems, historical impasses, and manifestations of social violence. Technical and economic progress is making its way amid political irrationality and planetary disorder, laying down a new challenge to the notion of total history, a notion according to which all levels of history evolve at the same rhythm along a single time scale. In this respect, two phenomena have probably played a fundamental role in breaking down the traditional barrier between ethnology and history: human space has become homogeneous even as time has ceased to be so.

The inhabited world has not only been explored, inventoried, and bounded; during the last few decades, particularly in the course of decolonization, it has been the locus of the irresistible spread of the European political model, that is, of the appropriation of *nationalism*. Thus, the entire inhabited world has been raised, like Europe, to the rank of national history. The countries belonging to what, on the basis of economic criteria, we call the Third World are all feverishly engaged in glorifying their origins, in which they are seeking a definition of their very identity, for these countries have ceased to conceive their differences in terms of space and have taken to enhancing them in terms of history.

Even the West, when it tries to counteract the intellectual spread of its most radical ideas, has no clear-cut frontiers left other than those provided by economic history, such as Rostow's model of takeoff. Perhaps this is an underhand manner of continuing to put oneself forward as an example by constructing a linear schema in which "postindustrial" society constitutes a horizon for mankind. At least it is a way of bringing mankind back into the realm of history.

Space has thus become historicized, but at the cost of a fragmentation of time. As history gradually absorbs the whole of mankind and becomes less Europocentric, it faces the ethnological challenge represented by the multiplicity of societies and cultures. This multiplicity undermines the notion of homogeneous time. Not only do societies evolve at different rhythms, but even within a given society the different levels of reality that compose it are not governed by an all-embracing and homogeneous temporality. "Change" has become a concept measurable in economic terms, in its various aspects; but it also reveals resistance to change. "Takeoff," "modernization," and the universalization of material progress and economic growth are thought of as the keys to the significance of contemporary history; but they clash with heritage, tradition, and the entire range of sociocultural patterns of inertia. Thus, by extending its field to the human world, history has discovered that it is also nonhistory: change reveals immobility. The great nineteenth-century historical tradition, inspired by both Manchester and Marx and predicated upon universal progress through economic development, is consequently being undermined by the crises of the contemporary world and by the application of its hypotheses to non-European areas. It is therefore no surprise that, while desperately trying to preserve its hegemony as a standard-bearer of "modernization," history is returning to ethnology as if it were aware of its own failures.

2. A second and probably less visible series of changes in the relations between history and ethnology is inherent in history itself and in its development as a discipline over the last thirty or forty years. I am referring to what is called in France, using a vague and moreover negative term, the replacement of a "history of events" (*histoire événementielle*) by a "non-event-oriented history" (*histoire non événementielle*).

Let us try to define these terms by abstracting them from the context of a pointless dispute. The history of "events" seems to me to be both a way of describing the past and a way of selecting events. Such history, which is informed by the desire to reconstruct "what happened" and to recount it in the narrative mode, chooses its material in accordance with these aims; in other words, the material—the celebrated events—is selected and arranged along the time axis in such a way as to give substance to the narrative as it unfolds. Change thereby becomes inherent in events, and the chain of events is supposed to give a meaning to the succession of changes. That is why history of this kind is marked, in contradictory fashion, both by the short term and by teleology. Since an event, a sudden irruption of the unique and the new into the concatenation of time, cannot be compared with any antecedent, the only way to integrate it into history is to endow it with a teleological significance. And as history has developed as a mode of internalizing and conceptualizing the feeling of progress, "events" in most cases constitute stages in an advent; for instance, of the Republic, of freedom, of democracy, or of reason. However patiently one tries, in accordance with the strictest rules of scholarship, to reconstruct an "event"—the quintessential form of historical "fact"—that event derives its significance only from a total history external to the event and independently defined. The temporal structure of this type of history consists of a series of discontinuities described in the mode of continuity: such is the classic substance of *narrative*.

History of the *non événementielle* kind rejects narrative—at least this literary type of narrative—as its primary concern is to define problems. Borrowing from the contemporary social sciences such as demography, geography, and sociology, it has renewed and redefined the scope of historical inquiry. First, it isolates the various levels of historical reality in order to focus on a small number of them, or on a single one, and describe them (or it) as systematically as possible, that is, separately. That is why it constructs historical "facts" that differ on two counts from those of "event-oriented" history: in most cases, they lie outside the classic field of major political changes, and they are defined no longer by their uniqueness but by the possibility of their being compared with earlier and later phenomena. A "fact" is no longer an event chosen because it coincides with a high point in a history whose "meaning" has been determined beforehand, but a phenomenon chosen and constructed on the basis of its recurrent character, which makes it comparable to other phenomena of the same kind over a given period. Documents and "facts" no longer exist independently but in relation to the series that precedes and follows them; it is their relative value that becomes objective and not their relation to an elusive "true" substance. By the same token, new topics and methods have been developed. Historical corpora are by definition so diverse that the historian can assemble them according to his preferences and skills and deal with them from an economic, demographic, sociological, ethnological, or linguistic point of view.

But there is no such thing as an innocent methodology. By his new approach, the historian has changed the nature of the problems traditionally dealt with by his discipline. The unique and noncomparable phenomenon cannot be handled by such a methodology, and the specialist of intellectual biography will not find it satisfactory, either. Nor will the historian of antiquity, who lacks and probably always will lack the serial data indispensable for a systematic quantitative treatment. Moreover, history that relies on serial data concentrates on a particular type of source, of problem, and above all of temporality. The sources must be, if not numerical, at least reducible to homogeneous and comparable units, a requirement that both restricts and broadens their scope, for while the "hapax" is no longer usable, an entire portion of the vast "reserve" of unwritten material that the historian has until now used so sparingly can be arranged in series; when handled in this way, even iconographic data such as photographic land surveys can represent more valuable historical material than the sempiternal literature of sempiternal witnesses. It is also natural that this type of serial source should serve as the basis for investigations or hypotheses that are more economic or ethnological in character than strictly political; such sources imply the reduction of individuals to equal units as economic or sociocultural agents. Incidentally, this explains how, by virtue of a misunderstanding, an encounter took place between the most "scientific-minded" type of history—the one with the fewest value judgments—and the most "democratic-minded" type of history, which aimed at rehabilitating the anonymous "little men," dwarfed by the great heroes of politics and yet indispensable to their existence.

Finally, the serial history described here is a history of long-term phenomena. Fernand Braudel, in his books and in an article that is now a classic, has demonstrated this better than anyone. Because it essentially describes repetitive and regular phenomena, serial history is of value only if it brings to light examples of historical evolution over a sufficiently long period for these repetitive and regular phenomena to change and fluctuate. Did the growth of the rural economy in the first two-thirds of the sixteenth century—a growth that can be charted by means of various indicators—betoken a decisive takeoff or merely a recovery from the terrible crisis of the period from 1350 to 1450? Only an analysis in the longer term, encompassing earlier and later periods, can provide an answer. Thus, by choosing identical indicators over a long period of time, historians can isolate phenomena according to their duration—short-term crises, longer recessions, cycles, and trends—and integrate them into a general interpretation. But this mode of selection puts greater emphasis on the factors that help to preserve a given system than on those responsible for qualitative changes. By adopting this approach, historians have rediscovered the long periods of economic stability and the social and cultural inertia that for a long time characterized societies studied by ethnologists. Historians, too, as Lévi-Strauss would say, have their "cold societies."

One could thus imagine a double-column inventory of what history owes to ethnology. The first column would list the changes in historical methodology, such as the systematic recourse to unwritten sources, the increasing use—as far as written sources are concerned—of statistical or prestatistical documents, or textual analysis of the "structural" kind (whether the model is provided, for example, by linguistics, psychoanalysis, or content analysis). The second column would list the new objects of history, developed in the wake of the momentous shift in historiographical curiosity described above: the substitution of anonymous men for great men, of nondevelopment for a model based on change alone, of the rudimentary forms of cultural life for the testimony provided by "great" literature, and so on. This list would, in fact, cover a considerable portion of contemporary historiography in France and elsewhere.

Actually, the dividing line between history and ethnology was never determined by epistemological criteria. It was based far more on the external conditions that shaped the development of these two fields and, later, on the conventional academic separation established between them. Today this boundary is disappearing like so many others and giving way to a configuration no easier to define than the disciplines of yesterday.

PART TWO

HISTORY IN SEVENTEENTH- AND EIGHTEENTH-CENTURY EUROPEAN CULTURE

5

The Birth of History in France

A Dual Tradition

The absence of history from the educational system, and thus its non-existence as a school discipline, in early modern Europe is due to the fact that it simply did not exist as a discipline at all. It was torn between two intellectual activities that ignored or even scorned each other: erudition and philosophy. The first was in the hands of the *antiquarii*, also known in old French texts as *antiquaires*, that is, specialists of things ancient and, naturally, of antiquity—men who confined themselves to a narrow, esoteric, and recondite area of knowledge and who were proficient in dead languages. This tradition gave birth, not to history in the nineteenth-century sense of the word, but to the notion of *historical facts* as the building blocks of history.

This old tradition, whose roots go back to the Renaissance, was not originally a critical tradition.[1] It did not deal with Scripture but with Greco-Roman antiquity, in which sixteenth-century Europe passionately sought a new identity. However, the antiquarians' interest in antiquity did not stem from a desire to rewrite the history of that period. The ancients had already written it, and who could improve on Thucydides, Livy, or Tacitus? The task of the "moderns" was simply to comment on ancient historians, to work in their margins. That was the meaning of *belles-lettres*. Alternatively, when they wanted to escape this mirror game they would write Roman (or Greek) "antiquities," not "histories." But these "antiquities" were themselves doubly marginal with respect to the royal way of history: they described nonliterary sources, and they ex-humed coins, stones, inscriptions, and portions of monuments—the ran-

First published as "La Naissance de l'histoire," *H-Histoire*, no. 1 (March 1979), 11–41.

dom remains of a fatal shipwreck. These vestiges provided subject matter for commentaries and studies that did not really qualify as history, since they dealt with customs, institutions, and art, whereas history consisted of the chronological analysis of political systems and governments.

Thus, the antiquarian was not a historian. But the second half of the seventeenth century witnessed the downfall of the notion of a universal history within which every particular history had been written for all eternity. At the same time, the antiquarian turned into a historical critic. The area covered by his "art" (the *ars antiquaria*) spread beyond classical antiquity to take in, for example, biblical antiquity. Above all, the antiquarian freed himself from the tutelage imposed on him by the historiography of antiquity, that is, by the model of the ancients. The antiquarian had not yet become a historian. But since the past had not been fixed for all eternity by Livy and Plutarch, he was now free to write *about* history.

In other words, the materials he unearthed and classified were no longer marginal. No less than literary sources, they now constituted the ingredients of history. And literary sources themselves were now subjected to scholarly criticism. The purpose of philology was no longer only to reconstruct them but to discuss their value. Coins, inscriptions, and fragments of arches and columns now served to corroborate the information contained in literary sources. Internal and external documentary criticism was born when the various types of sources were all integrated into the search for truth.

Thus, the second half of the seventeenth century did not mark the invention of history but rather a reworking of historical materials that led to a shift in the apparently immutable boundaries of the field. Bossuet was still able to write a *Universal History*, but he had difficulty making room in sacred chronology for the profane history of ancient peoples, a history whose limits had been pushed back by the discoveries of "antiquarians." Even biblical history itself, an intangible block standing motionless in the unending flow of time, was reexamined by modern chronologists. The Oratorian Richard Simon published in 1678 an *Histoire critique du Vieux Testament* that caused him to be expelled from the order.

Yet it was the church itself that set an example for scholarly research, even if it was not always able to control its development. Not only was the church caught up in the spirit of the age, but, in its struggle against Protestantism, it found itself obliged to undertake a systematic description of and to glorify the entire Christian tradition, particularly the first six centuries that constitute Christian antiquity and provide the basic interpretation of Scripture. Ecclesiastical scholarship focused primarily on the church fathers. It flourished at Port-Royal and above all in the work of Tillemont. Its central impulse came from the Benedictines of

Saint-Maur, who, more than a century before the advent of German historiography, laid down the canons of historical criticism.

The antiquarian's art thus culminated, at the end of the century, in the methodical undertaking of the monks of Saint-Germain-des-Prés, who set out to distinguish between truth, likelihood, and falsehood. In conformity with Mabillon's motto, "True piety loves nothing but what is grounded in truth," modern historical research was born of the application of the procedures of critical reasoning to the exploration of Christian antiquity. Consequently, pagan antiquity, which from this point of view was inseparable from Christian antiquity—because both were part of the same chronology—could henceforth be dealt with in the same manner.

But if the canonical division between sacred and profane history was thus becoming increasingly blurred, history itself remained distinct from historical research. It constituted a literary genre, one of whose rules was precisely to exclude all reference to a critical apparatus and to "proofs." Antiquarians published chronologies, "annals," "collections," and "memoirs." In contrast, history was a continuous narrative unencumbered by original documents. It was characterized not only by a moral lesson but by a regular and ornate form. While losing its rigidity of content, history preserved all its aesthetic and moral rules. It remained a writer's pursuit.

When Tillemont set out to publish what were to be his *Mémoires pour servir à l'histoire ecclésiastique*, he hesitated over the title to give to his work. In settling for *Mémoires*, he was guided by the fact that his expository method was that of the antiquarians: "It seems to be the most reliable and the most solid. It is like producing evidence in court: the reader need only judge for himself. But this method leads to lengthy exposition and frequent repetition. . . . It is rather the material of history than history itself." The same author, however, accepted the word *history* for the profane part of his work when, three years earlier, in 1640, he had published his *Histoire des empereurs*, under a title that is worth quoting in full: *Histoire des empereurs et des autres princes qui ont régné durant les six premiers siècles de l'Eglise, des persécutions qu'ils ont faites aux chrétiens, de leurs guerres contre les juifs, des écrivains profanes et des personnes les plus illustres de leur temps, justifiée par les citations des auteurs originaux, avec des notes pour éclaircir les principales difficultés de l'histoire* ("History of the emperors and other princes who reigned during the first six centuries of the Church, of the persecutions they conducted against the Christians, of their wars against the Jews, of the most noteworthy profane writers and individuals of their time, illustrated by quotations from original authors, with notes to explain the main difficulties in this history.") Thus, Tillemont was one of the first to combine history and erudition. But how apologetic he was in his foreword! Let us quote him once more in order to appreciate the tyranny of "genres" in the age of classicism: "For a long time the author wondered whether this work should not be entitled Mémoires, which is certainly the title that would suit it best, both because of the manner of its composition and because of the purpose for which it was compiled. The title of Annales has also been envisaged, because in fact the work follows as much as possible the sequence of periods and is even divided almost always according to year; moreover, a plain and unadorned style, such as will be found here, seems more suited to annals than to history. Nevertheless, the title of History was finally adopted as it is the one requiring the least justification, because it is the simplest, and because all narrative is in a sense a History. But the readers are asked to consider the title only in that sense of the word, and not to expect to find an ordered history here. The author never contemplated writing a history of that sort, and he would like to make it clear that he has always regarded such an undertaking as exceedingly difficult in itself and far beyond the scope of whatever talent and knowledge he may possess."[2]

The Impossibility of Teaching History in the Eighteenth Century

One might, however, infer from this excessive display of modesty that the gap between historians and antiquarians was narrowing. On the contrary, eighteenth-century French culture widened the gap by creating a vogue for "philosophical history," which drew away from antiquarian research, an activity it disdained.

Actually, it was the very advances in this research that backfired on it in the late seventeenth and early eighteenth centuries. Antiquarian research had criticized some traditional historical beliefs, for instance by debunking miracles, reducing the number of Christian martyrs, and revamping biblical chronology. As a consequence, rationalist individualism systematically challenged the very notion of historical fact. Bayle devoted an entire dictionary, from A to Z, to the destruction of the historical foundations of religious beliefs, but all he left to the rational individual was uncertainties. Fontenelle bluntly observed that it was impossible to write truthful history: "We have been so accustomed during our childhood to Greek fables that when we have become capable of reasoning, it does not occur to us to find them as astonishing as they really are. But if we shake off our habitual ways, we cannot help being frightened at the realization that the entire ancient history of a people is merely a heap of fantasies, dreams, and absurdities. Is it possible that all this could have been passed off as true? Why would it have been presented to us as false? How could men have been fond of blatant and ridiculous falsehoods, and why should they have stopped being fond of them?"[3]

But, above all, this historical defeatism was rooted in an obsession with modernity, that is, with the present. European elites had lived since the Renaissance with a cultural identity borrowed from antiquity, a period whose artists and authors represented unsurpassable models and whose literary genres constituted the authoritative canons of beauty and truth. Now Europe was raising the question of its cultural autonomy: the academic quarrel between "ancients" and "moderns" in France at the end of Louis XIV's reign ultimately centered on the notion that classical culture was not a past but a present and that history was not a new beginning but a progression. Consequently, history, too, began to structure itself around the perception of the present, thus making antiquarian curiosity obsolete.

Moreover, the *philosophe* historians incorporated nonliterary sources and "evidence" into their new history. Having shaken off the tyranny of political history as bequeathed by antiquity, and having abandoned the sequence of emperors, they turned to art, religion, and institutions. They were writing the history of "civilization," but in order to understand their own time. Montesquieu sought in Roman history the secrets of political stability or decadence. Voltaire compared the age of Pericles to that of Louis XIV. The eighteenth century turned to the history of the world's peoples not only to witness the spectacle of religions and customs in all their diversity but to find the key to a temporal flow emancipated from Holy Writ and now indefinitely open to progress.

In addition to the progress of civilization, philosophical history had another conceptual pole: the origins of the nation. Eighteenth-century Frenchmen searched their national history for the source of their "contract" with the king and of the nobility's legitimacy. The Germanic invasions were thought to have introduced an elective monarchy and an aristocracy of warriors into Roman Gaul. The dispute about Clovis is thus an expression, in its way, of French society's dramatic search for a self-representation. But Boulainvilliers's history—like Voltaire's—no longer had anything to do with "antiquarian" history. Eighteenth-century France did not have a Gibbon. An insurmountable barrier still separated French *philosophes* and *érudits*: the former were glorified, and the latter relegated to the ghetto of the Académie des Inscriptions. The tradition of critical research and the tradition of the great philosophical and literary narrative were to be reconciled only by the historians of the Restoration.

One need only glance at the bibliographies of the period to realize to what extent history represented a heterogeneous and fast-changing genre. Library classifications, for example, grouped under the heading of "history" an extremely vast area of knowledge. History encompassed everything that had to do with knowledge concerning human societies. As an epistemological heading, history expanded, thanks to all the scholarly or even simply descriptive contributions of European culture since the Renaissance. History presided over the whole, with its canonical division between sacred and profane, the cultural preponderance of antiquity, and the model of a moral narrative in the manner of Livy. But history subsumed not only the techniques and achievements of the *ars antiquaria*—chronology, paleography, archaeology, and so on—but also the inventory of space, that is the activity that preceded geography and was known as "travel." For the non-European societies, scattered across the surface of the earth and gradually described by travelers, also testified, in their own way, to history: the "savage" was man in his infancy. Space and time thus provided complementary perspectives for the developing study of evolution. And it is on the basis of this epistemological connivance that, in the later reforms of the French educational system, geography and history moved forward in stride and as if intertwined.

But in the eighteenth century, the ill-defined state of history as a field is sufficient proof of the extent to which the study of the past was still far from being a school discipline: if history was not taught, it is because it was not yet a *teachable* subject.

The two types of intellectual activity that composed history were too foreign to each other to constitute a homogenous discipline. Erudition was both too uncertain and too scholarly an art to be taught in the classroom. It was indulged in by gentlemen and by a narrow circle of specialists who discussed their discoveries far from even a cultivated public. How could one teach numismatics in primary or secondary school? As for philosophical history, it attracted many readers but represented too modern a genre, in every sense of the word *modern*, for it not to be, educationally speaking, a dangerous product. In the eighteenth century, it was still too recent a creation for its legitimacy to be recognized. Thus, it did not command the respect normally associated with subjects taught at school. Above all, philosophical history ran counter to the classical tradition, in which history was no more than an annex to belles-lettres, in other words, a fine story modeled on Livy or Tacitus. The Jesuit secondary schools (*collèges*) remained faithful to their late sixteenth-century charter, in which the model of antiquity constituted the cultural identity of Europe. Students learned history—apart from sacred history—only in the margins of Cicero.

There had been and still were exceptions to this rule. The elementary schools of Port-Royal turned history into a core discipline to which part of the daily schedule had to be devoted. But these schools were ephemeral—they were closed when Louis XIV persecuted the "Messieurs" of Port-Royal—and strictly elitist, since they took in only the children of the Jansenist upper bourgeoisie. The Port-Royal example, therefore, illustrates the exceptional rather than the regular presence of history in school curricula. The Oratorians, too, later regretted not having made enough room for history in their schools. And the military academies founded by the monarchy in the third quarter of the century, with a view to training professional soldiers, tried to include history in their curriculum. But, until the expulsion of the Jesuits from the kingdom, in 1762, it was their *collèges* that set the pace for secondary education. Although they remained conservative in their curricula—introducing Cartesianism, for example, only in the eighteenth century—it would be wrong to think that they were particularly "reactionary." The universities of the same period—especially the University of Paris—were still far more insensitive to the shifting boundaries of intellectual fields. At the end of the eighteenth century, the professors of rhetoric of the faculty of liberal arts in Paris found nothing to change in their traditional blend: a smattering of ancient history tacked onto sacrosanct Latin discourse.

The fact remains that the expulsion of the Jesuits signaled the beginning of a vast intellectual debate over the nation's educational system. The celebrated Jesuit schools, bereft of their teachers, were placed under the control of the Parlement of Paris, whose task was now to fill them with new professors and new ideas. Hence a flowering of educational schemes, the most famous being the one put forward by La Chalotais. In a report of 1768, the president, Rolland d'Erceville, tried to make a synthesis of these schemes. This was, in a sense, a Jansenist revenge, for the eighteenth-century *parlementaires* had never really accepted the condemnation of Jansenism by Rome, and they relished the political aspects of what had been a rare example of resistance to Louis XIV's absolute authority. Thus, it was also a revenge for history, which had been held in such high esteem at Port-Royal. But, for the *parlementaires*, the most detestable feature of the Society of Jesus was the fact that it was a foreign order, alien to the kingdom and totally in the hands of the pope. The *parlementaires* wanted a "national" educational system controlled by the state. This upper nobility of the robe, a passionately Gallican group, expressed in its own manner and in its own cultural terms the strong upsurge of a feeling of national identity rooted in a very distant past. These men wanted school curricula to include not history in general so much as the history of France, for it was this history that guaranteed the original contract between the nation and its king and was the depository of an imprescriptible tradition.

Actually, if one looks at the French secondary schools revamped at the end of the *ancien régime*, one finds that history had made occasional inroads into the curricula. At the celebrated Collège Louis-le-Grand on the Montagne Sainte-Geneviève in Paris, a compulsory half hour of history on "days off, Sundays, and holidays" was introduced in 1769. A number of historical topics were set as subject matter for "exercises," the public contests held on days off with the aim of testing the pupils' expository and reasoning skills. In 1772, an exercise at the *collège* of Arras was conducted in order to demonstrate that "the study of the history of France in particular can alone impress in the lawyer's mind the true principles of our government." In Lille, French history was included in the curriculum itself, beginning with the class of *troisième*, during which Gaul, the Germanic invasions, and the first two dynasties (Merovingians and Capetians) were studied, and continuing in *seconde* up to the sixteenth century.[3]

The best example, because it is perhaps the earliest, is that of the famous Collège de Juilly, the showcase of Oratorian education, attended by children of the kingdom's elite. As old rivals of the Jesuits, the Oratorians prided themselves on offering their "clientele" a more "modern" curriculum. By the end of the seventeenth century, an Oratorian was recommending that "heraldry, geography, some chronology, and history be taught with particular care, following the custom of this academy." These disciplines thus already enjoyed, in his view, an independent educational status. They were, moreover, emancipated from the exclusive relationship to antiquity. At Juilly, both the history of France and the geography of America were taught. The history syllabus was unusual for its time in that it was arranged in a chronological sequence culminating, so to speak, in the history of France. The syllabus progressed from sacred history to the history of France via Greco-Roman antiquity, from the junior to the senior grades. But it remained somewhat marginal in that it did not form part of the formal curricula of the grades themselves. History was taught in the *chambres*—that is, in the rooms where the various groups of students lived and studied (Juilly was a boarding school)—and outside official class hours. It also provided material for the public exercises, which, although held on rest days (Thursdays and Saturdays), were compulsory. However, they seem to have been very popular with the students during the eighteenth century.[4]

These examples—to which one could add a few more—show that, by the end of the *ancien régime*, the teaching of history had made some progress in the secondary-school system and was gradually ridding itself of the dual tyranny of sacred history and classical antiquity. But the change was slow and advances were modest. As a teaching subject, history remained in most cases a stowaway aboard official curricula. It was a source for dissertation topics; it was not a self-sufficient discipline. Moreover, history was absent from elementary schools, even from the most advanced of the period, the establishments run by the Frères des Ecoles Chrétiennes. At the other end of the educational system, even the highest teaching institution in Paris, the Collège de France (which practically specialized in innovation, since it was created in the sixteenth century to counterbalance the Sorbonne's inertia), had no chair in specialized history in the eighteenth century. The only innovation was a course entitled "History and Morals," which survived into the nineteenth century under the sixth subject-category of the program, "Moral and Political Sciences," alongside "Natural and Human Law," "History of Comparative Legislation," and "Political Economy." History at the Collège was thus freed from the yoke of ancient languages (which formed the second category of professorial chairs), but it remained philosophical history, divorced from erudition. The indirect and, so to speak, negative contribution of the Collège de France to the emergence of history as a distinct discipline resides instead in the definition of specific cultural areas. These were gradually detached from the common trunk of history because of their marginal position with respect to the European experience. An example of this is sinology.

The turmoil generated by discussions about educational reform and modernization contrasts with the slowness of pedagogic development. This shows that it would be dangerous to confuse the history of ideas on education with the history of education itself. The two histories do not advance at the same rhythm, nor do they follow the same chronology. It is true that they are not confronted with the same forms of inertia.

The Revolution: Break and Continuity

The preceding observation is particularly applicable to the period of the French Revolution. The Revolution enacted laws concerning national education far more than it lastingly transformed teaching institutions. That is easily explained both by the brevity of the revolutionary period and by the illusion—which was precisely typical of the period—that people and things were being completely transformed. In actual fact, secondary schools emerged nearly unchanged from the apparently universal collapse of the old institutions, and nothing resembles a *collège* of the *ancien régime* more than a *lycée* under the Empire. In particular, history remained a simple appendage to classical studies and to the teaching of Latin.

Yet it is worth casting an eye over revolutionary legislation in order to measure the development of attitudes and the aspirations of the new political elites. The Constituent Assembly waited until the last days of its existence (September 1791) to hear Talleyrand's huge report on education. The bishop worked into his report the ideas of the *parlementaires* of the end of the *ancien régime*. While preserving the structure of the classical secondary-school curriculum (grammar, humanities, rhetoric, logic), Talleyrand introduced history and geography. Condorcet, who took over from Talleyrand under the Legislative Assembly, was a direct heir to the men of the Enlightenment; he had a wide-ranging and penetrating mind; a mathematician and philosopher, he was obsessed by the division of knowledge into compartmentalized disciplines and the need to recognize the unity of human learning. The scheme he devised was guided by a totally different ambition, which was to reorganize the entire education system along the lines of a "philosophical" classification of knowledge, so as to place it at the forefront of intellectual innovation. From the very first year of secondary school, pupils were to study "the elements of all human knowledge," divided into four categories: (1) mathematical and physical sciences, (2) moral and political sciences,

(3) applied sciences (for example, comparative anatomy, midwifery, the art of warfare, and the principles of arts and crafts), and (4) literature and the fine arts (a category in which one finds—reduced to a very modest share—the humanities as taught in the old *collèges*). Thus, history was included under "moral and political sciences," which also comprised the analysis of sensations and ideas, morals, natural law, social science, political economy, public law, and legislation. History in this context was precisely what the eighteenth century had christened "philosophical history": a meditation on the evolution of peoples and civilizations, a study of the past that was indispensable for analyzing humanity's progress along the path of reason. It was accompanied by chronology and geography, two complementary tools for deciphering time and space.

From Condorcet, one can turn to Lakanal,[5] for the debates devoted to education during the Montagnard period were characterized by an obsession with the purely political aspect of the issue; moreover, they contribute nothing to our discussion. It was after 9 Thermidor that revolutionary political society reclaimed its rights, temporarily relinquished in favor of the Committee of Public Safety. The education act of Frimaire, year III (December 1794), presented by Lakanal, established a two-tier educational system, with primary schools for all pupils and *écoles centrales* to train the nation's elite. The *écoles centrales*, combining secondary and higher education, did away with the track system formerly used from the *sixième* to the *classe de philosophie*. The new schools introduced a set of parallel courses aimed at covering the entire span of human knowledge; pupils were free to move from one course to another. Each school comprised fourteen teaching chairs, representing the encyclopedia of knowledge imagined by Condorcet and revised by the Idéologues. One of these chairs was devoted to the "philosophical history of peoples." In the following years, the Thermidoreans, anxious to reestablish a higher-education system in the form of special schools each concentrating on a particular discipline, planned to set up a number of such schools devoted to history. Legislation, political economy, philosophy, criticism, and antiquities would also be taught there.

Thus, the Revolution, in the phases that preceded and followed the Robespierrist dictatorship, engineered the triumph of a concept of history developed by the Encyclopedists and systematized by Condillac and Condorcet. The ultimate aim was to turn history into a special testing ground for demonstrating the *meaning* of social life. Philosophical history was a secularized "discourse on universal history." The question arises as to why the revolutionary bourgeoisie, which committed itself with such energy and patriotic fervor to waging war on Europe, did not display greater fondness for the version of national history that had been developed by *parlementaires* and jurists and was very much alive at the end of the *ancien régime*. In my view, there are several explanations for this indifference. Some are of an epistemological nature: for Condorcet and for the Idéologues alike, history belonged to the realm of scientific reasoning, and the glorification of national identity did not square with a scientistic vision of the universe—a vision within which that identity constituted a sort of irreducible residue. The other explanation involves political ideology: the French revolutionaries did not regard their action as taking place within a narrow, national framework. In its struggle for liberty and equality, Jacobin and Thermidorean France constituted the vanguard of mankind itself. Even when its armies ransomed conquered countries, revolutionary France never abandoned the concept of universal democracy. Last, and perhaps not least, what was revolutionary France to do with the nation's interminable past, which belonged to the monarchy and to feudalism? The Revolution was associated only very briefly with the notion of a restoration of a golden age in the relationship between the monarchy and the nation. All the ideas about a popular contract, original rights, and a primitive constitution vanished as soon as the Revolution displayed its true colors. It was the Revolution itself that marked the starting point, established the original contract and constitution, and founded a new national history by wresting the French from their past. Since the Revolution cut French history in half, why did it have to recount that damnable part that belonged to its enemies? But the other part was still too short to constitute a past; it was only the celebration of origins.

Thus, for the French revolutionaries, history was not a genealogy, as it was to be for nationalist ideologies of the nineteenth century. Instead, it provided a universal reference chart against which the excellence and supreme rationality of the French experience could be measured. The French Revolution saw history as a laboratory for social science and as the agent responsible for organizing the materials for that science—not as a form of knowledge in its own right, built around the chronological study of the nation's annals. Consequently, the French Revolution bequeathed no enduring doctrine of history to posterity. The notion of "social science" lived on in the work of Saint-Simon and Auguste Comte but as a marginal, illegitimate, and suspect current in our culture. The encyclopedist concept was already obsolescent under the Directory, and it never passed into the educational system. As for national history—the prime area for the emergence of history as a discipline and for its legitimation as a school subject—the French Revolution turned it into a battlefield for an intellectual civil war. The French during the nineteenth century were a people who could cherish only one-half of their history: who could not love the Revolution without despising the *ancien régime*, nor love the *ancien régime* without despising the Revolution.

History Becomes a Discipline

Thus, history became an all the more burning educational problem and issue as its development—both epistemological and institutional—led it to focus on the genealogy of the nation. History therefore became less easy to teach to the French people as a whole. The First Empire was able to ignore the question and to reinstate the study of history as a mere annex to the study of Latin. This bracketing amply demonstrated the imperial regime's capacity and determination to forget, but it was not a durable solution. Even as the Restoration, personified by Louis XVIII and the *émigrés*, was bringing back to power the tangible forces of the past, history was consecrated as a full-fledged discipline both in France's school system and in its intellectual life. Guizot, nearly half a century after Gibbon (whom he translated into French), blended the antiquarian and the historical traditions. At the same time, he reconciled national history with the history of civilization. "Philosophy" had been the tribunal of the eighteenth century. History became the magisterium of the nineteenth century.

But precisely what history was it? The Restoration, the first regime to introduce a systematically chronological history syllabus, sought to give pride of place to its own genealogy, that is, to the monarchical tradition. A decree of 1814 drafted by Royer-Collard, and thus informed by constitutionalist and moderate attitudes, divided the history syllabus into chronological sections for each grade in the *lycées* and *collèges*: sacred history in *sixième*, Egypt and Greece in *cinquième*, Rome (up to the Empire) in *quatrième*, Augustus to Charlemagne in *troisième*, the Middle Ages in *seconde*, and the modern period and French history in *première*. It was an attempt to combine the old curriculum based on sacred history and antiquity with the requirements of a laicized chronology, more modern and more "national" in spirit. The new syllabus sought to emphasize France's dual tradition—Catholic and dynastic—and to train young minds in the ways of the monarchy as embodied in the Charte. History is never innocent; it was less so than ever in nineteenth-century French culture. But it is significant that the constitutional monarchy should have regarded history as an indispensable medium for diffusing its own values.

Indeed, history had difficulty surviving the hardening of the regime in 1820 and the fall of the Constitutionnels. Even if the cutoff in the syllabus was set in 1789, an explanation still had to be divised for the *terminus ad quem* represented by the French Revolution, which dominated the entire sweep of history that preceded it. But among the concepts that could have been used for such an explanation, the ultraroyalist Right was incapable of making intellectual room for progress, democracy, or the nation. All it could suggest was divine right and Providence—a return to Bossuet. Thus, when the ultraroyalists came to power, history became a suspect discipline, to be strictly watched over by the authorities, not only in the secondary-school system but also in the faculties of liberal arts, where lectures became political and social events. While history vegetated in secondary schools, Guizot restored the Sorbonne's prestige by attacking Villèle's government in the name of the third estate, the old monarchy, and the progress of civilization. Guizot's dismissal in 1822 represented a new blow struck against the established upper bourgeoisie of the third estate, against the Protestant tradition, against freedom, and against the values of 1789. The fall of Villèle in 1827 was thus the crowning point of history's revenge. Shortly after, history was completely emancipated from the tutelage of the humanities by the appointment of specialized teachers (soon to be recruited by a newly created *agrégation* in history) in the secondary schools.

But it was in 1830, with the July Monarchy, that the teaching of history entered a decisive period. No doubt one of the reasons was that two of the greatest French historians of the nineteenth century, Guizot and Michelet, were at the peak of their careers: Guizot was in the government (a fact that was to impair—unjustifiably—his reputation as historian); Michelet was a member of the intellectual and republican opposition at the Collége de France. But the main reason was that the Orleanist regime, a product of the Parisian insurrection, had no other legitimacy than the one it could derive *both* from the *ancien régime* and from the French Revolution. Unlike Bonapartism, Orleanism could not conceal the flimsiness of its legal foundations behind a legend or behind the notion of a prior consent given to despotism. It therefore had to take up a position at the exact point where the two liberal traditions of French national history—that of the nobility and that of the bourgeoisie—still stood side by side and strengthened each other. In other words, Orleanism had to set up 1789 as a new starting point, but this time as a link between past and future, not as a dividing line or a stake in a civil war. Louis Philippe turned the Château de Versailles into a museum of national glories and brought the emperor's coffin back to the Invalides. The history of France thus became the regime's highest legitimating authority. The July Monarchy lavished its attention upon history as if it were a beloved child, as evidenced by the extraordinary effort made during this period to preserve the nation's archival heritage.

This political determination also expressed itself in education policy. In 1838, Salvandy, the education minister, revamped the history syllabus by a "downstream" chronological shift: sacred history, Asia, and Greece in *sixième*; Magna Graecia, Macedonia, and the Jews in *cinquième*; Rome in *quatrième*; the Middle Ages in *troisième*; the modern period (1453–1789) in *seconde*; and the history of France from 406 to 1789 in *première*. One can already discern the outline of the academic chronology to which we are still subjected, since in the French historiographical consciousness the "modern" period ends in 1789, as if that were a universally valid terminus. Moreover, *première* was devoted entirely to the history of France—a demonstration that history had come to occupy a central pedagogic role, in contrast to the humanistic tradition. When Louis Philippe, in 1838, invited pupils from two Parisian *collèges* to the Château de Versailles, granting them the honor of visiting their past in his company, he made no mystery of his aims: "I wanted you to profit from all these fine examples of our history, all these glorious relics of the old French monarchy. The monarchy was certainly the equal of the Athenian and Roman republics, which take up perhaps too much of your time."

In this process, history as a whole, and not just the history of France, became one of the key issues in the French political and intellectual debate. Guizot's ecumenical and middle-of-the-road history encountered opposition on the Right from reactionary traditionalists haunted by the prospect of a politicized youth and on the Left from the two great democratic interpreters of national and European history, Michelet and Edgar Quinet. It would be outside the scope of this essay to recount the two professors' celebrated struggle against the Jesuits and against clerical control of the university; but, for the purpose of my argument, it is important to realize to what extent this battle *destabilized* a history that the July Monarchy would have liked to center on 1789 and its "remake," 1830. Guizot had seen the July Revolution as a new anchorage point for the accomplishments of 1789, as a sort of French 1688 that would open up for France an era of prosperity comparable to that ushered in by the Glorious Revolution in England. Michelet and Quinet countered with other references drawn from history: the dynamics of the Reformation, the unfinished character of the Revolution, and the boundless expectations aroused by democracy. The consensus of the French on their history does not seem to have run any deeper than their agreement about the July Monarchy. Both that consensus and that agreement vanished in 1848.

Yet the process begun under Louis Philippe was irreversible: however much history and the history syllabus continued to provoke strident political conflicts, they remained central to every change in education policy. Finally, the Second Republic (despite the grumblings of conservatives) and the Second Empire (despite its distrust of critical thinking) continued along the lines of Salvandy's reform. In 1848, Carnot added the 1784–1814 period to the syllabus of *seconde* and of the *classe de rhétorique*: the Revolution and the Empire had found their way into secondary education. In 1852, the decree establishing the "fork" between literary studies and scientific studies (another aspect of educational modernization) also reorganized the history syllabus. Biblical history was henceforth taught to the very young, in *huitième* and *septième*. *Sixième*, *cinquième*, and *quatrième* were devoted entirely to French history up to 1815. Finally, in *troisième*, *seconde*, and *première*, the syllabus consisted of the by-now-classic triad: antiquity, the Middle Ages, and modern times. But this reform, authored by Fortoul, was transformed in turn by the syllabus changes carried out by Victor Duruy in 1865. Biblical history was now taught in *huitième*, French history in *septième*. The introduction of French history into elementary grades was the sign of a growing consensus on the pedagogic need for this subject and on its content. In the higher grades, Duruy introduced a very modern division: antiquity from *sixième* to *quatrième*, the Middle Ages in *troisième*, the early modern period in *seconde*, the 1661–1815 period in *première*, and the nineteenth century up to the Second Empire in the *classe de philosophie*. Thus, Duruy won the battle for contemporary history, which he brought into secondary education. Not only did he raise the nineteenth century to the noble rank of history, but, in so doing, he broadened the history syllabus to include economic and social issues. For history was no longer simply the genealogy of the nation; it was now also the study of mankind's scientific and material progress. Thus, the groundwork was being laid, in these new circumstances, for the reconciliation of the nationalist and the encyclopedist philosophies.

For two sets of reasons, history appeared as the ideal medium for such a reconciliation. The first set was scientific in nature: reasons concerning the status of history as a type of knowledge and as a discipline. The mid-nineteenth century (or the last third of the century) was a decisive period for the development of historical studies in France—the most important, perhaps, since the Benedictines of Saint-Maur. Taine, Renan, Fustel de Coulanges, and Gabriel Monod put history once again on a scientific footing. In 1866, Victor Duruy founded the Ecole Pratique des Hautes Etudes with the aim of introducing German research practices into France, that is, of substituting the transmission from master to student of a rigorous method and of critical learning for the "social occasion" lecture favored by the universities.

But, if history appeared to be draped in the intellectual prestige of science, it essentially continued to represent—as far as social expectations were concerned—not what society knew about itself but what the nation knew about its past. This was another aspect of history's towering prestige. But after the few years of the *ordre moral*, a period that revived reactionary fears about the inherent dangers of history, the victorious Republic gave the French not only a regime on which they could reach a durable consensus, but a cumulative interpretation of their conflicting traditions. Unlike the July Monarchy, which sought above all to find a geometrical point common to the country's ruling classes, the Third Republic integrated Michelet's vision into Guizot's and provided the entire nation with a democratic history of itself. In this history, not all the kings of France were depicted as models of virtue or conscientiousness; but, on average, they were shown to have built France and to have contributed to its progress and prestige. The Revolution itself was guilty of excesses, but the Declaration of the Rights of Man and the armies of the year II made French history a sort of universal model. Thus, the two halves of French history were less conflicting than complementary—not, as Tocqueville had written, because they had in common a centralized administrative state, but because they shared the cult of the nation-state as instrument of progress. The fledgling Third Republic adopted all of the national heritage in the name of the people, because the Republic itself, at last, after nearly a century, was the French Revolution in power. That Republic, a provisional entity that nevertheless proved relatively long-lived, represented a conservative authority governing in the name of revolutionary values.

History's Magisterium in the Nineteenth Century

Henceforth, history was no longer just a subject in the secondary- or higher-education syllabi. It was also indispensable for very young children, who had to be trained early in patriotism and critical judgment. Once the general pattern of history had been made familiar—a pattern based on a history of France fitted into a universal history marked by the material and moral progress of mankind—the schoolmaster could forgo abstract ideas in the elementary grades. The general "philosophy" of evolution could be conveyed just as well by an anecdote, a detail, or, to use the very apt phrase, "by a story." Here, for example, is Lavisse, in his famous "Instructions" of 1890, recommending the teaching of ancient history (one can measure the road traveled since the days of the Jesuit *collèges*): "The history of Greece and Rome is already our history, since it already contains the origins of modern intelligence and of modern politics. These origins must be shown and explained to pupils, but practically without their being aware of it. They must not be treated to philosophical considerations or encumbered with details about institutions." Antiquity was no longer a model but an introduction to the history of Europe and France. It no longer gave the modern world its meaning but derived its own meaning from the modern world.

Lavisse's ability to write history at all levels—not in the same manner but with the same assurance (and, incidentally, with a great felicity of expression)—testifies to the extent to which history had become a form of knowledge and a discipline bordering on a sort of pedagogic classicism. Not that Lavisse was ever superficial—he was extremely well read—but he always knew where he was headed. A great admirer of the *Encyclopédie* and the eighteenth century, Lavisse wrote his own variety of "philosophical" history, dominated by an enlightened and learned bourgeoisie that was gradually emancipated from the church and the monarchy and soon brought to the entire world the conquests of science and progress. But there were two fundamental differences between this "philosophical history" and its predecessor. The new history had incorporated the *ars antiquaria* in the consummate form of positivism, and it had made the nation-state the central protagonist of evolution. In short, it had a method and an object. It had become what one calls a discipline.

I shall spare the reader a commentary of the famous "petit Lavisse," the textbook in which several generations of French people have acquired a lifelong knowledge of the basics of their history. It is certainly a crucial piece of evidence as regards the pedagogic and social usefulness of history in late-nineteenth century republican France, for it is at this level that the effects of historical writing must be particularly visible in order to have the maximum impact on young minds. But in his celebrated text of 1885 on history instruction in primary schools, Lavisse himself wrote a most explicit metahistory of his history of France for children. In this text he provided the best possible explanation of what he was doing. The fledgling Republic did not have a guilty conscience. Never was the general vision of the nation's history more limpid. First came the slow birth of France, made possible by the kings' struggle against feudal chaos. The decisive turning point was the Hundred Years' War.

> Once the English had been driven out, our France emerged. But, in this France, the central figure was the man in whom Joan of Arc put her hopes: the king. Because of the very fact that he had united his kingdom and reconquered it from the enemy, he, so to speak, concentrated all of France in his person. And here is what pupils must be clearly told: by the fifteenth century, when there were no more powerful vassals, when Louis XI had annexed the last great independent provinces, and when the communes had been disorganized by the king's agents and ruined by war, the king was no longer a suzerain and protector; he was a master.

The next phase was the development of absolute power—an ambiguous history, since it led France to European hegemony but also undermined the nation and oppressed the French people. The Revolution extended the "good side" of the monarchy while eliminating the bad side.

> It is an indisputable truth that the French Revolution made a heroic effort to replace the old monarchy by the reign of justice and reason. It is an indisputable truth that it ushered in a new era in the world and that nearly all of Europe was, as it were, reshaped by the Revolution. Thus, the schoolmaster can wound no conscience when he expounds the principles of this Revolution and shows how, by the force of our weapons and ideas, absolute governments were transformed everywhere and how new peoples, in the course of our contemporary history, acquired the right to exist.

But beware! The following warning was crucial for future citizens:

> It is an indisputable truth that the ideal regime dreamed of by the French Revolution is the most difficult of all to put into practice. The Revolution itself and the succession of coups d'état show this quite clearly. It is an indisputable truth [the

repetition of this introductory clause is in itself a telling indication of the fact that all these truths are precisely contested and
should not be] that these revolutions and coups d'état have
weakened France, and that further occurrences of them
would be fatal to her. Thus, the schoolmaster cannot mislead
any conscience when he teaches that any act of violence
against the law is an attack on the country, and that the
condition for France's survival is political stability.

Lavisse concludes with a thought for Alsace-Lorraine: "The schoolmaster who has recounted to his pupils the destiny of France, of all of
France—old and new—will be well aware of what one should think of,
and say about, the mutilation suffered by France fifteen years ago." The
aim of teaching history was as clear as the fact that school had become
secular, compulsory, and free. It was to train "citizens imbued with a
sense of duty, soldiers who love their rifles."

In secondary education, syllabi were broader and guidelines more
subtle. Above all, directives were designed to take into account the
pedagogic changes that were due not to republican ideology but to the
development of the discipline itself. In this field, the Third Republic
began by consolidating the work of Victor Duruy, which had been
imperiled during the *ordre moral*. Most notably, with the reform of 1902,
which reorganized the whole of the secondary-school system, the Republic once again modified the history syllabus. History was divided into two
cycles at the secondary level—a division that has survived to this day:
antiquity, the Middle Ages, the modern age (up to 1789), and the
contemporary period from *sixième* to *troisième*; and, once again, modern
history in *seconde* and *première* (but up to 1815: the no-man's-land
between 1789 and 1815 was still hard to label) and contemporary history
in *philosophie*. An interesting commentary on the background to this
reform was written by the man who played a crucial role in its preparation, Charles Seignobos. In fact, it is a general introduction to his
"course," which provided the substance for textbooks for all grades from
sixième to *philosophie*.

Seignobos does not distinguish between what he calls the "revolution"
in the approach to history teaching—a change dating from Lavisse's
celebrated "Instructions"—and the development of the discipline itself.
He does not clearly separate the two sets of phenomena—a separation
that strikes us today as obvious and necessary. For Seignobos, the pedagogic autonomy of history overlaps with its emancipation as a form of
knowledge. In other words, the triumphant entry of history into the
school syllabus in this period represents a consecration for a fully constituted discipline with its specific method, object, and social utility—the
three aspects being indissolubly linked.

History's "subject matter" was no longer confined to commentary on
great Greco-Roman literature, as in the Jesuit *collèges*, or to the analysis

of treaties and wars, as in the tradition of the Ecole Militaire. It no longer trained for a particular career. Its purpose was to make every Frenchman a citizen. "The study of science teaches us about the material world. The study of letters opens up the world of forms and ideas. History introduces the pupil to the social and political world. The humanities of old were oblivious to the world—and the world kept them at arms's length. But a Frenchman, who is destined to live in a democracy, needs to understand that democracy." The purpose of teaching history was, therefore, to build a general social science that would teach schoolchildren both the diversity of past societies and the general direction of their evolution. But the past remained "genealogical," chosen in terms of what it was sup- posed to portend or prepare: classical antiquity, the Christian Middle Ages, modern and contemporary Europe. The other societies, scattered in space, were abandoned to other disciplines. History honored by its interest only those societies that participated in "evolution"—another name for progress.

Hence the emphasis on the contemporary period, to the detriment of antiquity and the Middle Ages. Not only was there a desire to underscore history's hard-won independence from the humanities, but the contem- porary period was felt to make the past meaningful and thus to justify its study. "Modern times from the sixteenth century onward now form the substance of the history syllabus. Most of the facts that need to be known in order to understand the present state of the world date from this period." But even within "modern" history the traditional proportions were reversed: the seventeenth century, "in which no deep change took place outside of the revolutions in England," was whittled down—to the advantage of the eighteenth century, "which witnessed the formation of the great contemporary states, the Russian Empire, Prussia, the United States, parliamentary Britain, and revolutionary France," and the nineteenth century, "during which material and intellectual life was revolutionized by the definitive establishment of science, and political life was transformed by representative government and democratic equal- ity." History was not only a genealogy but also the study of change, of "upheaval" and "transformation," an area singled out for greater atten- tion than the stable features of the past. Moreover, genealogy and change were twin images: the search for the origins of contemporary civilization became meaningful only through the study of the successive stages of its development.

This enclosure of history's field involved a change in the nature of the facts to be studied and taught. It became imperative to abandon intermi- nable chronological lists, in particular the enumerations of kings, minis- ters, generals, battles, and treaties that needlessly cluttered pupils' memories. The main task was to emphasize two categories of facts: those pertaining to material civilization—because it formed the basis for civi- lization itself—and those that made it possible to understand the specific character of a period with respect to another, that is, to understand change. And these facts were, of course, to be located, dated, and described according to the method introduced by positivism—a method aimed at awakening pupils' critical faculties instead of appealing to their memory alone. Finally, the new way of teaching history, which was no longer to be a moral lesson or the occasion for literary commonplaces, had to give up rhetorical or philosophical style: "Now that history has begun to establish itself as a science, the time has come to break with the Roman and academic rhetorical tradition and to adopt the language of natural science."

A School for Citizenship

History's emergence as a full-fledged teaching subject in the late nineteenth century was due to an inseparable combination of a scientific method, a concept of evolution, and the chronological and spatial focus on Europe as a field of study. The basic rules of the *ars antiquaria*, codified by the positivists, made their way into secondary education via a provisional consensus on the meaning of history. To obtain this consensus, Lavisse and Seignobos revived the two themes of philosophical history since the eighteenth century: history is the nation; history is civilization. But they united the two themes in a far more organic manner than Guizot and the men of the July Monarchy had been able to do fifty years earlier. The Orleanists had remained trapped within a strictly bourgeois concept of evolution and "civilization"; by cutting off history in 1830—that is, in 1789—or even at the establishment of *habeas corpus* in England, they were offering too restricted a base for the historical field opened up by the French Revolution. The French were never sufficiently enthusiastic about representative government to make it the culmination of universal history.

In contrast, "the evolution of mankind," a` la Seignobos or à la Lavisse, offered the French a series of historical configurations on which they could more easily reach a consensus. The internal arrangement of these configurations involved three successive levels. First came "civilization," another name for the scientistic prophecy that prevailed in the late nineteenth century. Through intellectual advances, civilization led mankind to mastery over nature. The chief historical agent of this intellectual and material progress was the nation, or, more precisely, the nation-state invented by modern Europe. And the history of France, through the medium of absolute monarchy and the French Revolution, offered the prime example of the nation-state as vehicle of progress. For it is inaccurate to say that the republican historiography of the period was narrowly chauvinistic. With all its nationalism, it constantly made reference to the universal democratic ideal, following the Jacobin example. What made the history of France a choice topic was not only its particular value but its universal value. It took a hundred years for Mably and Condorcet to be united through the agency of the republican school system.

The other facet of this analysis would consist in looking at why and how this consensus has since broken down, especially after the Second World War, under both internal and external pressure—resulting from the evolution of historiography and of the social sciences in general and from the end of European ascendancy in the world. Although, or because, school syllabi always live on long after the circumstances that explain their birth have disappeared, there is a general awareness today that the teaching of history in France once again needs to be reexamined. And perhaps the first step, before putting forward any proposals, would be to understand what has come *undone* in the past hundred years. But one must understand beforehand the various elements of the total picture. One must first journey back through time. The following are what seem to me to be the main stages of the journey.

In order to become a school discipline, history has had to undergo several changes, so as to constitute an intellectually autonomous, socially necessary, and technically teachable field of knowledge. For history, by nature, lacks a particular object (since everything is "historical"), an autonomous language (since history is narrative), and assignable limits (since it exists everywhere and nowhere). It is, therefore, particularly hard to conceive history as a discipline, and all the more so as a school discipline. Either it is not teachable or else it is taught—as was the case for many centuries—as an appendage to classical letters. Even when it became a school "subject," its boundaries were laid down with painstaking care, out of fear that the pupil would be lost in the ocean of "historical facts" and fail to learn the language or method of history.

Since the seventeenth century, history's progress toward autonomy has followed two parallel and consequently independent tracks. Philosophical history won the battle of the "modern" against the "ancient" and eventually developed, thanks to Condorcet and the Idéologues, a doctrine of progress. For its part, the *ars antiquaria*—from Port-Royal to the Benedictines of Saint-Maur via the Académie des Inscriptions— constructed a method for locating and evaluating historical facts. But in the absence of a French Gibbon, the Enlightenment never united the two learned traditions. It bequeathed to the Revolution and to the nineteenth century a secularized discourse on universal history, along with a set of distinct techniques and descriptive forms of knowledge—chronology, paleography, travel, and so on.

It was these dissociated traditions that the nineteenth century thoroughly reshaped and redefined in order to produce, at the beginning of the Third Republic, the history taught to French youth. Reshaping meant, first of all, excluding. The age of classicism had shown the way by beginning to place outside history certain sectors of the vast spectacle offered by human societies. "Travel" began as an inventory of space, before developing into geography and anthropology. The study of past and present non-European civilizations, which required particular linguistic skills, generally evolved into distinct specialties. This trend continued under the Restoration and the July Monarchy, as evidenced by the highest teaching institution, the Collège de France. At the same time, the history of religion was also breaking away from the main trunk of history to become a special field of scholarship. Conversely, in the wake of the decline of Latin in the school curriculum, learned history gradually appropriated Greco-Roman antiquity as a subject to be taught as something other than a literary model. What had been a cultural identity for the Europe of letters gradually became its genealogy.

Indeed, the great transformation of history in the nineteenth century, and particularly in the 1820s and 1830s, lies in this shift. History was now the genealogical tree of European nations and of the civilization they bore. Guizot still regarded both France and England as models; for Michelet, France alone was the model. Once the encyclopedic discourse of the eighteenth century had been vested with that particular significance, national history was delivered from the curse of "feudalism" inflicted on it by the Revolution. The history of France represented both a choice image (but not the only one) of mankind's progress and a "subject" for study, a heritage of texts, sources, and monuments that made it possible to reconstruct the past accurately. It was at the confluence of these two notions that the positivist "revolution" took hold, giving to both of them the blessing of science. Henceforth, history had a field and a method of its own. On these two counts, it had become the main school for citizenship.

6

Book Licensing and Book Production in the Kingdom of France in the Eighteenth Century

For the historian, the book is always a perplexing object. Wrapped in its title as if in a timeless definition, the book is forever enclosed, and yet it never ceases to take on successive meanings. Although it is the product par excellence of individual effort, it presupposes a community of language and a complex system of social connections. It is doubly mysterious—as an invention and as a familiar object. Indeed, the study of the book crystallizes all the difficulties of the historian's craft: the passage from the individual to the collective, the relation between the intellectual and the social, time's judgments on time, the measure of innovation and inertia. Even though it has accumulated so many layers of criticism, human writing is far from having been deciphered in terms of history.

For the past century and a half, traditional literary scholarship has been tracking down the secrets of the book on two levels: internally, through the study of the texts themselves, and externally, through the biographical approach. Thus, traditional literary scholarship has been led to make assumptions about social and collective phenomena on the basis of evidence about individuals. It is precisely this approach that the historian would like to reverse. Not that he is obliged to settle beforehand the old debates about collective versus individual behavior or infrastructure versus superstructure. But the historian's raison d'être is to integrate accidental phenomena into a quantitative and intelligible framework. He must therefore isolate—in the extraordinarily bewildering mass of

First published as "La 'Librairie' du royaume de France au XVIIIe siècle," Comité International des Sciences Historiques, XIIe Congrès International des Sciences Historiques (Vienna, 1965), in *Rapports*, ed. Hanns Leo Mikoletzky (Horn-Wein: Verlag F. Berger, n.d.), vol. 1, *Grands thèmes*, 423–50. Reprinted in G. Bollème, J. Ehrard, F. Furet, D. Roche, J. Roger, and A. Dupront, *Livre et société dans la France du XVIIIe siècle*, vol. 1 (Paris and The Hague: Mouton, 1965).

creativity represented by books—a certain number of trends and constants. He must begin with those which, because they are external and measurable, are easiest to identify.

One can then venture a comparison with recent advances in economic history. Following in its footsteps, historians should be able to combine macroscopic and microscopic analysis, drawing up a general census of literary production in a society,[1] while conducting an ever-greater number of specific investigations into sociocultural circles and groups. It is only if the two types of research can be combined that one can attain a degree of historical certainty about major trends and their mechanisms.

But, in both cases, the analytical method involved is deliberately external to the unique melody of each book. These methods may therefore be suspected of leading to oversimplification. To avoid a pointless debate, suffice it to reply that if nothing can replace the study of the texts themselves, this type of research can bring to light with greater force—and with fewer theoretical presuppositions—the major points of convergence of a society and its written output. These investigations must be understood simply as a preface to, and a framework for, literary analysis proper—as nothing more, but nothing less.

As luck would have it, the historian of the printed book in the eighteenth century has a series of highly valuable quantitative sources at his disposal: the records of the royal book-control bureau, the Administration de la Librairie, recently unearthed by Robert Estivals.[2] By the Renaissance, the French monarchy had secured control of the kingdom's literary output. It kept a careful record of printed matter at the Chancellerie, which delivered printing licenses, and at the Dépôt Légal, which registered published books. This extremely thorough and complex bureaucratic accounting of book production has the posthumous advantage of making it possible to conduct surveys on a very large scale and thus to improve on later, incomplete bibliographies. It also offers the historian a more sophisticated perspective: the relation between a society and its own literary works. In this respect, the eighteenth century is an ideal period for study.

In actual fact, the French monarchy under Louis XV and Louis XVI was not the crude force of repression and censorship described *a posteriori* by the revolutionary liberation movement. Not that it is inaccurate, in a certain sense, to regard the Age of Enlightenment as a long struggle between the forces of intellectual innovation and those of conservative resistance. But the role of inquisitor devolved primarily, not on the central government, but on the Parlements, which happened at the same time to be the staunch adversaries of the royal bureaucracy. The king of France allowed more books to be published than the Sorbonne or the great magistrates would bear, as is shown by the crisis over the *Encyclopédie*. The truth is that the monarchic state, which put

Malesherbes in charge of the book trade for twelve crucial years as the first *directeur général de la librairie*, followed prevailing trends more than it directed them. The monarchy was not only very sensitive to pressures from civil society but receptive to contemporary ideas and to the concept of a more rational government. In short, it had become both weaker and more modern. This change puts into clearer perspective the official sources one can use to study the control of ideas. The technical and social value of these sources makes them a rather exceptional document produced by a society on the subject of its own writings.

Most of this society's literary output can be inventoried, since each work had to be granted a printing license by the *chancelier*. But even books that were refused a license were recorded on the register of requests, and these victims of censorship do not elude our general count. Traditionally, there were two types of licenses: *privilèges* and *permissions du Sceau*. The first, which was costlier,[3] also gave the applicant a monopoly on the work for a specified period. The second was not exclusive, but it saved the expense of a *privilège*. Both licenses were public and were explicitly mentioned in the books concerned; they were tantamount to government decrees. The book-trade code (Code de la Librairie) of 1723 restated this procedure, which was more than a century old. Both types of licenses were revocable, temporary, and renewable. When his *privilège* expired, the printer who wanted to keep his monopoly or reissue a work had to ask for a renewal or an extension of his *privilège*. The new license was recorded in the same register and is, thus, a likely indication of the work's success.

The tendency for printing licenses to be renewed was a boon for Parisian *libraires* (publisher-booksellers), who were in closer contact than their provincial colleagues with the authorities and with authors. It also fueled a long controversy in the eighteenth century. Provincial *libraires* were opposed not to licenses but to their renewal. In a famous text, Diderot came out in favor of the Parisian *libraires* in the name of property rights.[4] This debate, from which the modern notion of copyright gradually emerged, was resolved on 30 August 1777 by Louis XVI, who issued a series of important decrees. Henceforth, an author who secured a license in his own name and sold his work himself could hand down to his heirs a perpetual copyright for his work. But the transfer of the manuscript to a third party reduced the copyright to a life annuity, for the license granted to the *libraire* was valid only during the author's lifetime. (However, a ten-year minimum was stipulated if the author died within ten years of the issue date.) This marked the end of the renewal of *privilèges*, and these renewals ceased to appear in our registers.

In addition, the 1777 decrees seem to have led to a new type of permit, which did not bear the stamp of the Grand Sceau: the *permission simple*. The *Manuel de l'auteur et du libraire* of 1777 does not mention it, while the *Almanach de la librairie* of 1778 gives the following definition: "The *permission simple* gives no other right than that of publishing a work for which no license exists or for which the license has expired, under the provisions of the Council's decree of 30 August 1777 on licenses. *Permissions simples* are issued with the simple signature of M. le Directeur Général [de la Librairie].

"Any *libraire* or printer in any town can obtain a permit of this kind, but he must have it recorded within two months on the registers of the Chambre Syndicale [de la Librairie—the *libraires'* guild] in the *arrondissement* corresponding to his place of residence, otherwise his permit will be null and void."

Thus, the decrees of 1777, by placing more books out of copyright, made it easier to reprint them, especially for provincial *libraires*. However, these books slip through our survey, since the requests for *permissions simples* were handled not by the Chancellerie but by the *directeur général* alone.

Another type of printing license also appeared in the eighteenth century: the *permission tacite* ("tacit permit"). The best comment on it was made by Malesherbes, in his fifth *Mémoire sur les problèmes de la librairie*, written in 1759. First he discusses its origins: "As the tendency to publish on all sorts of subjects has become more widespread, and as private individuals, particularly the powerful, have also become more sensitive to being mentioned in print, circumstances have arisen in which the authorities have not dared to grant public permission to publish a book, and in which, nevertheless, they have felt that it would be impossible to forbid it. This is how the first tacit permits originated. . . ." Malesherbes added that they had been on the increase "for the past thirty years," but in 1788 he wrote that he did not know when they had begun.[5] His predecessor as supervisor of the book trade, the comte d'Argenson, who had been chief of police during the Regency and had been, since his very birth, familiar "with all the secrets of government," had always resorted to tacit permits. "I think," Malesherbes added, "that they began at about the time of Louis XIV's death." But the fact remained that they were illegal—under the laws then in force—because they were not public: "The only difference between these illegal permits and the others is that they are not handled by the Sceau and that the public does not see the censor's name. This practice was probably introduced to give *libraires* and authors some token authorization while protecting censors from complaints by hostile [i.e. unsuccessful] applicants. But a record of these permits is kept and the censor at fault is not immune from the rigors of official punishment."

These records are indeed preserved in the manuscript division of the Bibliothèque Nationale under the title "Registre des livres d'impression étrangère présentés à Monseigneur le Chancelier pour la permission de débiter." The first volume begins in 1718, but the series kept its fictitious title until 1772 in order to conceal the illegal character of the new practice by presenting these works as imports. The tacit royal license was confined to the distribution of the book in question; officials refused to accept any responsibility with regard to the act of printing. For the same reasons, a great many eighteenth-century works printed in Paris by tacit permission listed Amsterdam, London, Geneva, or even Peking as place of publication. It is only in 1772 that the registers of these licenses were labeled as what they really were: an interesting sign that the royal bureaucracy was no longer afraid of its own past and its own laws.

But, by the early eighteenth century, at the cost of a falsehood collectively agreed upon, the bureaucracy authorized and kept count of a literature that it itself designated as bearing the stamp of presumed nonconformism. The state accepted this literature as inevitable, that is, as the expression of a social and intellectual current that could no longer be repressed but only channeled. When in 1758 the weight of scandal led the *chancelier* to revoke the license for the *Encyclopédie* by government decree, Malesherbes got around the difficulty by issuing a tacit permit. But, more generally, authors or *libraires* who were seeking to avoid difficulties and reduce costs or who were speculating on the diminishing resistance of the authorities bypassed the administrative channel of the Sceau Public de la Chancellerie; they contented themselves with asking for a gesture of tolerance whose only guarantee lay in a consensus between public opinion and government. Among these somewhat suspect new titles, whose character was not concealed from the censor, manuscripts formed the largest but—as Diderot noted—not the only group: "One must distinguish two sorts of titles appearing by tacit permission alone: the first are the work of foreign authors and have already been published outside the kingdom; the second are the work of authors living in France and are in manuscript or have been published under spurious titles."[6]

Thus, there is a qualitative difference between the two major series of records relating to applications for printing licenses. In the eighteenth century itself, an external dividing line was drawn between two types of literature—a partition that is valuable for the historian, since it indicates the origin of the defenses put up by a society against its own culture. This aspect alone would be a sufficient justification for maintaining that dividing line and thus for studying *privilèges* and tacit permits separately. But the quantitative analysis of these sources confirms the need for this methodological approach.[7]

Between 1723—the opening date for the registers, following a gap between 1716 and 1723—and 1789, one finds 31,716 works submitted for a *privilège* or *permission du Sceau*. This figure is higher than the one given by R. Estivals, because he counts only published books, not licenses. The fact is that *libraires* or printers would sometimes include several books in a request for a single *privilège* or *permission du Sceau*.[8] Actually, the same is true for tacit permits, but there are far fewer works covered by this series for the whole century: only 12,610, or just over a third of the number of books in the first series.

This numerical gap is essentially due to the chronological difference between the two sources. Even though they dated from the Regency, tacit permits did not flourish in earnest before the 1750s. The practice did not become widespread until Malesherbes was appointed to the Direction Générale de la Librairie in 1751. The first register of tacit permits (1718–47) lists a total of 713 books over thirty years, that is, a very low average of 24 a year. The second register (December 1750–March 1760)—which, no less than the first one, is impossible to analyze on a yearly basis—includes 714 titles for a period of nine years and four months, that is, 126 a year. This almost decennial average is in itself only the starting point of a rising trend, since the next two registers reveal a very rapid increase in the annual average: 156 books a year between March 1760 and October 1763; 396 between October 1763 and November 1766. From 1767 on, the sources make it possible to calculate annual figures showing that there were nearly as many requests for tacit permits as for standard licenses (see chart).

While the two trends converged from the late 1760s on, only the second trend presents features enabling internal comparisons to be made from the beginning of the century onward, because of the relative stability of the annual figures. The yearly average for the period from 1723 to 1789 was 463 books; the figure works out to 456 before 1750 and 469 from 1750 to 1789. There is no trace here of the discontinuity that characterizes the registers of tacit permits. Thus, one cannot combine the evidence for two administrative practices that are not comparable, for one was an institutionalized tradition, and the other, which was for long time unavowed and unavowable, did not flourish before the 1760s.

Moreover, the problem remains of determining if and how, in earlier decades, the hundreds of titles a year belonging to a category officially recognized only later were actually printed. In his fourth *Mémoire sur les problèmes la librairie*, which can be dated to early 1759, Malesherbes noted that "over the past thirty years the use of tacit permits has become almost as widespread as that of public licenses." "Over the past thirty years"? Since the 1730s? The statement is surprising if one compares it with the huge disparity in the annual figures revealed by the two series of licensing records spanning the first half of the century. Yet it is difficult to reject this statement out of hand, coming as it does from a man who was ideally placed to know. One can assume both that the statement was exaggerated[9] and that nevertheless, during this period, a considerable number of books were granted permits so "tacit" as to leave no written trace. Indeed, Malesherbes himself implied as much in his fifth *Mémoire sur les problèmes de la librairie*, quoted earlier, when, having distinguished between tacit permits and simple acts of tolerance of which no trace remained, he added, "The first tacit permits to be granted were no doubt of this sort; similar permits are sometimes still given, owing to the lack of well-established principles enabling the censor to regard himself as immune from reproach. But true tacit permissions differ considerably from these acts of tolerance or perhaps of connivance."

Thus, it is probable that until the 1750s a wide variety of illegal literature—distinct, however, from clandestine literature proper, hunted down by the royal police—was simply tolerated by the authorities, without our being able to find a written trace of it in the licensing registers.

An example dating from the midcentury shows the extent of jurisprudential uncertainty surrounding the matter. In 1748, Montesquieu had *L'Esprit des lois* printed in Geneva without an author's name. Its immediate impact in France indicates how widely it was distributed. Both the Jesuits, in the *Mémoires de Trévoux*, and the Jansenists, in the *Nouvelles ecclésiastiques*, devoted two articles to it the following year. The Jansenist journal, which fulminated against the book, concluded its second article, dated 16 October 1749, by openly accusing the authorities: "Orders will be given for the executioner to burn the *Nouvelles ecclésiastiques*, whose sole and perpetual aim is to confirm men in the possession of truths that make both a true Christian and a faithful subject of the king; and permission will be granted for the sale of a disgraceful work that teaches men to regard virtue as a useless principle for a monarchy, and all religions, even the true religion, as political issues, as being solely the product of climate, etc. May we be allowed to say so: is not one act a punishment for the other?" In August 1750 the Sorbonne intervened in its turn to make up *post eventum* for the official clearance that had not been requested for the work. The Sorbonne suggested a certain number of cuts, which Montesquieu refused by appealing to public opinion: "All of Europe has read my book, and everyone agrees that it was impossible to tell whether I preferred republican government or monarchical government. . . ." Actually, if Malesherbes is to be believed,[10] Montesquieu's book, in its original form, obtained a tacit permit that immediately paved the way for numerous reprints, none of which bear any traces of the Sorbonne's demands.

The very complexity of this example shows that it is hard to assess the precise bibliographical value of the two series of licensing records described above. As comparisons cannot be made with the two most readily available sources—the Dépôt Légal, which is less exhaustive, or the alphabetical author catalog of the Bibliothèque Nationale, which does not list anonymous titles—the simplest procedure is to summarize the contents of the two registers in order to point out what they do not contain.

1. The registers of *privilèges* and *permissions du Sceau* contain three sorts of applications. The largest category concerns new manuscripts. But before the decrees of 1777, which put an end to the need to apply for

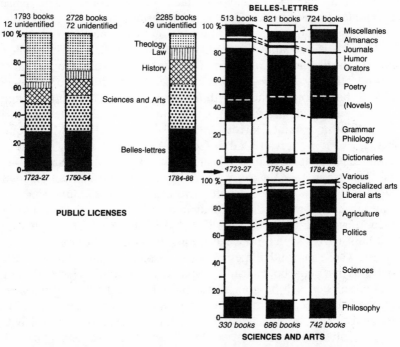

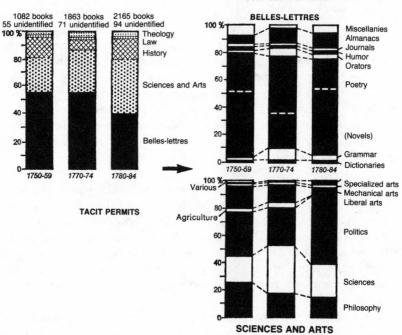

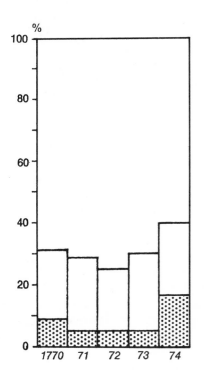
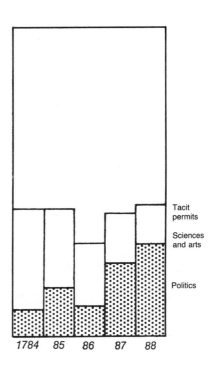

Tacit
permits

Sciences
and arts

Politics

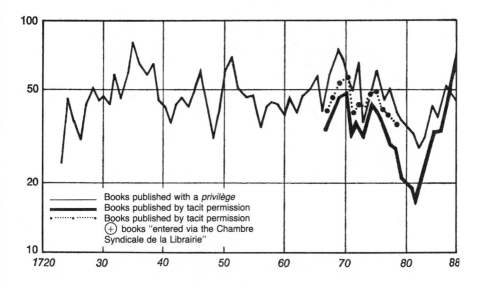

Books published with a *privilège*
Books published by tacit permission
Books published by tacit permission
⊕ books "entered via the Chambre
Syndicale de la Librairie"

renewal of *privilèges*, one also finds applications for such renewals by authors and printers wishing to prolong their monopoly. These requests indicate the likelihood that the book was popular and that the *libraire* intended to reprint it in the near future. Finally, new editions of previously published books—as distinct from manuscripts—also had to be vetted by the royal censors: these instances would involve a *libraire* basing his claim on a license that had already been issued for an earlier edition and had expired or a competitor invoking the original character of the new edition in order to seek permission to publish an author who was not yet on his list. The latter sort of applicant could save money by requesting a *permission du Sceau*. The registers for the first half of the century make fairly frequent mention of these reprints (maked by an *R*), which were considerably greater in number than applications for renewal of *privilèges*. But the records were kept too carelessly—the *R* markings actually disappeared in the 1760s—for an accurate count to be made. Finally, from 1778 onward, the introduction of *permissions simples* led to less frequent listings for reprints.

New editions almost always concerned the same categories of books: Latin classics, seventeenth-century masterpieces (especially plays), the great legal handbooks, devotional and liturgical works, and what can be called, for lack of a better term, "popular literature"—almanacs and short novels issued by the Bibliothèque Bleue de Troyes and other specialized *libraires*. While the frequency of reprints can lead to double counts in the general census, they are valuable indicators of book consumption. In this respect, the registers of *privilèges* not only make it possible to measure the volume of traditionalist literary output; they also reveal the areas of consensus in public taste and the sense of a shared culture, that is, of a common past.

But these records also teach us that even the present could become "classical." Time and success could temper the subversive character of a book first published abroad. Dangerous ideas could become commonplace. In some cases the book in question was granted a license later on and so found its way onto the very official licensing records. Such was the case with Voltaire's *Henriade* and *Siècle de Louis XIV*, and the same happened to the *Lettres de Madame de Maintenon*, a sort of secret history of Louis XIV's reign, which, according to Malesherbes, was first published abroad and was allowed to circulate in France by the chief of police: "For if the authorities had not wanted the book to appear, the persons most connected with the court would not have provided the publisher with information. . . . One had to be in the know in order to make sure that the king would not object to the publication of the book, in which Louis XIV's secret marriage, whose existence had until then been in doubt, was fully described." In short, already under Fleury's premiership, the court was secretly taking its petty revenge for its great humiliation. But from the 1750s on the book was quite openly mentioned in many guises in applications for licenses—which, moreover, it readily obtained.

2. Nevertheless, tacit permits were the refuge par excellence of new titles, since that was their very function. Some tacit permits were also issued for reprints—generally described in such a way as to give the impression that the books in question had been totally rewritten—but instances of this are far less frequent than in the registers for *privilèges*. For the most part, tacit permits concerned manuscripts and new books for which anonymous approval would compromise neither the censor nor the authorities. That is why these permits sometimes concerned books that had been removed from the public circuit of *privilèges*. While the registers tell us next to nothing about the first half of the century, they are increasingly informative from Malesherbes onward. Helvetius, Condillac, Mably, Condorcet, and Beaumarchais, for example, all get a mention. These sources are all the more valuable for listing rejected manuscripts.

Finally, this paralegal administrative bibliography also gives a chronological listing of another category of books—those that came from abroad already printed, did not succeed in avoiding controls, and reached the Chambre Syndicale de la Librairie in sealed packets. These works are mentioned in applications for tacit permits between 1767 and 1778;[11] as with "domestic" manuscripts, permission was being sought for their distribution in France. A separate count was made for these volumes, in most cases at the end of each register; these figures can therefore be added to the total of authorized publications.

One can also reverse the question: What sort of publication bypassed applications for printing permits, whether public or tacit? Basically, three categories of books.

No doubt the least important one includes a share of provincial publications. In the eighteenth century, most new books published in the provinces with official permission seem to be works of local interest— items commissioned by local government bodies, bishoprics, courts of justice, academies, or universities. That, at least, is the conclusion drawn from Madeleine Ventre's study of the Languedoc,[12] and her data seem to correspond to what we know about the rapid decline in provincial publishing as early as the seventeenth century.

Actually, in the eighteenth century, a considerable number of provincial *libraires* and printers had taken to dealing directly with the central government, especially for matters that did not concern official orders from local authorities. The prevailing trend was toward centralization, and the appropriate habits were spreading. But the fact that our registers contain few applications for licenses from the provinces substantiates and justifies in retrospect the endless complaints by eighteenth-century provincial *libraires* against their Parisian colleagues, who exercised a dual hegemony over the book market owing to the renewal of their licenses (which prolonged their monopoly of previously published books) and owing to the proximity of most authors (which gave them a monopoly of new titles). The example of the Languedoc shows that the decrees of 1777 gave a small stimulus to provincial publishing without seriously threatening Parisian ascendancy.

In practice, a Parisian *libraire* would be deprived of a manuscript only if the author, fearing even the censorship of tacit permits, preferred the circuitous route of having his book printed in the provinces or abroad and deposited at the Chambre Syndicale. But even in this case the work would be mentioned in the registers of tacit permits under the heading of "books introduced through the Chambre." Thus, the Parisian and centralized character of the sources concerning official control of the book trade is probably not a major drawback, at least for the eighteenth century.

The two other categories of missing books pose a far greater problem for an exhaustive census of eighteenth-century publications. First, some books were simply tolerated by the police without ever being mentioned in official documents. "I do not know," wrote Malesherbes, who discussed these publications at length, "what to call these sorts of licenses, which have become common practice. Strictly speaking, they are only assurances of impunity." It was, for example, an authorization of this kind that Montesquieu's Paris publisher claims to have obtained—prior to any tacit permit—from the comte d'Argenson for *L'Esprit des lois* as early as the beginning of 1749.[13]

We have seen that the very graph of the number of requests for tacit permits is a sufficient indication of the extent of this practice before Malesherbes took office. But, conversely, the increase in tacit permits from 1751 onward strongly suggests that the first *directeur général* succeeded in establishing as a standard administrative practice the doctrine he described to the dauphin in 1759, when he asserted that he knew "only one way of enforcing prohibitions, namely, to enact as few of them as possible." One can also observe that his successors remained faithful to his doctrine.

However, it is unlikely that simple tolerance disappeared altogether. Too many anecdotes testify to the contrary, and in 1761 Malesherbes himself found no other solution than to allow Rousseau's *Emile* to circulate at its own risk, without being able to grant it a tacit permit. But when one considers the spread of tacit permits from the 1760s onward and when one observes that Restif de la Bretonne and Mirabeau requested and obtained them, one can assume that this practice very largely replaced the secret acts of tolerance of the first half of the century.

Nevertheless, the Parlements and the clergy continued to threaten even authorized books with scandal and legal prosecution. They intimidated not only authors but also censors and royal officials. It is their pressure that explains to a great extent the existence of the last category of books to elude our grasp—those that enjoyed no permission or tolerance whatsoever and, whether printed in France or (as was more often the case) abroad, were quite simply clandestine. Police records and legal sources for the history of the book trade under the *ancien régime*[14] are so scattered that it is virtually impossible to make a count of such books. Thus, by definition, they fall outside the scope of the present study.[15]

All the same, by using the applications for *privilèges* and tacit permits, we have been able to count up slightly more than 44,000 book titles. This is a considerable figure if one compares it, for example, with the 25,000 titles published in Paris during the sixteenth century (according to Lucien Febvre and Henri-Jean Martin), even if it is true that we are dealing with requests for publication and not with the published books themselves. But we have seen how the statistical value of this count is unevenly distributed: nearly 13,000 licensed books up to 1750, and only a few hundred tacit permits. Thus, it is above all on the strength of the 30,000 works dating from the second half of the eighteenth century that the sources studied here accurately reflect their titles and provide a realistic census of the publications of their period.

Let us imagine for a moment that all these books could be placed in a library arranged in a temporal sequence—a doubly fictive library, in that successive reprints would stand alongside never-published manuscripts and in that no cultured individual in the eighteenth century would have deprived himself of the major works published abroad and banned in France. But this imaginary library remains to a great extent, as we have seen, that of an entire society. It is richer and more representative than the partial bibliographies compiled late in the century. We have tried to reconstruct it according to subject by means of chronological samplings.

Works have been classified according to eighteenth-century criteria. The Bibliothèque Nationale contains a wealth of inventories of eighteenth-century private libraries, in which books are arranged according to the five major categories in use at the time: (1) theology and religion, (2) law and jurisprudence, (3) history, (4) sciences and arts, and (5) belles-lettres. Moreover, bibliographical manuals such as those of Durcy de Noinville or Cels-Martin provide detailed information on the guidelines for such inventories, thus making our own classification easier. The following is the scheme adopted here:[16]

I. Theology and religion[17]
   A. Scripture, Bible, interpreters of the Bible[18]
   B. Church fathers, conciliar literature[19]
   C. Theology and apologetics
      1. Catholic[20]
      2. Non-Catholic

D. Liturgy and devotion[21]
II. Law and jurisprudence[22]
    A. Canon law and ecclesiastical law[23]
    B. Civil law[24]
        1. Ancient law
        2. Natural and public law
    C. Jurisprudence and practice
III. History[25]
    A. Ecclesiastical history[26]
    B. Profane history
        1. Ancient
        2. Modern (by state)
        3. Ancillary sciences (genealogy, numismatics, paleography, etc.)
    C. Geography, travel, and cartography
IV. Sciences and arts[27]
    A. Philosophy
        1. Ancient
        2. Logic
        3. Ethics
        4. Metaphysics[28]
    B. Science
        1. Physics
        2. Mathematics
            a) Astronomy
            b) Mechanics
            c) Algebra, arithmetic, geometry
            d) Applied sciences and mathematics
        3. Natural sciences
            a) Botany
            b) Mineralogy
            c) Zoology
            d) Chemistry
        4. Medicine, surgery, pharmacology[29]
    C. Political economy[30]
    D. Agriculture and agronomy[31]
    E. Liberal arts[32]
    F. Mechanical arts[33]
    G. Specialized arts[34]
    H. Various
V. Belles-lettres[35]
    A. Dictionaries[36]
    B. Grammar and philology
    C. Poetry
        1. Poetry
        2. Drama

    3. Novels

    4. Correspondence[37]

D. Orators

E. Humor

F. Journals and periodicals

G. Almanacs[38]

H. Miscellanies

As with all classifications, the rigidity of the scheme above involves certain difficulties. The first problem is the relation of the title to the work itself. The tradition of long and detailed titles often yields sufficiently accurate information about a book's contents, but occasionally, and in particular in the first half of the century, a neglectful scribe would omit part of the title, replacing it by a mere *etc.* In such cases, we are generally left without the explanatory subtitle—the semantic equivalent suggested by the author himself—which was so common in the eighteenth century and is so valuable for the historian. For example, in 1750 an application for a *privilège* was submitted for a work entitled *L'Art de vérifier les dates, etc.*, which was actually published in Paris that year by the *libraire* Desprez. The abbreviation of the title conceals the fact that the work was a polemical theological treatise, written from a Jansenist and Gallican point of view and based on a chronology of the errors of various popes, such as Honorius and Liber. Patouillet's dictionary classifies it among the more pernicious works.

Generally speaking, these incomplete titles have been easier to identify—using the catalogs of the Bibliothèque Nationale—than simply ambiguous but complete titles such as *Promenades d'un solitaire* or *Lettres de Monsieur X à Monsieur Y*. In all these cases, several hundred checks have been made, enabling us to establish the virtual absence of any misleading title aimed at concealing the true contents of a book. Besides, the fact that the censor was obliged to read the work eliminated any possibility that such a subterfuge might be effective. However, the practice does seem to have been commonly applied to prohibited books circulating clandestinely. But our listings still contain a few ambiguous titles that we have been unable to identify at the Bibliothèque Nationale—whether in the author catalog, the catalog of anonymous titles, or the eighteenth- and early-nineteenth-century bibliographies.[39] Consequently, these books, which were either lost or never published, are impossible to classify. They are slightly more common in the records of tacit permits than in the registers of public licenses, but never exceed 5 percent.

After these investigations, a final difficulty remains, owing to the imprecision of bibliographical criteria for a certain number of works. The title of the book itself can cause hesitation: is Rousseau's *Discours sur les sciences et les arts* (1750) "philosophy" or "politics"? At least it clearly belongs to category IV. A very small number of titles raise the problem of whether form or content should be the criterion. For example, should *Le Bonheur*, a poem by Helvetius, come under the heading of "poetry" or "ethics"? In all these cases we have been guided by eighteenth-century criteria: the theme for Rousseau's *Discours* was suggested by a resident member of the Classe de Morale of the Académie de Dijon, and most contemporary libraries classified the work under "ethics." In the catalog of Malesherbes's library, *Le Bonheur* is listed under "ethics and morals," an extremely rare exception to the tyranny of nomenclature—a product of classical aesthetics—which quite often manifested itself by the juxtaposition of a genre label to the title.

The slowness of identification procedures for these books naturally made it impossible to classify all the 45,000 works mentioned. In order to eliminate annual fluctuations and attempt to measure the general trend, we have made three five-year samplings (1723–27, 1750–54, and 1784–88), each involving some 2,000 works, in the registers of *privilèges*. The registers of tacit permits, which can be used from 1750 on, have also been divided into three periods: the first is a ten-year period (1750–59), so as to obtain a reasonable number of books; the other two are five-year periods (1770–74 and 1784–88). All the figures have been converted into percentages to allow for comparisons. In absolute terms these figures represent highly diverse units—since nothing is more different from one book than another book—but in relative terms they are quite comparable, if indeed reckoning in large numbers eliminates similar disparities within each time period.

The bibliography of the *privilège* registers of the 1720s reveals the fundamental importance of the supernatural underpinnings of the social world—in consonance with the hierarchy of the time. More than a third of the works were concerned with religion[40] in the broad sense, However, under this general heading, they were very unevenly distributed among the traditional categories. One finds few commentaries on Scripture, and even fewer on the church fathers, in an age dominated by the Augustinian obsession. But it would be wrong to conclude that the Jansenist current had been eliminated by official fiat. A society cannot enforce an administrative ban on its own religious sensibility. When examined individually, the theological and devotional works of this period show the extraordinary penetration of Jansenist ideas, which one must be careful to distinguish—as the royal censors did—from Jansenist politics. The Unigenitus Bull was a law of the realm; all comment on it, even favorable, was forbidden. Similarly, censors would invariably refuse all titles containing such words, expressions, and names as *missal for laymen, grace, predestination*, Port-Royal, *knowledge, council, exposition*, or even Embrun, Tencin, Senez, Soanen, Auxerre, Montpellier, and so on. However, one can observe the authorized development of an abundant popular religious literature of a Jansenist strain, representing more than half the religious works in our sample.

This enduring tyranny of the sacred was the source for the legal and jurisprudential regulation of the two realms of human activity: first, the church, as a temporal organization; second, the civil and political world. Hence the considerable importance of canon law, ecclesiastical law, and jurisprudence. The first two categories constituted a model and, as it were, a guarantee for the rest. Jurisprudence was a matter of publishing, updating, and adapting legal procedure; it attests to the justifications gradually elaborated by learned royal jurists with a view to unifying customs and customaries, defining status and rank, and building the foundations of political society. These books were by definition weightier than small devotional works. They were also more esoteric and, thus, far less numerous, but they continued to embody in exemplary fashion the monarchic absolutist civilization.

The following categories involve an ultimately less fundamental area of knowledge, since it was in a certain sense of secondary importance. This area was the ornament and almost the pleasure of life; it did not cover the rules of life. But it already represented a majority of published or reprinted books. Most of the history books in our sample deal with profane history; only a quarter of them are devoted to ecclesiastical history. The accent is on the modern period, but the outlook is both quite international and almost exclusively European (France, England, Spain, Italy, Russia, Poland, Sweden, and so forth). The extra-European world was the province of travel accounts, which transformed the view of the present not through time but through space. But geographical curiosity was also linked to history by a kinship more secret than the fraternity of faraway time and faraway space: travel unveiled the past contained in the present by revealing the existence of infant mankind in other parts of the human world. As Servan explained in 1781: "It has always seemed to me that the discovery of America has contributed not insignificantly to the progress of ethics. . . . For previously we knew nothing about the infancy of our species." Thus did history and geography begin their arduous cohabitation. The interest they aroused goes back a long way. By the early eighteenth century, these two fields accounted for a considerable number of works.

But profane knowledge was essentially constituted by "sciences and arts," a classic label designating every intellectual activity connected with knowledge and beauty. Even before Boileau, the parallelism between arts and sciences—one of the fundamental theses of French classicism— had been declared to be the logical consequence of their common origin: reason. "The common feature of arts and sciences," wrote Le Bossu at the beginning of his treatise on epic poetry (1675), "is that they are founded on reason, and that one must be led to them by the wisdom that nature has given to us." Thus, belles-lettres themselves were only an especially important area of sciences and arts: it was their volume and above all their degree of "nobility," more than their special character, that justified their being classified separately.

The *privilège* registers of 1723–27 point to the great social importance of sciences, arts, and belles-lettres, all of which together represent nearly half the total. Within the "sciences and arts" category, ethics and metaphysics predominate in philosophy, and medicine dominates the sciences. The "liberal arts," consisting mainly of music, have a crushing numerical superiority over agriculture and mechanical arts, which retain the stigma of manual activities. Apart from the *abrégés de paix perpetuelle*, almost all "political" books consisted of manuals of commercial practice.

In belles-lettres, classical aestheticism still prevailed: many grammar and philology books perpetuated and taught the science and rules of noble language. "Poetry," in the wide sense of the word, was by far the largest category, bearing witness to the persistence of the main classical genres: verse, drama, and correspondence. There were also many books in Greek and even more in Latin. But one can already note the relative importance of novels, which were more common than verse compositions and tragedies.

Such, then, were the broad bibliographical outlines of a great traditional classical culture in the early eighteenth century and the balance between its various elements. One can proceed to a comparison with the two samplings for the 1750s and the late eighteenth century based on the *privilège* registers alone.

The later samples reveal continuities as striking as the signs of change. One finds a comparable mass of works in law, history, and belles-lettres, indicating a persistence throughout the century of a classic style of writing and of a social demand for such writing. The "law" category expanded to take in the developments of jurisprudence, attributable both to the increase in individual litigations and procedural "briefs" and to the great national effort to rationalize juridical practice. In the course of the century, history lost part of its substance. Books on ecclesiastical history fell from 25 percent in 1724–28 to 15 percent in the 1750s and 11 percent in the 1780s. But history remained faithful to the general principles visible at the very outset: a common past made Europe an intelligible and worthy object of historical study, while the rest of the world was in most cases dealt with by ahistorical travel accounts. As the century wore on, the increasing number of books devoted to early France, particularly to the Carolingian period, pointed to the rise of an antiabsolutistic national consciousness, which originated as a nobiliary nostalgia for Frankish assemblies and turned into a lesson in constitutional government.

"Belles-lettres" remained an extraordinarily stable category, not only with respect to the others, but also in terms of the distribution of works according to classical literary genres: orators, poetry, theater, novels, grammar, and so forth. The aesthetic formalization of classicism survived the century unscathed, Diderot and Rousseau notwithstanding; it had become too rooted in public taste for it not to enjoy a long lease of life. Classical aestheticism revealed the persistence of the *style noble* in which revolutionary eloquence was to flourish before dying out.

Yet there were two new elements in late-eighteenth-century belles-lettres. One was the proliferation of dictionaries, a well-known aspect of the encyclopedist fanaticism of the Enlightenment and of the zealous efforts to classify and fence off the realms of knowledge. The other element is more surprising and can be discerned only by reading the titles themselves: it was the virtual disappearance during the 1780s of Latin classics, which were still quite common in midcentury.[41] It is hard to find a cultural reason for this change in an age still dominated by neoclassical aestheticism. More probably we are dealing with an administrative side effect of the law of 1777 concerning the renewal of *privilèges* and with the effects of the spread of the new *permissions simples*.

But although, through its books, the whole of eighteenth-century French culture gives us the impression of continuity and of well-established social habits, two bibliographical categories exchanged their respective dimensions between 1724 and 1789: "theology" and "sciences and arts." This dual trend seems to have been very gradual and fairly steady. It does not bear out the hypothesis of Daniel Mornet, for whom the great battle against religion was confined to the first half century.[42] The trend we have observed was already established by the middle of the century and, if anything, it accelerated until the end of the *ancien régime*—an interesting sign of the rhythm of desacralization in the eighteenth-century world.

In actual fact, the main types of religious books to disappear were liturgical and devotional works. Catholic theology and apologetics were characterized until the end of the century either by a Jansenist approach or by a traditionalism that in the 1780s seems to have been infected with "philosophy."

"Philosophically demonstrated" Christian truths were adapted to prevailing fashions. Moreover, such works were by then hardly ever written in Latin. But the relative scarcity of liturgical books and devotional tracts commissioned by dioceses is perhaps an indication of a slackening of public demand. Does this not confirm the existence of an urban anticlericalism that was mentioned by so many eighteenth-century authors since the great crisis over the *vingtième* tax and, thus, seems to have developed well before the Civil Constitution of the clergy voted in 1790? The Jansenist, or even Richerist, roots of this movement no doubt explain *a contrario* the persistence of a sizable theological culture.

But, by the end of the century, "sciences and arts" had become the largest category of books produced. The two terms were all the more significant for having taken on new meanings: they no longer designated, as in the seventeenth century, a harmony between social activities and divine order—a harmony variously expressed by the notions of truth and beauty or nature and reason. In 1750, in the very middle of the century, Rousseau brutally divorced society from nature. Sciences and arts lost their innocence; henceforth they were damned or blessed. They had come to resemble the neoclassical façades built at the end of the century and lost in nature à l'anglaise—an expression used to characterize nature's alien and secret essence. Sciences and arts had become the prime agents of history and mankind, or, as Condorcet was to say, "of the progress of the human mind." The controversy over sciences and arts, as well as the naturally connected debate about luxury, was thus at the very heart of Enlightenment society, for which these debates symbolized the split in its own self-awareness. Hence the extraordinary impact of Rousseau's first discourse, which, from the literary point of view, was more commonplace than the intuition that informed it.

The *privilège* registers bear witness to the increasing number of books in the "sciences and arts" category—the messengers par excellence of a more civilized, richer, and more human world. The percentage of these books doubled during the course of the century. These figures represent, as it were, a vast collective compensation for the disappearance of devotional works. However, the distribution within the "sciences and arts" category remained fairly stable. One finds the same percentages for "philosophy," although "ethics" increased with respect to "metaphysics." The percentages for scientific books remained comparable: the major heading was "medicine," dominated by the obsession with venereal disease—an obsession whose psychological hold was fully revealed here. Books about agriculture and especially about politics were increasingly numerous. The nature of political works also changed, shifting from economics to politics proper. One can see by their titles the effect of the crisis of the last years of the *ancien régime*.

Among the "liberal arts," there was a proportionate increase until the 1750s in the number of books on painting, architecture, and the art of warfare. At the end of the century, the decrease in the total percentage for this category was due mainly to the decline in music books, which were very common between 1750 and 1754 and very scarce between 1780 and 1784. It may also be that, after the decrees of 1777, the regulations concerning public licenses became laxer for works as innocuous as music books.

The most surprising feature in this classification of arts and sciences is the consistently negligible share of books about the "mechanical arts"— arts that the eighteenth century often prided itself on having restored to their proper rank. But our bibliographical statistics point perhaps less to a falsehood than to a confusion. If Enlightenment society did indeed attempt to revive the mechanical arts, it was not so much through a study of the manual tradition of a preindustrial world that did not have much to teach it. Instead, the Enlightenment sought to raise these arts to the level of the *style noble* and to include them—in the name of universality—in a hedonistic utopia. The cities of happiness depicted by Ledoux are perhaps more significant than the famous plates of the *Encyclopédie*.

But, in contrast to this vast traditional output, what do the tacit permits tell us?

Comparisons can be made only for the second half of the century, but the three soundings carried out in the tacit-permit records are proportionately larger than the samplings of public licenses for the same period. The tacit-permit samples indicate that by the 1750s the share of religious and legal works dropped to about 2 to 3 percent of the total—a figure that remained unchanged until 1788. This confirms both the traditionalist character of books in these categories and the particular purpose of tacit permits. One finds an artificially larger share of intellectual innovation and of what we would today call "fashion," as opposed to intellectual and social habits.[43]

Why, then, does one find religious works at all, even in very small numbers? Liturgical literature disappeared, and devotional works became very scarce. "Theology" was the dominant category and was generally contending with the "prevailing errors" of the age and with the *philosophes*. The numerous samplings carried out among these books—when they exist in the Bibliothèque Nationale—generally reveal once again the influence and vocabulary of Jansenism. For example, a book entitled *Pensées morales adaptées aux figures de l'Ancien Testament qui représentent Jésus-Christ*, which was granted a tacit permit in 1788, turns out to have been written by an anonymous author in a rigorist style evocative of the great period of the *solitaires*. The violence of his antiphilosophical polemic is also reminiscent of the *Nouvelles ecclésiastiques*.

But apart from these religious and legal works, too scarce to warrant anything but individual comment, tacit permits almost exclusively concerned history, sciences and arts, and belles-lettres. The boundaries of these fields are more elastic than in the *privilège* registers, not only because there are greater variations in the percentages obtained for each major category, but especially because the internal structure of each field seems to have varied considerably from one sampling to another and to have been more dependent on time—that is, on fashions. Within an enduring pattern of great classical aesthetics, one can read the exaggerated signs of short-term variations and of longer-term changes.

The main feature of these trends is already familiar: the rapid increase in the number of books about sciences and arts, up from 25.6 percent in the 1750s to more than 40 percent in the 1780s. The prerevolutionary character of this trend is evidenced by the specific increase in the number of political works, which by the end of the century represented more than half the titles in this category. Naturally, we are dealing with the crisis of the *ancien régime*—that is, the short-term crisis, for if one looks at the 1784–88 period year by year, one finds a fairly constant proportion of books in the sciences and arts, while the percentage of these books that were devoted to politics rose sharply from 1787 onward, specifically after the Assembly of Notables in February, which triggered the spate of revolutionary literature. A similar but opposite phenomenon no doubt explains the relatively shrinking volume of political books between 1770 and 1774 in comparison with the 1750s: the early 1770s were the period of the Triumvirate, the last great attempt at neoabsolutist government by a king of France. At any rate, the percentage for "politics" rose suddenly in 1774 with the death of Louis XV, Turgot's liberalization, and the return of the Parlements. Thus, the registers of tacit permits not only confirm the exuberance of science and art so deeply characteristic of the Enlightenment; they also record the shorter-term variations of this phenomenon, which reflect the turning points charted by traditional history.

Hence the greater instability and the more marked character of percentages within the category. The most revealing perspective is obtained by adding philosophical and political works together; their proportionate volumes vary, but they have many internal connections in that the philosophical category is dominated by the moral works of contemporary philosophers. Indeed, it is not the twentieth century but precisely the eighteenth century—with Abbé Baudeau—that invented the expression "moral and political sciences." One can thus measure their numerical superiority over conventional sciences, a superiority that does not appear in the public *privilèges*. The tacit permits forcefully demonstrate the upsurge of interest in a wide range of social issues. However, certain features are common to both sets of sources: the predominance of medicine in the scientific category,[44] the relative importance of agronomy, and the infinitesimal percentage of works dealing with mechanical arts.

Toward the middle and end of the century, history seems to have represented a percentage of tacit permits very close to its share of *privilèges*. It is hard to explain the intervening drop during the 1770–74 period. However, an examination of the titles clearly shows that the historical works submitted for tacit approval were of a slightly different character from those listed in the *privilège* records: alongside genuine historical narratives, one can observe an increase in historical documentary literature, especially in more or less authentic memoirs of more or less famous figures of the past. The term *memoirs* is in itself a sufficient indication of the ambiguity and novelistic overtones of this genre. During the eighteenth century, which novelized history and historicized the novel, heated discussions took place about the similarity between the two genres.

Moreover, the novel, a perennial suspect for classical aesthetics, was taking shelter behind history. For this was one of the means it had found—along with the artificial exoticism of Persian or Turkish travel and the device of "letters"—for freeing itself from the burden of poetry and for setting out in its quiet way to describe the real world. Titles like *Mémoires de Monsieur X* or *Histoire de Mademoiselle Y*, which were so common, often betray a move away from pastoral toward realism and from collective idealization to particular truth. Such was the wish expressed by Diderot in his *éloge* of Richardson: "This author does not make blood drip from the walls; he does not expose you to the danger of being devoured by savages; he does not shut himself up in clandestine dens of iniquity; he never gets lost in fairyland. His setting is the world in which we live. His drama is rooted in truth; his characters are as real as can be." There is no better way of saying that, in the eighteenth century, a certain type of English-style novel destroyed the aesthetic formalization of classicism.

Thus, it is not surprising that tacit permits were a shelter par excellence for the novel. The statistics point unequivocally to the invasion of the "poetry" section by the novel. Novels represent between 25 and 50 percent of belles-lettres titles as against 15, 13, and again 15 percent in the three soundings in the *privilège* registers.[45] Admittedly, the share of belles-lettres declined among tacit permits, owing to the sharp drop in ancient and modern classics and, above all, to the expansion of sciences and arts. But the internal proportion of novels remained very high.

These figures prompted us to undertake a comparison for the periods 1740–45 and 1750–55 of the novels recorded in the licensing registers and those listed by Daniel Mornet in his classic edition of *La Nouvelle Héloïse*.[46] We have had to rearrange in chronological order the works classified by Mornet according to genre. But the comparison remains shaky, since Mornet's bibliography lists novels that were actually published or reissued (and of which copies are still extant), whether printed in France or abroad. In contrast, applications for printing licenses concerned only the novels for which permission was sought in Paris from the *chancelier*. Some of these titles were reissues, but they also included, in the mass of manuscripts, a certain number of novels that were simply planned or that may possibly have been lost. Certain of these books can be identified only tentatively or with difficulty.[47] Moreover, there is an irreducible time lag between the two sources being compared, because of the variable delay between the request for permission to print and actual publication. Nevertheless, the figures seem interesting enough to warrant inclusion here:

	Manuscripts		
	Privilèges	Tacit Permits	Mornet
1741–45	74	18	205
1751–55	123	193	199

Thus, the novels listed in the manuscript records of the royal bureaucracy were less numerous than those in Mornet's bibliography in the 1740s and considerably more numerous during the 1750s. This contrast is primarily due to the rise in tacit permits, whose representative character is therefore demonstrated for the post-1751 period. Many—but naturally not all—of the novels listed by Mornet as having been published abroad are to be found in the requests for tacit permits. Conversely, Mornet's list omits many titles of novels mentioned in the official records.

But quite apart from this comparison—which will have to be examined in a less general perspective than that of the present study[48]—the comparison between the two series of licensing records underscores the considerable proportion of novels among books submitted for tacit approval. This relative importance is all the more striking as, in midcentury, the number of books per year submitted for tacit permits was three times lower than the figure for *privilèges*. Thus, in the 1750s, France does not seem to have been exclusively obsessed, as Voltaire claimed in a well-known passage, with the debate about grain. One can only conclude that the novel must have been a much-demanded commodity, since it seems to have monopolized the "belles-lettres" category. The origins of this phenomenon are more remote, and must also be sought in the long aesthetic and literary quarrel chronicled by Georges May. But the tacit permits of the second half of the century bear witness to what was now the dominant role of the novel in literary innovation.

The soundings we have carrried out confirm the basic features of the two sources—features emphasized in all contemporary accounts: without tacit permits, the book-licensing records of the *ancien régime* would give no indication of the fascination exercised by the novel over French society at large. But, without the public licenses, these records would obliterate all trace of the Latin culture and traditional aesthetics on which every eighteenth-century generation—even that of the Revolution—was brought up.

These two radically divergent series are valuable for the historian. Not only do they help to mark the boundary between innovation and tradition, but, by assembling at the outset the conditions for their contradictory development, they appear as complementary at the end of the process. The proportions differ, but the trends are identical.

The persistence of legal works indicates the vitality of a political society engendered by the great royal jurists. This continuity points both to the proliferation of private interests and to the yearning for the abstract and univocal arbitration of legal codes. The persistence of books on history is as ambiguous to interpret as history itself, which in the eighteenth century was, all at the same time, a conventional form of recitation, an undiscriminating form of curiosity about time and space, and an awakening of national consciousness. The Age of Enlightenment preserved the traditional balance between history as rhetoric, as knowledge, and as justification.

The bookshelves of our imaginary libraries also reveal quite clearly the continuing importance of belles-lettres and the survival of the major genres. The eighteenth-century world was still that of the grammarians and normative critics of the French classicist period. The culture of antiquity, oratory, poetry, and theater retained its privileged status and its audience. It is through the novel that Beauty sometimes took on a new form, freed from the constraints of *le grand style*. But novels often preserved the appearances of that style by disguising themselves under the traditional headings of "pastoral," "morals," "travel," or "history." Such devices were no doubt less a precaution than an homage of sorts to prevailing public taste. This general pattern is not without significance, in that the quest for what the Revolution owed to Enlightenment philosophy still goes on. Perhaps it would also be interesting to examine what the Revolution owed to classical rhetoric: Robespierre and Saint-Just wrote verse before their speechmaking days.

Finally, throughout the century, there is the large-scale decline of religious books coupled with the rise of "sciences and arts"; the variations in this trend are visible indications of shifts in collective interests and in receptiveness to new ideas. At the most general and unsophisticated level of analysis, this trend expresses the well-known phenomenon experienced by contemporaries as the attempt by the *philosophes* to eliminate the supernatural from the human world. It is no coincidence if so many eighteenth-century texts speak of "sciences and arts" and "mores and religion" as opposing categories. The desacralization of French society and culture was expressed through the old unifying concept of classical nomenclature.

But sciences and arts were not only the instruments of secularization. Well before the spectacular successes of industrial efficiency, they already appeared to be vested with the attributes later assigned to them by optimistic liberalism and its Marxist inversion: sciences and arts were no longer ornaments or even mere forms of knowledge, but mankind's specific implements, the equipment that would make its adventure a success. The great idea that presided over the rationality of the modern world thus originated in classical culture from the very accumulation of reflections on sciences and arts.

The fact that this idea emerged well before the process of industrial transformation no doubt explains the specific features that it displayed in French history: the weakness of technological research, the relatively slow development of science itself, the persistence of classical modes of thought, the predominance of social welfare as an intellectual preoccupation. Sciences and arts were no longer a joint study of Truth and Beauty as concepts spontaneously attributed to the eternal order of the world. Sciences and arts already expressed the awareness of a dichotomy and of a history—not so much the history of man's relationship to nature as the history of human knowledge, the *progress* of which was both recognized as a fact and transfigured as a value.

In this advancement of learning, ethics and politics carved out the lion's share. The two fields were not only concerned with technical observation and with correcting "abuses"; they also aimed at reconstructing the entire polity. A vast social upsurge expressed itself through the twofold language of experience and vision. The most innovative currents of Enlightenment thought espoused both an ambition and a utopia: the ambition of power and the utopia of happiness. The Enlightenment was a conquest, an enlargement of human knowledge, but at the same time a clandestine effort to forestall the dangers of a now open-ended history. It bequeathed to modern France a pair of alternatives that for the past two centuries have never ceased to infuse passion into her cultural and political history.

7

Two Historical Legitimations of Eighteenth-Century French Society: Mably and Boulainvilliers

The eighteenth century asked two questions of history: What is a civilization? What is a nation?

The two questions were independent of one another and never overlapped. The first was connected with the strong feeling of progress that characterized the century and with the development of a linear scheme of human history. "Civilization" was seen as the peak of moral, literary, and artistic perfection, its model provided by Greek and Latin antiquity. The Europe of the Enlightenment was a new illustration of the benefits of such perfection. Between Voltaire and Condorcet, civilization even ceased to be thought of as a cyclical embodiment of the model of antiquity and came to be regarded simply as the more advanced phase of the "progress of the human mind." All societies had to go through civilization at some point. Civilization was an ideal for societies that had not yet attained it and a blessing for those that were flourishing in it. In any case, history—now that its direction was clear—insured that all societies, sooner or later, would experience civilization.

The second question had nothing to do with this prophetic rationalism—at least not until the French Revolution. On the contrary, it originated in the uneasy relationship of French society with absolutism. It is therefore understandable that the first signs of preoccupation with the question can be discerned during the wars of religion and the Fronde, that is, during the two earlier crises of absolutism. A civil society that was asking itself "What is the nation?" was expressing a sense of autonomy with respect to government. This question also involved the notion of *rights*: if a kingdom was a gathering of subjects, a nation was a community

First published as "Deux légitimations historiques de la société française au XVIIIe siècle: Mably et Boulainvilliers," *Annales: économies, sociétés, civilisations*, May–June 1979, 438–50. I thank Mona Ozouf, coauthor of this essay, for allowing me to reprint it here.

of citizens. A kingdom was a property; a nation was a contract. The function of history was to rediscover the clauses of that contract, to assert its imprescriptibility, to insure that it was being carried out, or to denounce its abandonment. Acting for, and on behalf of, defaulting Providence, history was entrusted with the broad task of verifying titles: those of the king and those of the nation. History was either the repository of the original contract or it was merely a chronology of despotism—another way of saying that the nation embodied freedom.

But just what was that nation? That was the core of the problem. For although French society stridently displayed very early in the century—by 1715—its determination to transform its relationship with royal authority, it was unable to think of itself as a political community.

French society had been not just tamed but truly shattered by Louis XIV's tyranny, whose memory it never exorcised. For intellectual, political, and fiscal reasons, and by a variety of means—which were based on different principles but converged in their results—the Grand Roi mixed all ranks of society. Through wholesale servitude, the sale or renegotiation of titles and privileges, and arbitrary bureaucratic promotions, the nobility was robbed less of its role than of its very essence. But, while the absolute monarchy destroyed the principles of the society of orders, it preserved and even "castified" the appearances of this society. The inflexible court protocol actually dissimulated a state and a society that had ceased to share a common legitimacy.

Moreover, the intellectual conditions for developing a new legitimacy had changed. By the early eighteenth century, politics and society had been included in the sphere of critical thought. The providentialist and organicist justification of social hierarchy was no longer sufficient to rebuild a consensus. This hierarchy had ceased to be taken for granted. Rather, it had to be made compatible with natural equality among men. It had to reveal and express the social contract, and no longer a divinely ordained plan. Lastly, it had at all costs to lay the basis for participation in government, that is, for a rudimentary form of citizenship.

These complex imperatives, at once social, psychological, and cultural, could be justified by arguments drawn from the boundless resources of French history. The history of France had replaced God as the guardian of the original contract, of the rights of the French, and of the secrets of the social compact. It was now the supreme legitimating authority, whose task was to answer the question, What is a nation? The reference to history served as the basis for political theory, for claims to citizenship, and for a discourse on inequality. It is striking to see history being invoked in the same terms by men as different as Boulainvilliers and Mably, so often contrasted as the exponent of nobiliary ideology versus the exponent of democratic ideology. We should like to show in this essay that their constructs are contradictory but comparable, having been obtained by the handling of identical historical data and identical conceptual building blocks. Through Boulainvilliers and Mably, one discovers that in the eighteenth century the same history could be written from contradictory points of view—all it took was the demands of immediate circumstance for that history to become overladen with unexpected significance.

As observers of their own times, Boulainvilliers and Mably were struck by the debasement of political freedom. What they regarded as the most decisive development of their age was, however, stubbornly overlooked by men around them whose task was to understand the present. The *intendants*, for example, were supposed to describe conditions in France, but their reports, which were filled with references to royal rights, were silent about the rights of the French. "They do not conceive, or refuse to conceive, of any principle of government other than the despotism of a prince and his ministers,"[1] wrote Boulainvilliers indignantly, having resolved there and then to condemn the authorities. As for Mably, he was distressed to read a history of France by Père Daniel: "From Clovis to our times," Père Daniel led his reader on "as if he were dealing with the very same monarchy."[2] Only those who took the present for granted could display such peace of mind; but a present experienced in such a manner was, of necessity, unintelligible. Only dissatisfaction with the present could give meaning to the past.

For both Boulainvilliers and Mably, the present in all its features bespoke the abuses of despotic kingship, while contemporary observers did not even seem aware of the fact. This twofold diagnosis lay at the heart of the two authors' pursuit of history, which they regarded as a necessity. So similar was their need for history that Mably had to resist those of his friends who wanted him to title his observations *Histoire de notre gouvernement*. *Histoire de l'Ancien Gouvernement de la France* is what Boulainvilliers had called his great work a half century earlier—a telling sign that the two men shared an identical belief in history as a meditation on the origins of power and as a remedy for fascination with the present.

To confess to such beliefs was obviously to break with the providentialist view of history. Boulainvilliers did so more forcefully than Mably, because for him the model of Bossuet, however repulsive ("one of the most shameful demonstrations of the indignity of our time"),[3] was also closer and more constraining. Boulainvilliers still felt it necessary, before undertaking a historical project, to state that God may have given man natural wisdom without controlling the use man would make of it. "He has abandoned the world to our contest": this strong statement, which emancipated history from metaphysics, opens the *Abrégé d'Histoire universelle*, written around 1700 for his children. Fifty years later, Mably did not regard this *laissez-passer*—this *laissez-penser*—as indispensable, even as a rhetorical precaution.

There was still another kind of history from which the very logic of their undertaking diverted them: the history of princes written for princes. Nevertheless, in keeping with tradition, Boulainvilliers wrote history primers for the duke of Burgundy and Mably for the infante of Parma. But neither author remained faithful to the content or tone of this type of history, designed for a traditional purpose. Erudite minutiae concerning "idle and lazy kings who contributed nothing to human happiness"[4] seemed superfluous to both. There should be no trace of sycophancy in a work aimed at being thoroughly critical. As a revenge on despotism, history could bring monarchs before its tribunal. Mézeray and Père Daniel, for their part, had been gripped by panic when popes and kings appeared on the stage. But their pusillanimity was precisely a telling sign of what their work was worth.

Neither Mably nor Boulainvilliers wanted to break with erudite history—another variety of history for which tradition provided a model. Following the teachings of Bayle, they still regarded history as a continuing effort to correct errors. But this demanding form of history, requiring vast quantities of archives and preoccupied with checking facts, was wholly dependent on the present. It was the present that guided the historian in the necessary selection of events from the abundant stores of the past. It was in the name of the present that the two authors disdained the "succession of feats of arms and wars," "quirks," and "prejudice," in order to focus on the crucial issues: the source of authority, the extent and limits of power, the rules of government in France, and, lastly, the "principles"[5] that determined the entire sequence of events leading up to the detestable present.

For both Boulainvilliers and Mably recounted a process of deterioration. Theirs was a history of how "self-evident principles" were worn down, adulterated, and transformed beyond recognition. The history of France was a story of decay. Boulainvilliers made the point in his empirical and realistic way by excusing himself—when, for example, he had to discuss "the most unpleasant reign in the history of France,"[6] that of Charles VI—for having to dwell so often on the disgrace of the state. Mably described the same situation with the more tragic accents of a man who viewed all of history as a decline. "History is an almost unbroken succession of miseries, disasters, and calamities."[7] What was there to be gained from such a black tale? Mably and Boulainvilliers shared a somewhat intermittent belief in the pedagogic value of misfortune.

Yet the true value of history did not lie in these negative lessons, but in giving prominence to a continuous transformation, in which the past was constantly present in the present. Mably and Boulainvilliers—unlike Voltaire—firmly believed in history as a process of perpetual change. Neither thought it possible to divide the flow of time into periods that would constitute strongly individualized and relatively autonomous wholes. Thus, their history, which linked interminable transformations to one another and displayed the ubiquitous role of differences, was both a war machine against centralizing government and a remedy for the doctrines of centralization and fixity. Its peculiar virtue was that it enabled the historian, thanks to the well-established connections between successive transformations, to work his way backward to a point of origin.

Hence, for Mably and Boulainvilliers alike, the very essence of the historian's activity was to provide the French with a description of "their old government." They were counting on the powerful emotional significance of this return to origins to counteract the superficial notion—so widespread among the French—according to which the present was mistakenly credited with the solidity of what had always existed. They wanted to cure the French of the frivolity that prevented them from concentrating on "ideas about government"[8] and to combat their compatriots' prodigious ability to forget. Indeed, the French were guilty only of having forgotten. The severity displayed by Mably and Boulainvilliers toward a nation inconsiderate enough to have forgotten that "it once had a Charlemagne"—their positive and shared hero—was thus tempered by hope, for forgetfulness was not quite the same thing as ignorance. Even if stifled, the "old notions of society and order" did not have to be instilled so much as revived. History was a reminiscence. Thus, it was hardly necessary to offer the French a new interpretation of their past. It was enough to show them their past for their memory to be reawakened. After so many "memoirs for a perfect history," the task was to write histories for a perfect memory.

It is easier to understand now the role played within their interpretation of history by the flattering description of primitive barbarity, a very strange attitude on the part of men so obviously attached to the contemporary values of the Enlightenment. How could the unpolished customs of a tribe of fully armed roughnecks roaming the Germanic forests constitute the breeding ground for liberty and equality? Why did Mably and Boulainvilliers, like their "Germanist" contemporaries,[9] so readily equate barbarism with energy and regard savagery as a portent of independence? What was their purpose in describing cruelty as the very mark of a "proud soul"? One can understand such sympathy only in terms of their need to evaluate contemporary abuses. Without going back to the primitive savagery of the fledgling nation, no one could judge the present for what it was or be fully aware of the "gaps" between French society and its historical traditions. The unsophisticated comradeship of the Franks and their jealous attachment to their independence helped to highlight the illegitimate growth of despotism and its retinue of servility. The concept of origins, which led to a lesson in comparative history, was thus a governing concept.

But it did not imply any sanctification of origins. Neither Mably nor Boulainvilliers considered a nation's first laws to be its fundamental laws. No one, said Mably, is so ignorant as to confuse the former with the latter. And he demystified the Golden Age. Mably's "early Greeks"[10] did not live bedecked by myrtle wreaths in pastoral peace. They, too, like the Franks, advanced in arms, with determination. The tale of origins was thus curiously tempered by realism. This approach is more explicit in the work of Boulainvilliers, who, feeling a greater need than Mably did to legitimize the society of orders, was obliged to admit that violence was indeed the root cause of social distinctions. Without a doubt, society originated in viciousness. The Angoulême manuscript notes that the nobility "is hateful, so to speak, because of the fearsome violence that desolated the earth." But this violence in no way justified going beyond its assertion to seek for an innocent and more primitive starting point. The feeling that retrogressive historical analysis had to stop somewhere certainly determined Boulainvilliers to draw the line where he did. But he was also guided by a sense of realism free from any illusion: "The antiquity of origins thus gave way, with reason, to the superior force of conquest. . . ."[11] That is why the strenuous efforts of certain historians to camouflage the Capetian usurpation seem to Boulainvilliers to be totally absurd: was a 700-year-old tenure such a mediocre claim to legitimacy?[12]

To temper the surprise one feels at seeing a man so representative of the "early Enlightenment" blithely equate law and fact, one ought to remember that he was an assiduous reader of Spinoza. Familiarity with a system in which God's right is equated with his power and in which every individual enjoys rights exactly proportionate to his might undoubtedly taught Boulainvilliers not to put right on a par with ideal ends. Like the Spinozist polity, Boulainvilliers' society was the outcome of an interplay of forces. Historical description was for him only the expression of an empirical situation, and it excluded axiology altogether. Boulainvilliers's realism expressed itself most fully in the Angoulême manuscript: "There is in fact no more authentic nobility than that acquired by right of conquest, just as there is no greater distinction among men than that between victor and vanquished. . . ."

Mably, on the other hand, was not prepared to grant any right to the victor. While he agreed about the state of the French before the conquest, he refused the crude statement that seemed to him to summarize the history of origins as written by Boulainvilliers: "Every Frenchman was a nobleman, and every Gaul was a commoner." But Mably was no more convinced than Boulainvilliers that one could proceed backward in history indefinitely. One could never move from history back to nature. The "most ancient monuments of history" represented already decayed societies. Nevertheless, they had to be dwelt on.

But the purpose of such attention was to improve one's understanding of history, not to relive it. Tradition was a stimulus for intellectual and moral energy, but not an invitation to reverie. There was no nostalgic note in the description of origins, for the description of each period balanced its advantages and drawbacks, so that even the fallen nobility depicted by Boulainvilliers could not simply complain "of having lost the superior and incommunicable rank that it enjoyed for so long during the centuries of ignorance and coarseness." Similarly, Boulainvilliers thought it would be indecent to criticize the third estate and the magistracy indefinitely for what they initially were; it would be insane to believe that one could downgrade the representatives of the third estate "to the rank of serfs"; it would be absurd to attempt to restore the turbulent equality practiced by the pillaging horde.[13] Mably was somewhat less sure: with a little luck, and by acting in time, one could have succeeded in going back to origins. Sometimes Mably indulged in a vision of such a return, playing the role of the legislator intent upon reforming a society that had not yet reached the point at which the accumulation of vice and prejudice becomes irreversible. His description then takes on the ethereal quality of utopia: "I have visions of citizens divided into different classes. . . . everywhere I can see public stores containing the riches of the Republic . . . And the magistrates, true fathers of the homeland. . . ." But the opportunity for returning to the primitive state had unquestionably vanished. "Wisdom comes too late, when mores have been corrupted."[14]

Prediction, however, was not impossible. The unfolding of a tight-knit temporal sequence in effect committed the historian to "horoscopes"— the term is Mably's. The fact that each period was so closely linked to the past and enmeshed in a network of effects and causes that left so little room for chance was no doubt an encouragement to make forecasts. But, by the same token, this vision quashed the hope of a leap forward as effectively as it eliminated the prospect of a return to the past. Social change could never take place except gradually and unobtrusively. Boulainvilliers contented himself with expressing a desire to see the states general reinstated and endowed in particular with financial powers. Mably wanted to revive the assemblies of the Champs de Mars and the Champs de Mai under the name of the Estates General. But the recourse to "this forgotten practice" would create only an illusion of change if the degenerate nation was unfit to "take advantage of the event." The prophetic overtones ascribed to Mably's work owe a great deal to its proximity to the Revolution. His *Droits et devoirs du citoyen*, written in midcentury, was published in 1789. But in reality there was no messianic spirit in Mably any more than in Boulainvilliers. Neither author regarded the present as the locus of an imminent restoration—and even less of a revolution.

Thus, Mably and Boulainvilliers shared a common notion of history. But they also used the same material and developed identical themes. It was not to retrace the progress of civilization that Mably and Boulainvilliers examined the passing of time, but to discover the lost origins of the nation and the reasons and the stages of this eclipse. Only the Germanist thesis with its emphasis on Frankish conquest gave them the means to conduct this investigation, for it alone enabled them to wrest the history of the nation from the yoke of the Roman *imperium*. It alone could conjure up from the forests of Germany the warriors who brought the original contract to France. It alone turned the French people into a free nation. Everything had already been said in the late seventeenth century with the words *free nation*.

History was thus the repository of the greatness of origins and the secret of usurpations. It constituted a purely immanent reference system that substituted for the unfolding of a providential plan. But Boulainvilliers used history to justify a "discourse on inequality" that was exactly the opposite of Mably's.

Yet for the comte de Boulainvilliers—and this once again proves how much of an eighteenth-century man he was—men were originally free and equal in rights. The problem for this intellectual so obsessed with his noble status was, therefore, how to interpret and justify the traditional social hierarchy according to the values of a cultural world already dominated by the Enlightenment—that is, a world cut off from any transcendental reference point and suffused with the concept of natural equality among individuals. The task of history, in this cultural setting marked by the notion of natural equality, was to explain the emergence of inequality, the product of a conquest that turned the victors into nobles and the vanquished into non-nobles. But Boulainvilliers did not stop there, for history could undo what it had wrought. Race was the element that would preserve history's achievement. The original distinction between statuses, which was by and large accidental, became a necessity when perpetuated through the blood. Thus, far from being archaic, the concept of "race," as Louis Dumont has suggested, seems to have been linked to the birth of egalitarian ideology. Indeed, this concept made it possible to replace the old organicist justification of inequality with a historico-biological theory that was not only compatible with "natural" equality but allowed the notion of equality to be integrated into an inegalitarian construct. Nobles were different from (that is, superior to) commoners, but all nobles were equal among themselves. Equality was a basic element in Boulainvilliers's vision of the nobility, and it was what made him so different from Saint-Simon, obsessed with the preeminence of dukes and peers.

For Boulainvilliers, the military caste created in the wake of the conquest was a society of equals. He never failed to stress that among the free conquerors who had come from Germany, "the now-prevalent distinctions based on titles were totally unknown." But this egalitarian society was also a closed society. While conquest conferred a rank then perpetuated through the blood, nothing else could confer it in its place—not even, and least of all, royal favor. Boulainvilliers was therefore intent on emphasizing the closed character of the nobility (the idea of establishing once and for all a general inventory of noble families of the realm was another aspect of that intention)[15] and the strict equality prevailing within that exclusive group.

This model, which reinstated equality in an inegalitarian framework, did involve a major difficulty, for the argument based on heredity seemed to Boulainvilliers as unconvincing when applied to the king (all the misfortunes that befell the state were due to the hereditary monarchy) as when applied to the people (while virtue could indeed "appear" among commoners, it remained strictly personal and could never be transmitted to their offspring). Yet heredity guaranteed "incommunicable nobility"—a privilege that Boulainvilliers justified by some shaky statistical arguments: virtue was *more* widespread in good races than in others; furthermore, noble birth was *the most* common way of exploiting and honoring virtue.

In addition, two contradictory dangers threatened this curious arrangement. First, the inequality of status might be challenged from the outside: it was therefore necessary to resist the rise of the third estate and of the magistracy. Second, equality might be compromised within the privileged group itself: it was vital to prevent the proliferation of new forms of inequality within the system of second-degree equality established amid inequality. Thus, the nobility had as much to fear from expansion (that is, from the sovereign's power to ennoble, which introduced spurious equals into the group of equals) as from separation (that is, from the prospect of new and more marked distinctions within the group of equals). That is why Philip the Fair was the great villain of French history, according to Boulainvilliers. Philip the Fair was the first to "claim the power to ennoble the blood of commoners and, by a somewhat similar abuse—although different in kind—he was the first to create new peerages."[16] It is significant that the two actions should be described as identical and as being the product of the muddle-headedness inseparable from despotism. Philip the Fair was guilty on two counts: for having introduced, first, a measure of equality into inequality (since "newly ennobled commoners came to believe that they had attained genuine equality") and, second, a measure of inequality into equality, by establishing a peerage that had no historical justification (since "peers, princes, and hereditary nobles alike all sat with the nobility in the assemblies of state"). The only argument capable of tempering Boulainvilliers's opposition to Saint-Simon in the dispute over dukes and peers was that, since the possibility of purchasing office had opened the doors of the magistracy to "even the most modest bourgeois," there was no reason for "royal favor not to be displayed toward some nobles as well. . . ." The fact remained that the two practices were, as far as principles were concerned, equally heinous.

What was to be done, then? Boulainvilliers ultimately aimed at counteracting the apologetics of absolutism by building another model of national history, one founded on "feudal" society. But it must be noted that Boulainvilliers was not a "feudalist" in the sense in which the term was used during the Enlightenment and the Revolution. He criticized the church and scholasticism, as well as the crass manners and the ignorance of his time. He hailed the sixteenth-century Renaissance of arts and letters[17]—an uncommon periodization in histories of France of this epoch and in eighteenth-century culture in general.

In truth, what Boulainvilliers sought to give back to a nobility that had so completely forgotten its origins as to be unable to define itself was the awareness of its own existence. The fact was that the nobility would nearly have lost that awareness were it not for the greed of commoners. The "inordinate passion" of the latter for "entering the nobility by royal patent" still kept alive within the nobility the feeling of corporate identity, with its dual aspect of exclusion and equality. Boulainvilliers dreamed of a less external basis. But the feudal regime that provided him with the model was simply an ideal type of the relationship between civil society and the king of France. This ideal type presented two features: a society founded on inequality of status and on equality within each status; the independence of nobles from the king, conceived as *primus inter pares*.

Mably's problem was quite different. Like Boulainvilliers, he postulated a primitive state of equality, rooted in "a nature that had no enclosed fields." But he was not out to legitimize at any price a metaphysically unacceptable social hierarchy, for he regarded it, in any case, as having no genuine historical foundation. On the contrary, Mably developed a radical critique of heredity. He was challenging the concept not as applied to kings alone, but as applied to all of mankind. As long as vassals were granted personal distinctions, all was well in Mably's history: nobility was not transmitted through the blood, the children of the nobility remained in the common class of citizens, and there was a single order with two classes. History went wrong when these two classes (which were constantly disintegrating and being rebuilt according to individual talent and virtue) were turned into fixed orders. Mably's villain was not Philip the Fair, but Clothar II, who, by establishing hereditary benefices, introduced a privileged order into the nation.

This order at once became the mortal enemy of equality—if only by the fascination it exerted on the third estate, which it prevented from having a sense of its own corporate identity (one can observe here the complete reversal of Boulainvilliers's thesis). Mably dated its birth to a still remote period. But his basic aim was nevertheless to demonstrate that the nobility had not always existed, thereby depriving the privileged order of the prestige of an original state. This point was so crucial for Mably that, in order to prove it, he did not hesitate to challenge the authority of Montesquieu and to call to the rescue—only once, it is true—the arguments of the opposite camp, that of Abbé Dubos: "I do not imagine that Monsieur le Président de Montesquieu believes that nations had noblemen from the start." Thus, Mably found no trace of political feudalism in the origins of the nation. In his borrowings from the *germanistes*, what counted for Mably was the structure of the "old government." A king who was more of a captain than a monarch and who commanded soldiers far more than he ruled subjects; a collegial executive power exercised by the king and the notables in council; a legislative power in the hands of a general assembly, the Champ de Mars—these were the basic features of Mably's system.

One must add to it a vision of the conquest borrowed from Montesquieu, halfway between the absurd idyll of the relations between Gauls and Franks imagined by Dubos and the watertight separation imposed by Boulainvilliers. For Mably, as for Montesquieu, the vanquished, having been freed from the Roman *imperium*, rallied to their conqueror. Mably saw this rallying less as an effect of habit than as the result of a voluntary, conscious, and public choice—a solemn declaration, an oath. Official renunciation of Roman law was the price that the Gauls had to pay in order to "begin to enjoy the same prerogatives," to obtain the same legal settlements as the victorious Franks, and finally—the obvious triumph of assimilation!—to be admitted to the Champs de Mars.

Thus, Mably rejected inequality on two counts: it was neither the product of race (since, unlike Montesquieu, he did not believe in the existence of an original Frankish nobility) nor the fruit of conquest (since, unlike Boulainvilliers, Mably postulated the intermingling of the victors and the vanquished). Inequality was a perversion, the first link in a long chain of vices. It stimulated the growth of private wealth, the loss of attachment to freedom, and—worst of all!—irregular attendance at the Champs de Mars. In Mably's view, therefore, the only possible foundation for society was equality.

But one must be clear about the exact nature of equality as Mably saw it. Mably did not believe, any more than Boulainvilliers did, in an undiscriminating form of equality, whose model was once again provided by despotism: "The closer one gets to despotism, the more social ranks become indistinguishable."[18] Mably—who also invoked the authority of Montesquieu—inherited from Boulainvilliers the notion of a farsighted despotism that saw things from too far and too high to perceive any differences. But Mably did not advocate the type of equality that would be fatal to dependency, for "only in Turkey or some other despotic state can one believe that the subordination necessary in society is incompatible with equality."[19]

This time the aim was therefore to reestablish inequality within an egalitarian system, and Mably did his best to devise such a scheme. Actually, a few adjustments were enough to make inequality tolerable. Could one preserve inequality of wealth? The Swiss example showed that wise sumptuary laws succeeded in preventing the anarchic proliferation of wealth. Could one admit the inequality of power? Yes, if it were based on competence, that is, if one claimed power less as a sovereign than as a magistrate. Therefore, since it was impossible to return to primitive equality, one could preserve all the features of unequal status, provided one took certain precautions, some of which were reminiscent of the "hidden hand" in Rousseauism: subjects would obey "without sorrow and without humiliation sovereigns who, by copying their simple, unostentatious, and thrifty bourgeois habits, would *conceal* the fact that they constituted a privileged order."[20] As for the nobility, in order for it to enjoy a fully justified status, all it had to do was to bear in mind that "the spirit of servitude is the most demeaning behavior for a nobleman."

One category was excluded from the benefits of this system: the "populace, which lacked all credit, esteem, and fortune and was incapable of acting on its own." Admittedly, some of Mably's writings imply that every man should belong to an order and enjoy genuine rights within it: every man should be declared free. But it did not necessarily follow that every man should participate in government. While the artisans in the *Entretiens de Phocion* were regarded as free men in the eyes of the law, they had no political existence and did not take part in assemblies. "It is important for the very masses themselves, who are demeaned by their work and occupations, not to take over the government."[21] This is not a far cry from the terms used by Boulainvilliers to describe the subject nation, similarly excluded from political assemblies "because its role was to work, to cultivate the land, and not to partake of the honors of government." Boulainvilliers excluded a larger category than did Mably, but both used the same criterion for exclusion.

In other words, Mably's version of history is essentially a justification of the society of orders. Like Boulainvilliers, he was obsessed by the feeling that societies were perpetually deteriorating, and he sought to halt the interminable drift of history. He therefore wanted to preserve social orders but also to prevent the encroachments, the challenges, and even the transfer of individuals from one order to another that heralded new upheavals. This aim could be achieved by assigning a fixed amount of wealth to each order:[22] individual wealth could increase or decrease, but the total wealth of each order had to remain unchanged; thus, none of them would "fall prey to contempt." The effort to provide social orders with an insurpassable "constant condition" was to be accompanied by the education of the community. Mably was as severe as Boulainvilliers toward those who tried to infringe upon the rights of the neighboring order. For example, Mably criticized the *parlementaires*, who stubbornly advocated the notion that "the clergy and nobility were admitted only as a favor to the assemblies of notables, primarily composed of magistrates." He was not optimistic about the future of a kingdom "in which no one wants to remain in his place and in which everyone's ambition is to join an order that refuses to let him in," for vanity would then become the major concern of every citizen.

Thus, Mably's great innovation was not the reversal of the concept of nobiliary liberalism—what one might call his democratic version of Germanism—but its extension to include the third estate alongside the clergy and the nobles in the nation's assemblies. Mably also linked the ideal of equality to the preservation of "ranks." This linkage—which, incidentally, shows how risky it would be to oppose the liberal current and the democratic current in the eighteenth century—could be achieved, according to Mably, thanks to a legislation devised as a harmonious system.

Indeed, the idea that is new in Mably, and that one would look for in vain in Boulainvilliers, is that of harmony. The organicist metaphor is obviously useless in describing a society split between victors all enjoying equality through privilege and vanquished all equal in servitude. However, the metaphor is indispensable to a pluralist notion of the body social. It guarantees the dignity of each section of society ("each class of citizens understands that it can be happy without oppressing the others") and insures that they will take part in the effort to reach a common goal—the "public good"—which can be attained providing there is a general acceptance of a hierarchy of social functions. That is why, for Mably, the most admirable sovereign in the history of France was Charlemagne, the orchestrator of harmony, the mediator who brought social orders closer together and made them forget their old quarrels. The work of the ideal legislator is to hold the balance between the various orders—a balance that "is today the only imaginable equality among men." Consequently, the legislator's task is easier when there are more orders: they balance each other out and, in addition, it is a finer achievement to make them all contribute to common happiness. Four orders are better than three, and five better than four. Such multiplicity would therefore, according to Mably's wish, mean the triumph of harmonious plurality, which he regarded as the ultimate constituent factor of the nation.

Thus, the discussion on the history of France was one of the liveliest features of eighteenth-century French culture, because it was rooted in civil society's drive toward power and in the search for a legitimacy intended not as a substitution—since absolutism was a usurpation—but as a *restoration*. Boulainvilliers and Mably represent two decisive moments in the debate, for they were writing respectively the nobiliary version and the roturier version of the same history, that of the nation. What separates them is important as far as their opinions are concerned: Boulainvilliers was an exclusionist aristocrat, while Mably brought the third estate back into the national fold. But in other respects their differences were virtually negligible. Both authors joined in the social demand for a liberalization of the regime—a demand for which the nobility, at the end of Louis XIV's reign, acted as a natural spokesman. Above all, both authors were writing what was intellectually the same history, built on the same institutions, and enacted by the same cast. Their concept of "nation" enabled them to deal simultaneously with the social and the national dimensions, unlike their nineteenth-century successors, who restricted their vision to the national dimension alone. By combining the social sphere and the national sphere, Boulainvilliers and Mably wedded society to its own myth.

In the years immediately preceding the French Revolution, the historical theme of nationhood acquired a particularly momentous political significance. It occurs very often in the prerevolutionary pamphlets published between the Assembly of Notables and the opening of the Estates General (late 1787–April 1789). These pamphlets, most of which were anonymous, testify to the spread of the Boulainvilliers-Mably version of French history among the educated classes of the eighteenth century. They contain many references to the origins and history of the nation.

In these improvised writings, so closely connected to contemporary events, such references present the advantage of making the political demands quite explicit; they also show the extent of the triumph of Mably's "democratic" thesis over Boulainvilliers's aristocratic thesis in public opinion. When one of these pamphlets defends the orders of society as one of the building blocks of the monarchy, it is in the name of tradition or of the Constitution, never in the name of race. Far from being a possible foundation for a new legitimacy that would have benefited the nobility, the notion of race was used as an argument against the nobles in Sieyès's *Qu'est-ce que le Tiers Etat?*, in which he advocated sending back "into the forests of Franconia all the families that cling to the absurd pretention of being issued from the race of conquerors and of having inherited their rights."

In actual fact, "Germanic liberties" had become the mythical heritage of the entire nation, now waging the decisive battle for the restoration of those liberties. The centerpiece of this construct was the king-and-nation dyad—two powers that were not defined by a conflict but were the two indispensable elements of legitimate public authority. Their theoretical definition was not contradictory but complementary. The king, enjoying a historical right attested by filiation, embodied the state. The nation was both a historical and a mythical human community—a depository of the social contract, a general will whose origins were shrouded in the mists of time, a promise of fidelity to those origins. Between king and nation there existed an apparent relationship of subordination, which was actually a binding obligation to cooperate. The king was the head of the nation, but his rule was legitimate only if he respected the rights and laws of the nation.

When he did not respect them, it was because nefarious elements thwarted that cooperation. The culprits were either ministerial despotism, as had been the case since Richelieu, or usurpation by the nobility, as during the feudal period. Thus, the battle waged during the years from

1787 to 1789 was thought of as a campaign for the nation's reconquest of its own rights and for the reestablishment of communication between king and nation, to be symbolized by the rule of law. An age-old legalistic current triumphed in this new secular religion, intended as the foundation of a revamped monarchy.

Thus, the French Revolution, before it became the zero point of French history, the myth of origins of our contemporary society, was the culmination of our remotest past, the restoration of the national community to the fullness of its rights. Ultimately, the two visions—the Revolution as a culmination or as a point of origin—are informed by an identical desire to abolish time (an aim inseparable from the revolutionary ideology) and by the same emotive power that created modern nations.

8

Civilization and Barbarism in Gibbon's History

In the Paris of the Enlightenment, from which Gibbon drew much of his intellectual inspiration, the century had begun with the so-called quarrel between the "ancients" and the "moderns," a literary controversy that seems to have run its course by Gibbon's time but that nevertheless went to the heart of his intellectual life. At issue in the quarrel as it began toward the end of Louis XIV's reign was the nature of the cultural identity between ancient and modern thought that had constituted the common heritage of the European intelligentsia since the Renaissance. The moderns did not deny their ties with antiquity and its heritage, but they rejected the notion that their own contribution should be limited to the rediscovery of a Greco-Roman model. They declared the modern to be superior to the ancient, especially in regard to the progress of knowledge, the rigor of reasoning, and the quest for truth; in doing so, they broke with the classical conception of history as cyclical and replaced it with a belief in the creative value of time, which would progressively separate truth from error.

This detachment of the concept of "modern" from its ties with antiquity gradually allowed the development in the course of the eighteenth century of an evolutionary history and a theory of progress. After the providential histories of churchmen, after the cyclical histories of the humanists and the Reformation, now history could be opened up infinitely into the future. The fears that were latent in the notion of an infinite and unknown future were conjured away by the spectacle of a continuing advance in the arts and sciences, which seemed to promise a more general progress.

First published in English, under the present title, in *Daedalus*, Summer 1976, 209–16. Reprinted here with corrections, by permission of *Daedalus*, Journal of the American Academy of Arts and Sciences, Boston, Mass.

The ideas of the moderns were given their definitive form for the eighteenth century in d'Alembert's *Discours préliminaire* and Condorcet's *Esquisse d'un tableau historique des progrès de l'esprit humain*. In them we find that "civilization" was a process before it was a state; its purpose was to make "civil," to "police" the uncivilized. The word *civilization* itself, which dates from this period in both French and English, was invented to express this drive of enlightened society toward what ought to be, the conviction of being on the right road, the certitude that the future was in fact infinite and that history had a purpose.[1]

But, in many respects, Gibbon wrote a history very different from others of his century; his history was at once more "ancient" and more "modern": more ancient because Gibbon was a professional antiquarian and familiar with the learned and the scholarly societies of Europe in the seventeenth century, into whose proceedings his mastery of French permitted him easy access; more modern because he integrated this erudition with the art of retelling the past and, in so doing, invented the historical panorama that was to become so important in the romantic era. Gibbon was somewhere between Tillemont and Renan, but this "somewhere" constituted more than just the philosophical consensus of the Enlightenment; it was also an original vision of the past and present in Europe.

His own biography already reveals some of this vision in the studious, retiring years in Lausanne undertaken by an English gentleman who had tasted the charms of the salons of Paris and London. For, on the banks of Lake Geneva, in those Franco-German confines that were so crucial for the transformations of European culture, Gibbon saw only a retreat where he could continue his work. A place of exile in his youth, Switzerland became a shelter in his maturity. By choosing Switzerland, he avoided belonging to any of the nations of Europe and thus signified that his only loyalties lay with his two universal homelands: historical erudition—that most international of cultures—and Rome, the mother of Europe. The revelation of 15 October 1764 had given a meaning to his life amounting almost to a religious conversion. Freud entered Rome only after he had already become Freud and was ready to confront the classical studies of his youth, which constituted at the same time the world of the gentile. But Gibbon did not become Gibbon until that day in October when he trod "with a proud foot upon the ruins of the Forum." He received from Rome more than his idea of civilization; he received from it his cultural identity.

Between Rome and Gibbon lay the same link that connected the European intellectuals of the Renaissance to antiquity. It was a romance, complete with the same delight in discovery and the same freshness and joy in the recapture of lost secrets. Yet, since the Renaissance, education had put Rome into everyone's store of knowledge: the Latin and history that one learned from Cicero and Tacitus continued to be the basis of the scholarly apprenticeship expected of future gentlemen. Thus, when Gibbon discovered Rome, he was familiar with it already. It was the most classical topos of European culture, the basis for its theater, its art, its moral philosophy, its historical reflection. What is strange is that his meeting with a place already so heavily charged with significance should still contain any surprise at all, much less one amounting almost to an existential conversion. In contrast, when Montesquieu had visited Rome in 1729, though he could hardly have been accused of indifference to Roman history—he had written his *Essai* (1716)[2] before his famous *Considérations* (1734)[3]—precisely because ancient Rome was for him a legitimate subject of study, he retained in his reactions to pontifical Rome something of the attitudes of an intelligent tourist—an observer of customs, politics, and the arts.[4] Thirty-five years later, Gibbon saw only the *urbs* in Rome: "Each memorable spot where Romulus stood, or Tully spoke, or Caesar fell, was at once present to my eye; and several days of intoxication were lost or enjoyed before I could descend to a cool and minute investigation."[5]

This traveler's sentiment, which anticipates the emotional investment the romantic writers were to bring to history, also reflects Gibbon's devotion to European humanism and to the tradition of the sixteenth and seventeenth centuries. According to this tradition, Rome was a model of civilization that had never been surpassed. For Gibbon, however, this was not a philosophical proposition. He did not theorize about man in society, about natural law, about the social contract; he had no interest in that essential question of his time, What is a "savage," and where does one place him in the history of humanity? He was instinctively and totally the historian; that is, he was an empiricist, a narrator, and completely and unquestioningly Europocentric in the midst of a world where only Greco-Roman antiquity, the Judaeo-Christian tradition, and their offspring—Europe—counted.

The superiority of Rome was, therefore, not something that had to be demonstrated. It was in the order of evidence, a fact. It was a unique experience that had only to be described and had nothing to do with historical laws. Gibbon had read and admired Montesquieu, but in the end the two works had little in common. For Montesquieu, Roman history was merely a "case study" for a general typology of political regimes. The reasons for Rome's greatness were at the same time the reasons for its fall: the expansion of the Empire necessitated a monarchical government incompatible with the laws that had nonetheless made it necessary. Gibbon, though he intermittently echoed his predecessor's theory, was not given to rigorous conceptualizations. He was eclectic, and he multiplied not only the possible explanations for Rome's greatness and fall, but even the kinds of explanations. For him, Roman history was not just another collection of human experiences; it was quite simply, in the second century after Christ, the highest point in human history, "the period in the history of the world, during which the condition of the human race was most happy and prosperous."[6] It was a unique moment, which did not fit into any general concept of historical change.

This view of second-century Rome as representing a privileged moment in human history was impossible to integrate into a linear view of humanity's progress, such as the one Condorcet wrote later on (1793). But such a conception was typical of cyclical histories, according to which civilization had no purpose toward which the cumulative progress of mankind was heading but rather consisted of a series of intermittent "happy and prosperous" periods. In this conception, second-century Rome represented the crowning of history's most splendid cycle—and to such a degree that the hope Gibbon assigned to eighteenth-century Europe was not to surpass this model and the values it bore but to constitute a less fragile vessel for them.

It is difficult to determine very precisely or securely the reasons behind Gibbon's worshipful admiration for the Empire. Nowhere does he present a systematic description of Roman civilization. He is so permeated with the idea of its superiority that he feels no need to discuss the reasons for it nor to take stock of its elements. The famous judgment from chapter 3 of the *Decline and Fall* quoted above, regarding the exceptionally happy state of humanity during the Antonine period, is supported only by some rather brief justifications relating to the virtue and wisdom of the emperors who came after the civil unrest in the first century. The loss of freedoms—those famous Roman freedoms that nourished so many of the century's books—was more than compensated by the exercise of an equally enlightened despotism.

Gibbon was, in fact, indifferent to the political philosophy that so excited many of his contemporaries. He wrote, as did his masters in antiquity—Thucydides, Cicero, and Tacitus—moral history. For a period to be great, it was necessary, but also sufficient, for it to have produced a certain kind of man. The emperors of the second century were his *exempla*; they were at once a culture and a moral.

Nevertheless—and not surprisingly—Gibbon's history of Rome is also a history of Gibbon. The cult of the Antonines reflected the views the historian held toward his own present. In this respect, Gibbon was an entirely original writer. He did not, as did the men of the Renaissance, have to rediscover Rome beneath the medieval sediment, for that work had been done for him. But neither did he believe, as did the artists and men of letters of the seventeenth century, that Rome could truly be imitated. He was already too much of a historian, in the nineteenth-century sense of the word, not to conceive of history as flux, never representing the same situations—or the same successes—twice. The cycles of civilization that history presented were not comparable, and they were transient. The *Decline and Fall of the Roman Empire* is dominated throughout by the romantic notion of the uniqueness and transience of the great periods of history. It is an extraordinary example of that moment when the old cyclical conception of history hung in balance with nineteenth-century historicism.

Gibbon, we must remember, did not write a history of the Roman Empire; he chose to write a history only of its decline and fall. In the very years when impeccably neoclassical ruins contributed their note of controlled sadness to the parks of aristocratic castles, Gibbon joined his powerful voice to the melancholy chorus of European scholars: far from being history's promise, civilization was the historian's nostalgia. The clearest expression of this comes at the end of chapter 38, in the famous "General Observations on the Fall of the Roman Empire in the West," which forms the only genuinely analytic commentary on the problem that gave the *Decline and Fall* its title. As we know, Gibbon, after having summarized the causes of the fall of Rome, proposed to draw from them lessons for his own time. Does this mean that he found a similarity between eighteenth-century Europe and the Roman Empire in its years of fading splendor? Yes and no. Yes because he points out, at the risk of appearing unpatriotic, that he considers Europe a great republic, united precisely by its participation in the same civilization, for all its inhabitants have attained "almost the same level of politeness and cultivation." By this he means that the European elite of his time, regardless of the vicissitudes in power relations among nations, displays a "state of happiness" and a "system of arts, and laws, and manners" common to all nations, and these are what constitute a civilization. There is nothing in this attitude that cannot be found in Enlightenment thought of the most classic kind. At the same time, however, the comparison with the civilization of the great Roman period was made only with references to external dangers: Roman history no longer constituted the basis of Europe's cultural identity, but a lesson for Europe's defense.

In short, what fascinates Gibbon about Roman civilization is not so much that in it lay the foundations of Europe but that it was so fragile, as fragile perhaps as Europe's civilization now was. As he looks upon the ruins of Rome, the humanist gentleman asks the future about the chances of survival for the things he loves. Gibbon's feeling of belonging to a special but threatened moment in history does not come from an analysis of the inner contradictions of European civilization. On the contrary, he says that the fact that the majority of nations carry on this civilization and emulate it is, in his view, a source of strength, not of weakness. He does not even suspect that, within this community of European culture, nationalism would become an element of disintegration. He reasons only in terms of a possible barbarian (or, more precisely, "savage") menace, as if the invasions had been the sole cause of the dismemberment of the Western Empire (though several pages earlier he expressly blamed its excessive size and the disintegrating influence of Christianity) and as if the multinational Europe of the eighteenth century could be compared to the extended Roman frontiers (though a few pages later he points out that northern Europe, once a stronghold of barbarians, had little by little been civilized).

The comparison, in fact, comes out in favor of eighteenth-century Europe. Gibbon lists the elements militating in favor of a relative stability for the civilization it has attained—its geographic extent, its national diversity, its mastery of the art of war, the undeniable distinction of its inventions and basic technology—and in the end he even advances the idea of a continuous progress of humanity "since the first discovery of the arts." But it was still the case that Europe's civilization, even if it was probably indestructible, remained subject to the challenge of the "savage nations of the globe." It could be seriously threatened, forced to retreat, to become expatriated "in the American world." In a century that had witnessed a rapid acceleration in the Europeanization of the globe, a phenomenon that had characterized history everywhere since the Renaissance, Gibbon discussed the reverse hypothesis drawn from the Roman example. It was not that he thought it likely, but that his concept of civilization already included a threatening reversal, a permanent exterior menace—the savage world.

Savage or barbarian? Generally speaking, the Enlightenment distinguished between these two terms by defining them as two different steps in the evolution toward civilization. The *Encyclopédie* (1751) still confused them, however, for in it "savages" were described as "barbaric people who live without laws, without government, without religion, and who have no fixed habitation." But it then adds, "There is this difference between savages and barbarians, namely, that the first form scattered little nations that have no desire to unite, whereas the barbarians often unite, and this happens when a chief submits to one of the others. Natural liberty is the sole concern of government among savages; along with this liberty, nature and climate are almost the sole forces that prevail among them. Occupied by hunting or pastoral life, they do not burden themselves with religious observances and do not make their religion a basis for organizing their lives."

Some time later, the *Dictionnaire* of Trévoux (1771), although it followed the *Encyclopédie* very closely, took pains not to use the term *barbarian* as a synonym for *savage*. The latter term "is also used for those people who wander in the forests, without fixed habitation, without laws, without government, and almost without religion." Thus, the two dictionaries agree with Montesquieu in distinguishing between savages and barbarians by stating that the first "live scattered about, retreating into the forests and the mountains, without uniting, while the second often unite and sometimes live under a chief to whom they have submitted."[7] Ferguson (1767) writes that the savage, in America, has neither property nor government nor judges, while the barbarian, in Europe, had property and obeyed a chief.[8] De Pauw (1768) clearly distinguished different stages in history when, for example, he differentiated between the treatment of prisoners by "the most savage," "ordinary savages," "semibarbarous peoples," and "the least barbarous" nations.[9]

Thus, the Enlightenment, in France and in England, constructed a three-stage progressive scheme of history: "savage-barbarian-civilized." Just after Démeunier,[10] Robertson, in 1778, defined the same three stages of evolution but this time according to more materialistic criteria: the savages had neither writing nor metals nor domesticated animals (America); the barbarians had metals and domesticated animals (Europe, Mexico, and Peru); the civilized nations had industry and the arts.[11] To this materialistic classification, destined for a great future in the following century, the eighteenth-century thinkers usually added philosophico-political criteria: the savage belonged to the natural order. He was without fixed habitat, without religion, without laws, without customs, the embodiment of human origins. Yet he was capable of acceding to history and to a policed society so long as his natural character was not corrupted by contact with Europeans. The barbarian, however, already belonged to history: he formed nations and he established states; but he did not enjoy the protection of regular laws, and his knowledge and customs remained, or reverted to being, crude. For barbarism was what preceded, threatened, or came after civilization. "Nations have all oscillated," wrote Diderot, "from barbarism to the policed state, from the policed state to barbarism, until unforeseen causes have brought them to an equilibrium that they never perfectly maintain."[12]

Gibbon, however, did not distinguish between the savage and the barbarian. In this respect he was behind the times, still fixed on the historical dichotomy of the beginning of the century. For he was not really interested in man in nature, the concept of the savage that so engaged the philosophers of the Enlightenment. His perception was more historical than philosophical; it was perhaps entirely historical. The fall of the Roman Empire is played out between a civilized society, on the one hand, and those outside this society, on the other. Ultimately this former reader of Thucydides and Tacitus adopts the classical distinction between Greek and barbarian or Roman and barbarian: the barbarian is the one who is on the other side of the frontier. But Gibbon also calls him "savage," in part at least because the word was so commonly used in the eighteenth century, but also to emphasize the gap that separated him from civilized man.

One has only to read chapter 9 of Gibbon's history, which is devoted to the Germanic tribes, to become convinced of this. Here Gibbon closely follows Tacitus, his master and model. He wants to understand what has made those "wild barbarians of Germany" Rome's most formidable enemy. No cities, no letters, no arts, no monetary system—such are the negative traits that define what he calls a "savage state." When he comes to the famous theme of the Germanic freedoms, so important in the historiography of the period, especially in Montesquieu and Mably—

whom Gibbon had read attentively—the description of the system of assemblies and the independence of the soldiers do not arouse any "democratic" sympathy in him. To his way of thinking, the backward state of German customs, letters, and arts carries its own condemnation; on several occasions he refers to the Germanic tribes as "savages," until he arrives at the following perception, which more precisely defines his thought: "Modern nations are fixed and permanent societies, connected among themselves by laws and government, bound to their native soil by arts and agriculture. The German tribes were voluntary and fluctuating associations of soldiers, almost of savages."

An extraordinary judgment for a writer so passionate about the historiography of his time, a witness of the central controversy of French historiography over the origins of the nation: were they Roman or Frankish? At no time did Gibbon seem interested in what had constituted in Europe since the sixteenth century one of the raisons d être of history and the fundamental impetus for it: the quest for origins, the original contract from which a nation arose. Of the two questions that the eighteenth century asked of history—What is a nation? What is civilization?—Gibbon was interested only in the second. He had read Boulainvilliers, Montesquieu, Dubos, and Mably, not as their heir but purely as an erudite, as an ethnologist of the Franks. As a result, he deprived the Germanic people of their basic dignity; they existed only as "near-savages."

The same sort of judgment can easily be found when Gibbon deals with other peoples whose movements threatened Rome. In chapter 26, for example, Gibbon describes the nomadic tribes of the Far East, whose growth would ultimately affect the Empire by driving the Goths to the West, along with "so many [other] hostile tribes more savage then themselves." In discussing those populations of nomadic shepherds, Gibbon says that what makes the study of them so simple is their proximity to animality:

> . . . it is much easier to ascertain the appetites of a quadruped than the speculations of a philosopher; and the savage tribes of mankind, as they approach nearer to the conditions of animals, preserve a stronger resemblance to themselves and to each other. The uniform stability of their manners is the natural consequence of the imperfection of their faculties. Reduced to a similar situation, their wants, their desires, their enjoyments, still continue the same; and the influence of food or climate, which in a more improved state of society, is suspended or subdued by so many moral causes, most powerfully contributes to form and to maintain the national character of Barbarians.

Consequently, barbarians are savages. Gibbon recognizes neither natural man nor the "noble savage." There is only historical man, and certain of his manifestations, unchecked by reason, remain bogged down in a dependency predicated upon natural conditions, stagnation, and the absence of a policed society. At the other end is civilized man, who is not necessarily the conqueror: the fall of the Empire proves that point. The paradox is that Gibbon was so interested in the victory of barbarism over civilization.

This paradox is resolved when one realizes that Gibbon wrote a second history alongside the first, but distinct nonetheless; this second history is that of Christianity. Gibbon was the first historian to treat the history of Rome and the history of religion together. This innovation lies behind the chronological distortion to which he subjected Roman history: he was trying to comprehend not just the secrets of the greatness of Rome, not just the collapse of that greatness, but beyond that the passage from imperial Rome to papal Rome. If the fall of the Empire encompassed all the Middle Ages, it was because the historian sought to describe more than the fall of a civilization invaded by barbarians. Ultimately he says so, with a disarming directness: "I have described the triumph of barbarism and religion" (chapter 71).

"Barbarism and religion"—the phrase clearly indicates that if, in the dramatic history of Rome's fall, the two phenomena contributed to the same result, they nevertheless remained distinct. Religion helped barbarism to win, but it was not itself barbaric. For the religious phenomenon was multiform because it was rooted in that fear and ignorance which were inseparable from human society. Gibbon was an enthusiastic disciple of Bayle, who perfectly reflected Enlightenment thinking on the subject. But he goes further than Bayle. He was the first historian systematically to place religion in a relative position in human events, which hardly means that he reduced its importance—on the contrary, he paid particular attention to it—but that he integrated it in all its many forms into the societies and empires whose history he outlined. There is, thus, in Gibbon a historian of paganism, a historian of the cults of the ancient Germans, a historian of Islam, and a historian of Christianity. Religion is a cultural phenomenon that he examines with great care, even to details of its refinements, as the chapters devoted to the theological controversies of the first centuries of Christianity demonstrate.

Religion thus becomes a part of the great social and historical drama of the fall of the Roman Empire. But when Gibbon writes that he has described "the triumph of barbarism and religion," he means only one religion: Christianity. The analysis of the religious phenomenon, of the generic, becomes specific. In the same way that, in the eyes of this gentleman-scholar, there have been several societies in history that have attained the status of, and embodied, civilization, though none so perfectly as the Roman Empire, so, too, inversely, have there been many religions in human history, though probably none of them quite so noxious as Christianity. Here we reach the second major theme in the

Decline and Fall. The first revolved around the external confrontation between Rome and the barbarians, the second around the internal disintegration of the Empire at the hands of the Christians. It is a Rome weakened by "the spirit of Christianity," we might say, borrowing from Montesquieu, that is finally conquered by the barbarian invasions. And the real victor, as the history of both the Eastern and Western Middle Ages shows, was Christianity.

This is perhaps the reason—or the existential impulse—that led Gibbon to write, not a panorama of Roman civilization, but an account only of its fall. Of course, like his contemporaries, Gibbon was sensitive to the transience of history's great successes, but this feeling hardly justified his having extended his account as far as the fifteenth century! If he wished to encompass the entire Middle Ages into the fall of Rome and under what was, in that context, a very strange title, it was because Christianity's history fascinated him as much as, perhaps even more than, that of Rome. He invested his account with his hatred, not of the Christian faith, but of the church, the priests, and monks; he committed to it his struggle against intolerance and fanaticism; he deployed for the purpose the whole anticlerical tradition of the French Enlightenment.

He was too good a historian, however, to say—and he never did say—that the Christianity of the established churches for which he professed no love was a form of "barbarism." On the contrary, he seized every opportunity to show how Christianity was in fact the important reconstructive principle of his historical world—the Europe built upon the debris of the Roman Empire. On the one hand, he wanted to express, through the three-dimensional historical space in which civilization, barbarism, and Christianity evolved, his preference for a pre-Christian civilization rather than a Christianized barbarism. But, on the other hand, he constantly—and more radically—showed that what motivated his worship of Rome, its values, its "spirit," and its moral figures was the existence of a civilization in its chemically pure state—and that meant without the Church.

PART THREE

AMERICA AND THE IDEA OF DEMOCRACY

9

From Savage Man to Historical Man: The American Experience in Eighteenth-Century French Culture

In order to interpret America, along with the rest of the non-European world, the Europeans of the seventeenth and eighteenth centuries resorted to the conceptual opposition between the civilized world and the savage world. This device enabled the Europeans to translate into epistemological terms the new regions discovered since the Renaissance, the new-found peoples of the globe—in short, a world that offered the three unusual features of being neither European nor Christian nor national. The "savage" world was described and inventoried by travelers, not by historians. It was a world without laws, without arts, without governments—in a word, without history. For an implicit scale of values still placed time, the dynamic creator of laws and nations, above space, the passive distributor of immobile societies.

The Savage Man

The misfortune of the savage was sometimes equated simply with his backwardness. Such was the view expressed by travelers who, in providing the reader with accounts of the mores of distant peoples, were seeking

Originally delivered as a lecture in October 1976 at the William L. Clements Library, Ann Arbor, Michigan. First published in French in *La Révolution américaine et l'Europe*, proceedings of the Colloques Internationaux du Centre National de la Recherche Scientifique, no. 577, Paris-Toulouse, 21–25 February 1978 (Paris: Editions du CNRS, 1979), 93–105; reprinted in *Annales: économies, sociétés, civilisations*, July–August 1978, 729–39. This study, as will be seen, is greatly indebted to two classic works: Bernard Faÿ, *L'Esprit révolutionnaire en France et aux Etats-Unis* (Paris, 1924); and D. Echeverria, *Mirage in the West: A History of the French Image of American Society to 1815* (Princeton: Princeton University Press, 1957). My analysis is an attempt to modify the conclusions reached by these two authors, but it is based very largely on the material they have provided.

to popularize the picturesque aspects of otherness but were also bringing back an image of the past from an area of the contemporary world: the savage was man in his infancy. But the curse that afflicted the savage could also be the incurable consequence of permanent factors such as climate, natural environment, or race. This famous and influential thesis was advanced in the late eighteenth century by Cornelius de Pauw, who invoked Buffon's authority when presenting his *Recherches philosophiques sur les Américains*.[1] This extravagant compilation of geographical and biological data was aimed at combating two ideas: that the European colonization of America was a good thing and that the inhabitants of America were happy and thriving in the savage state. De Pauw, on the basis of a fundamentally pessimistic analysis of American savagery, called instead for a systematic European withdrawal.

For de Pauw, that savagery, an object of study for the "history of natural man," was not a social state; it was a curse of nature—and more precisely of climate—that had led to the appearance of biological features of inferiority with respect to European man. De Pauw regarded America as a recently emerged continent, colder and moister than the Old World, covered with forests and swamps, and filled with degenerate, and thus all the more dangerous, animals. Its human inhabitants suffered from the same handicaps stemming from the same causes. They were lazy, amoral, sexually and intellectually idle, hairless, and devoid of intelligence. They represented not a sort of happy childhood of historical man but, on the contrary, a degenerate state in comparison with European man:

> Is it not surprising that the only men found on one half of the globe should be beardless, devoid of intelligence, contaminated by venereal disease (for syphilis, which Europe calls the French disease, has become the American disease), and so fallen from the human state as to be incapable of being disciplined—which is the complement of stupidity? The fondness that Americans have always displayed, and still display, for savage life proves that they hate the laws of society and the constraints of education, which, by taming the most intemperate passions, are alone capable of raising man above the animals. . . .[2]

De Pauw's theory of the nefarious influence of the American nation on man also applied to the colonizers—first to the Spaniards since the sixteenth century, then to the emigrants who peopled the English colonies. The Dutch theoretician cited the case of the Creoles, but his demonstration applied also to any American of European origin—whether immigrant, son, grandson, or great-grandson of Europeans. The "debased genius of the Americans" (title of section 1, part 5) had a rapid effect and caused immigrants to degenerate, although somewhat more slowly than animals taken from the Old World to the New, for men could "protect themselves against the immediate impact of climate"; all the same, the end result was inevitable.

Thus, the immigrant enjoyed no long-lasting privilege. All Americans were or had become savages. The European who left Europe was abandoning civilization for savagery. The most astonishing feature of this bleak conceptualization of the American enigma is its blindness in face of the facts, its ignorance of the most recent historical developments. De Pauw was writing at about the time that the decisive political crisis erupted between the British colonies in America and their motherland, a crisis that brought typically European values into play and turned the principles of the European Enlightenment against Europe itself. But de Pauw's blindness fed primarily on the tremendous cultural and affective commitment of European elites to their civilization, which they quite simply regarded as civilization *tout court*. In the European consciousness, this civilization presupposed the existence of an external or inverted world always regarded as somewhat threatening: savagery. De Pauw carried the commitment to civilization to its most extreme—and also its most archaic—form, for he argued that civilization was underwritten for all time by nature, that it was a product of natural history and not of human history. If climate and geography were indeed the determining factors of civilization, Europe was, for all eternity, on the right side of the fence.

During the same period, however, two factors of a very different nature modified the outline of this traditional image, which comforted the good conscience of Christian or seventeenth- and eighteenth-century Europe. The first factor was political: the American Revolution. The second was intellectual: the mirage of "nature" in European culture.

On the American Revolution and its impact on opinion in France (and elsewhere), I shall not dwell at length. This is the best-known aspect of the history of ideas about America, and it has also become a topos for a certain type of Franco-American rhetoric. The political and military events that marked American independence crystallized images of America that emerged on different levels. For enlightened opinion, these events embodied both the political ideas of the *philosophes* (conveyed in particular by the Quakers) and the agrarian state envisaged by the physiocrats—a fusion of which Benjamin Franklin was the living symbol. But, on a broader level, no doubt—and especially in France, in the climate of anglophobia—the accession of the thirteen colonies to nationhood destroyed forever the image of a savage continent and integrated America into the history of Europe, that is, into history *tout court*.

At the same time, the concept of "savagery," with reference to the new nation, gave way to the concept of nature. Actually, since the Renaissance, the concept of "savage" in European culture had never ceased to be ambiguous. It referred either to man bereft of the benefits of civilization or to man in the state of nature that preceded the social contract. In this second usage, the savage embodied primitive natural law, whose principles had been corrupted by social life and had to be revived and respected by the social contract. The savage was a matrix for true civilization. For Rousseau, this civilization had degenerated by virtue of its very development (arts and sciences, luxury, and pleasure); for most other authors, civilized man remained the symbol of perfection, but the barbarian replaced the savage as his antonym. Thus, in the tripartite scheme being developed in the eighteenth century—the savage, the barbarian, and civilized man—the savage represented the origin of mankind (in the temporal sense and in the principial sense), civilized man the end of his history, and the barbarian the cyclical corruption of this history. The savage, if he emerged from the natural order without having been corrupted by the Europeans, combined the benefits of nature with those of history and served as an example to mankind.

The French View of America

It is precisely this fundamental notion of a natural order turning into a historical order—that is, of a history for once congruent with nature—that the young American nation came to embody in the eyes of enlightened eighteenth-century opinion and more particularly, owing to the Franco-American alliance, in French opinion.

First, America had to be removed from the category of "travel" accounts—from the inventory of space—and accede to the higher, temporal order of history. This shift was brought about by the War of Independence and the break with England. This war in itself already had a familiar ring for Europeans. But, because it was waged against a European power (England) with the help of another European power (France), it was a doubly effective agent for integrating America into the exclusive circle of "historical" nations. Finally, the war was the high point in the birth of a nation—and the nation was the supreme form of civilized societies. On all these counts, the war constituted a historical entity, that is, the description of a memorable event and the testing ground for a primordial experience.

Accounts of the American war proliferated in France, especially as the participation of the French and the victorious outcome of the conflict provided national pride with revenge on England and on the 1763 treaty. On this elementary level, the history of France provisionally identified itself with that of the thirteen colonies. The high points in the progress toward American independence—the struggle with Parliament over taxation, the Boston Tea Party, the Declaration of Independence, the major military battles—found their way very early into French historiography: a common fund of reminiscences was being constituted at the same time as a corpus of full-fledged historical material. The earlier period of Franco-Indian collusion against American settlers was totally forgotten.

This common fund relied—even more than on military victory or anglophobic glee—on philosophical ideas. For educated opinion in France, independent America embodied an alternative society and an alternative state, a world whose presence was so keenly felt only because America existed by *default*, as an imaginary recourse against what was soon to be called the *ancien régime* and as a compensation for the impossibility of destroying or transforming that old order. America did not make a sudden and glorious appearance on the stage of history merely in the role of a new nation; its chief role was that of a model country, which, because of its youth, its expanse, and the circumstances surrounding its birth, had succeeded in escaping from the curses of the Old World. America was both a Europe and an anti-Europe: a Europe because it was founded on the ideas of the Enlightenment—a language common to both sides of the Atlantic—and an anti-Europe because its inhabitants had precisely fled from religious and political intolerance in order to invent a new historical memory, free from persecution and injustice. The sentimental attachment of the French to the fledgling United States was thus a disguised way of expressing concern with domestic politics, one of the manifestations of the vast drive of civil society toward political power that characterized the last years of the *ancien régime*. The "American discourse" that flourished in those years was in fact a discourse on French society and on the French Constitution.

As this is one of the best-known aspects of this history, I shall not dwell on it here. From La Fayette to Chastellux, from Mirabeau to Brissot, from Mably to Condorcet, from subtle argument to polemic, the commentary on the young United States became a new discourse on human equality and on the right way to govern societies. America, which had embodied the infancy of mankind, had not yet become mankind's future but was already an example to it. America existed primarily as a semi-imaginary, semi-real phenomenon discussed by the French in a prefiguration of the debates on their revolution. It is especially striking to see how the mechanism of rhetorical escalation in the name of democracy—a process that was to become so important during the struggles for power between 1789 and 1794—was already at work, though as yet without a political dimension, in discussions about America. Brissot's critique of the book by the marquis de Chastellux is a case in point: it reads like a *girondin* attack on the *feuillants*![3] The unfortunate marquis, despite his having fought for America, was soundly rebuked for having contrasted the American people, who enjoyed a freedom equal to that of ancient republics, with the people of Europe, more inclined toward inequality and servitude:

What is clearest in my mind is that your argument is far more favorable to the cause of mankind's true oppressors; for by telling them that the people today are neither worthy nor capable of freedom, that men and nations are degenerating at an increasing rate, and that this degeneration would not cease even if the circumstances that provoked it were to disappear— by imparting to them these alleged truths, you will encourage them to keep their slaves in irons.

But nothing is more contrary to the truth. The American Revolution proves it. Those who made the Revolution descend either from Englishmen tyrannized by the Stuarts, or from enslaved Germans.

You think you are doing the Americans a great honor by likening them to the Romans and Greeks; actually, I think they are far superior to these ancient peoples. But this is not the place to prove it. I shall limit myself here to advancing this proposition, whose demonstration will be found elsewhere, in order to show you that men today, far from being degenerate, can, in the right circumstances, surpass their ancestors.[4]

But independent America was also, and at the same time, a laboratory for constitutional experiment. The discussion about principles and the heated arguments concerning the best possible society were to lead to considerations on the mechanism of power: the history of America was an object lesson. The debates that later took place in the Constituent Assembly originated in the debates on the government of the United States. On the subject of voting rights and eligibility, for example, the French debates of 1789–91 contributed nothing beyond what was already contained in a book by Mazzei, a friend and correspondent of Jefferson.[5] Mazzei's work, published in Paris in 1788, was probably the best compendium of historical and political information on the United States to appear in its time. Between the American described by Cornelius de Pauw and the one described by Mazzei, a nation and a people had entered history.

But the redemptive character of this history stemmed from the fact that it was inseparable from nature. Until its appearance, the culture of the Enlightenment had oscillated between two incompatible beliefs: the superiority of history over nature and the corruption of nature by history. The young United States came as the unexpected reconciliation between human industry and fidelity to nature; America was the first to give an impulse, in this laicized form, to a feeling that was destined to a great future: revolutionary expectation.

No book demonstrates this better than that of Crèvecœur, a Norman nobleman for many years an expatriate.[6] *Letters of an American Farmer*, written in English and translated into the French *style sensible* then fashionable, gave a Marie Antoinette-like description of the "frontier" epic. But the agrarian idyll of the American smallholder was considerably more than an additional variant of the old theme of natural happiness. Far from being a sort of exotic reference lost in space—that is, harking back to a very ancient past—it inaugurated a new historical epoch and constituted a promise. The union of the thirteen colonies represented "an unforgettable moment in the annals of the universe. This moment can be regarded as a rebirth of nature, as a new gift it has bestowed on the Old World, as a second creation; for everything we see today bears the stamp of youth and is only just unfolding."[7]

Thus, America was a new origin of humanity, but a thoroughly historical origin, since it was contemporary. This logical paradox was possible because the American *homo novus* brought about a radical change in European man—a rebirth at once geographical and cultural. It was geographical because it was initially a consequence of the availability of space, in contrast to the "overcrowding" of European societies, but it was especially a consequence of man's return to the earth, the mother of moral and civic virtues. Crèvecœur's American foreshadows Robespierre and Saint-Just's "patriot," who also owned a parcel of his homeland's soil. Landownership and agriculture enabled man to be at one with nature and with history. Indeed, the man of the "frontier," living on the outer *limit* of cultivated land, was for Crèvecœur a sort of transitional, ambiguous figure, caught between the virtues of new man and the two sources of corruption threatening those virtues: the European heritage of violence, conveyed by every newcomer, and contamination by the savage state, which wrested the settler from agriculture and drew him toward hunting.

For only educated and enlightened men could fully enjoy the blessings of space and land. The United States was doubly fortunate in having been peopled by European dissenters, fleeing from intolerance, prejudice, and persecution, and in having been born precisely in a later age, enlightened by science and philosophy. Far from being, like the Europeans, burdened with and corrupted by the weight of the past, Americans were predisposed by that very past to rid themselves of its inertia, since they were the first to have fought and escaped its violence. Their relationship to history was in the nature of a rebirth, in which their late appearance on the American scene made them benefit fully from the progress of knowledge and reason. It is this shortcut that brought them back to the state of nature, which, instead of acting as an abstract reference, thus became a historical period, the rebirth of society on a rational basis. Provided it remained faithful to this exceptional origin, America was destined to be the central laboratory for human history. It was thus to America, and not to Greece and Rome, that the "learned men" of Europe were invited to turn in order to acquire new knowledge—that is, to the "primeval germ . . . of an enlightened and new people," since it is "more enjoyable to find oneself at the origin of things than at a sad review of the fragments of the past."[8]

In this happy history, what was the role of the two figures excluded from the new society, the Negro and the Indian? The Negro was either happy under the patriarchal authority of a good master or on his way to emancipation. He had no real existence in a world built on equality; indeed, there was almost no conceptual room for him. The Indian played an ambiguous but crucial role. On the one hand, as a primitive, he bestowed nature's blessing on the settlers. While de Pauw had regarded the settler as being trapped in the brutish state of savages, for Crèvecœur, on the contrary, the settler imitated their simple and natural virtues. On the other hand, although the Indian was untainted by European corruption, he embodied a society inferior to that of the settlers: Indian society was fragile and unenlightened; it was based on hunting and had no agriculture, arts, or sciences. Europe represented history without nature. The Indian embodied nature without history. Only the American reconciled the two principles.

Therein lies the secret, in my view, of the assimilation of the "American dream" into French culture. Before the outbreak of the French Revolution, which acted as the focal point for the belief in a new beginning—a regeneration, as the French were to put it—of mankind, it was American independence that crystallized the idea of a history-as-origin, by means of which society would once again conform to nature and reason. That is the deep connection between the two revolutions. The idea of revolution in its 1789 sense originated for the French in the birth of the United States.

The End of the "American Dream"

But this link also explains precisely why the French Revolution put an end to the "American dream" in French opinion. Not that America ceased to exist as a political and philosophical point of reference. The American example was still cited in revolutionary speeches and newspapers, particularly in connection with constitutional problems. A systematic study[9] would probably show that references to America were specifically made by the *girondins*, and in particular by Brissot and Condorcet, who remainded faithful to their youthful passion. But that the "American discourse" should have been a feature of the most cosmopolitan intellectual and political family of the Revolution—the only family, in fact, with any "international" character at all—already indicates that this discourse had become quite alien, if not suspect, to a great many actors in the French drama, from the members of the Constituent Assembly to the *montagnards*.

The reason is that from 1789 on, the French had their own dream, which made a substitute unnecessary. From the very onset of the Revolution, they were obsessed with their own example, narcissistically fascinated by their own history. If one reads the countless pamphlets that flooded the old kingdom between 1787 and 1789 or if one examines the interminable and monotonous evidence of the *cahiers de doléances*, one will find few references indeed to foreign examples. Tocqueville, who was well versed in this literature, had understood the phenomenon:

> Among all the proposed schemes that had just blossomed at the time the government seemed to put the Constitution up for contest, one finds hardly a single one that deigns to imitate what was happening abroad. The major concern was not to take lessons, but to give them. . . . Thus every single Frenchman was convinced that the Revolution would not only change the French system but also bring to the world new principles of government that could be applied to all peoples and would reshape the entire face of human affairs; and every single Frenchman was also convinced that he held the key not only to his country's fate, but also to the very future of his species.[10]

Accordingly, the American experience lost the central historical position it had occupied since independence. American became once again peripheral. It continued to represent the opportunity afforded by a *tabula rasa* and by an absolute beginning, but *for that very reason* it became relatively alien to the French revolutionaries, whose primary concern was to articulate the new nation's connections with its own past. And the two modes of dealing with this past—compromise and refusal—removed America from the French Revolution.

The moderate revolutionaries understood this at once, and Mounier, on 9 July 1789, provided the best statement of their position in the course of the first debates on the Constitution:

> We shall never relinquish our rights, but we shall not use them to excess. We shall not forget that the French are not a new people just emerged from the depth of the forest to form an association, but a great society of twenty-five million men—a society intent on strengthening the ties that exist between all its parts, and on regenerating the kingdom, a kingdom for which the principles of genuine monarchy will always be sacred.[11]

Mounier, like Mirabeau somewhat later, and like so many members of the Constituent Assembly, was hoping for a compromise with the king, that is, with the country's past. On this point, the United States of America could offer Mounier no guidance. The Revolution was a face-to-face encounter between the French and their own history.

But as the Revolution unfolded, entering into conflict with the Catholic church, waging war on the kings of Europe, and sending Louis XVI to his death, it became an expression of the French people's rejection of their own history. There are two reasons why the Jacobin break with—or eradication of—the nation's past was incompatible with an admiration of the American example. First, Jacobinism was predicated on a total psychological and ideological commitment to the French Revolution, now the sole embodiment of liberty and equality, of the great beginning of human emancipation. There was no room in Jacobin thinking for two pilot nations. Second, the secret of social happiness rediscovered by France was no longer thought of as a gift of nature but as the stake in a domestic and international conflict. In America, equality and independence resulted from consensus. In revolutionary France, they were seen as the outcome of a long and bloody conflict. This, it seems to me, is where the two myths of origins parted ways and made the political and cultural life of the two nations so alien to each other after several years of considerably fraternal relations. Furthermore, from 1793 on, it is what I would call the "conflictual messianism" of French Jacobinism that, in its turn, had an impact on American politics via the Republicans. However, Jacobinism failed to constitute an effective ideological model for America, for the two experiences had become as remote from each other as the physical distance that lay between them.

America, the Observation Ground

Even as America ceased to be a myth for the French Jacobins, the shattering of the revolutionary political illusion after 9 Thermidor led the survivors of the terrorist adventure to a critical reexamination of that illusion. The Thermidoreans, as exemplary heirs to the Enlightenment, put the burden of blame not only on Robespierre's Supreme Being but also on the American dream, which had fed their hopes during the Constituent Assembly. Back in 1791 and 1792, liberals such as La Rochefoucauld, Démeunier, and Talleyrand, disappointed by the turn of events in France, had forsaken the homeland of freedom for a rough and difficult America, where they led an unhappy and, incidentally, not always blameless existence. After Thermidor they returned fairly promptly to France, where they became additional witnesses to the end of the revolutionary dream on both sides of the Atlantic. For the moderates, too, America was no longer a dream; it was a friendly but foreign country. And for the intellectuals among them, such as the Idéologues, America became an object for dispassionate study.

A representative of this attitude is Volney, former member of the Constituent Assembly, who sailed for the United States in the year III (summer 1795). Volney was a seasoned traveler and scientifically minded observer, a pioneer in the use of questionnaires and social statistics, and a member of the Institut—of the academy of Idéologues who became the spiritual mentors of the Thermidorean republic. Less than ten years had elapsed since Brissot's visit, yet how the tone had changed! Volney was the first Frenchman to visit the United States not in search of nature or freedom, or the two together, but in order to study one of the manifestations of historical man. In passing, Volney counseled diplomatic caution to his Parisian friends, at a time when the Directory wanted to concede Louisiana to Spain. But his journey was above all that of a postrevolutionary intellectual: America had entered the social science of the Idéologues. Consequently, it was no longer a model, but a varied ground for observation:

> Roughly speaking [wrote Volney to a friend on 14 January 1797], my itinerary has included Virginia, Kentucky, Wabash, Fort Detroit, Lake Erie and some of what is called here the North-East: Genesee country, Mohawk, and the Hudson; in particular, I have been able to sample the four most diverse areas of this great continent. In the South, I have seen the slave system and its moral effects; in the West, the condition of a nascent society; in Canada, Frenchmen of the age of Louis XIV who have become half-Indian; in the East, Englishmen of the last century—already an old nation, the only one here to have a developed character. That, my friend, is the knowledge I have acquired for you and for our Institut National.[12]

Thus, Volney's America had ceased to be a unique and comprehensive image of the human condition. It was fragmented into distinct objects of knowledge, according to the character, history, and situation of the various societies that it accommodated. America was no longer a focus of ideological commitment but a mosaic of historical experience.

The only book that Volney actually wrote as a result of his American travels was *Tableau du climat et du sol des Etats-Unis* (1803), a study confined to physical geography. Of the projected second part of the book—which was never written and was to have been devoted to the population, mores, and history of the United States—Volney left us a general outline, the preface, and some detailed analyses in the appendixes.

Volney's general argument was that the young United States was not free from the drag of European history, in which it had originated. Hence a frontal attack against the founding myth of origins, constructed and kept alive by certain writers of the 1780s. Volney had specifically planned to study—after the climate and soil—"the size of the population; its territorial distribution; its composition according to work and occupation; the habits, that is, the *mores*, resulting from these occupations; the combination of these habits with the ideas and prejudices dating from the earliest origins."[13] There follows this crucial passage:

> By retracing these origins through history, language, laws, and customs, I exposed the fanciful mistake of writers who described as a *new and virgin people* a gathering of inhabitants of old Europe—Germans, Dutch, and above all Britons from the three kingdoms. The organization of these traditional and diverse elements into political bodies led me to outline the history of the formation of each colony; to show that the character of their founders contained the spiritual ferment that acted as the driving force for almost the entire pattern of behavior of their successors, in keeping with the insufficiently recognized moral truth that, in corporate bodies as in individuals, the earliest habits exert a predominant influence on the remainder of their existence.

In other words, the British American remained a Briton, the German American a German, the French Canadian a Frenchman, and so on. The origin of the United States was no longer the blessing of liberty bestowed on a new people but the weight of European history, that is, the various "spirits" (in the sense in which Montesquieu spoke of the "spirit of laws") of nations and peoples as constituted by their respective traditions.

Thus, for Volney, America had lost its political superiority and its exemplary value. Instead, America had a history in which, as in the European history it reproduced, founding principles were corrupted by a combination of money, ambition, and passion. The American Revolution, exactly like the French Revolution between the Constituent Assembly and the Convention, had regressed from its initial promise to a situation of strife and civil war.

> I should then have examined [Volney went on, describing the section he never wrote] from a moral point of view the conduct of this people and of its government, from 1783 to 1798; and I should have proved by incontrovertible facts that, in proportion to the population, the volume of business, and the multiplicity of combinations, there existed in the United States neither a greater restraint in financial matters, nor a greater degree of good faith in transactions, nor a greater decency in public morality, nor a greater moderation in the partisan spirit, nor a greater care displayed in upbringing and education, than in most of the states of *old Europe*; that whatever good and useful achievements the United States has to its credit, whatever has been accomplished in the realm of civil liberty, and in protecting persons and property, has been due more to popular and individual habits, to the need to work, and to the high cost of all forms of labor, than to any

ingenious measure or policy devised by the government; that on nearly all these counts, the nation has regressed with respect to its founding principles; that in 1798 only the absence of a particular set of circumstances prevented a certain party from usurping power and resorting to violence of a totally counterrevolutionary character—in a word, that the United States has owed its public prosperity, the affluence of its state and its inhabitants, far more to its insular position, to its distance from powerful neighbors and from all theaters of war, and, finally, to the general ease of its situation, than to the fundamental goodness of its laws or to the wisdom of its administration.

Thus, the United States came once again under the common-law jurisdiction of history. The American Revolution was subject to the same erosion of principle by passion as the French Revolution had been, and it became the object of the same disenchantment. Whatever advantage still accrued to America was due solely to geography and chance.

In order to complete his demonstration, Volney also had to demolish the last American myth: that of a harmonious and happy savage state, enshrined in the natural order before the institution of property. In short, Volney had to exorcise Rousseau. He did so in one of the very few fragments of this part of his book that he actually wrote. These fragments were published as appendixes to the *Tableau* under the title *Observations générales sur les Indiens ou Sauvages de l'Amérique du Nord*. Volney's savage no longer played the leading role on the philosophical stage where the natural order and civilization confronted each other. Although, as in Rousseau, the savage predated the creation of property, he ceased to be an abstract entity à la Rousseau and became the object of empirical observation. Volney's savage embodied not a principle but a historical society, whose weakness lay precisely in its having predated property and agriculture; consequently, it was vulnerable to the slightest contact with "civilization." The savage was neither a utopian creature, as in Rousseau, nor a foil, as in de Pauw. Savagery was a primitive society, a still-rudimentary history, destined—condemned, even—to become civilized through the introduction of property. Thus, it was one of the several elements in American history, but a secondary element, set for assimilation or destruction, and subject to the merciless law of development. Savagery had been removed from the poetic world of origins and returned to the prosaic world of social life. By losing its "savages," America was all the more thoroughly reabsorbed into the ordinary flow of history.

By a chronological coincidence, at almost the same time, or just a short while earlier, the greatest of all French writers went—or pretended to have gone—on the same journey as Volney. Actually, it is of little importance that the itinerary was for the most part invented, for Chateaubriand introduced America, not into French philosophy or politics, but into French literature—and with what a stir! *Atala* and *René*—together with *Les Natchez*, published later but cast in the same mold—revolutionized the novel and aesthetic sensibility. Admittedly, Chateaubriand incorporated traditional descriptive elements such as the good savage, the antithesis between savagery and civilization, and the luxuriance of nature; but he added the feeling that Europe would never again move out of its confines, that it was a prisoner of its past, and that the American dream of happiness lay beyond its grasp. Of all the imaginary travelers in search of the new man, René was the first to experience the burden of time and the impossibility of casting off the old man. France under the Consulate shared in this feeling. All it discovered in the American forest was the "genius of Christianity"—its own past.

Thus, between 1780 and 1800—twenty years during which French history moved at such a rapid pace—the American dream shifted from revolutionary messianism to social science and met its death in literature. The myth of a reborn humanity at last faithful to its origins—a myth so enduring in American culture—did not survive in France after the Jacobin experience. The French replaced it by the myth of an egalitarian nation, composed of both peasants and soldiers, a nation engaged in an endless battle to deliver mankind from an invincible past. I do not feel that, since this period, the two nations have ever again experienced the ephemeral sense of cultural community that had brought them so close together for ten or fifteen years. That is perhaps why these ten or fifteen years are being celebrated with such loquaciousness and such solemnity. Deep ties are generally silent.

10

The Conceptual System of
"Democracy in America"

The genesis of Tocqueville's visit to American is shrouded in mystery. When did the idea first occur to him? When did the project materialize? And why America?

Neither the known facts nor the available documents provide a satisfactory answer to these basic questions. The facts are clear, but they illustrate only the secondary aspect of the American voyage: the mission to study the American penal system. When Tocqueville and his friend Beaumont sailed from Le Havre in April 1831, the two young magistrates had been entrusted with the mission of examining American penal institutions.[1] This mission, requested by the two magistrates themselves, was unpaid but official; a formal report was duly presented to the authorities and later published.[2] But this investigation, whatever appeal it may have had for Tocqueville (who displayed an abiding interest in French prison reform), was obviously, on the intellectual level, only a side aspect of his momentous visit.

The available sources do not provide irrefutable evidence regarding his deeper motives. For example, the correspondence between Tocqueville and Gustave de Beaumont contains only one allusion to the matter in a letter of Tocqueville's dated 14 March 1831, that is, shortly

First published as a preface to Alexis de Tocqueville, *De la démocratie en Amérique* (Paris: Flammarion "G.F." paperback series, 1981), 1:7–46. References to the original of *De la démocratie* are to this edition. References to Tocqueville's other writings are to the *Œuvres complètes*, in progress (Paris: Gallimard, 1951–). [The passages from *De la démocratie* quoted here are taken from Alexis de Tocqueville, *Democracy in America*, ed. J. P. Mayer, trans. George Lawrence (Garden City, N.Y.: Doubleday, 1969). References to this edition are given in brackets and preceded by the letters *GL*.—Trans.] I should like to thank my friend André Jardin, the foremost contemporary specialist on Tocqueville, for having read this essay in draft and having made many valuable suggestions.

before his departure.[3] Moreover, this letter mentions only the incidental reasons connected with the 1830 revolution—an event that placed the two applicants for the mission, as scions of legitimist families, in a "difficult position." Besides, even if one were to accept this type of "diplomatic" explanation, why America? Many other countries could satisfy the curiosity of two friends and provide a legitimate excuse for their absence. At the time, the young American republic represented the ideal for an intellectual orientation quite alien to the tradition in which the two young aristocrats had been brought up: the orientation of the liberal opposition under the Restoration—liberals of every hue, freemasons, and republicans, all assembled in a pro-American camp under the symbolic aegis of La Fayette.[4] But it is true that Beaumont was distantly related to La Fayette and that in family circles the young Alexis had met former "Americans" such as Chateaubriand, Hyde de Neuville—the agent of princes during the Revolution, former ambassador to Washington, and close friend of the comte Hervé—and Monseigneur de Cheverus, archbishop of Bordeaux and former bishop of Boston.[5]

If Tocqueville and Beaumont were searching for the secret of free institutions, they could have gone to study them in countries less radically alien to their tradition and more spontaneously dear to their hearts—Switzerland and England in particular. But Switzerland, according to classic political theory, was considered a republic only in consequence of its smallness; England, then regarded as being on the verge of collapse, was not, in any case, a democracy. However, Tocqueville did visit England in later years, and his correspondence from the pre-1830 period, even as he was attending with passionate interest Guizot's course at the Sorbonne, shows his concern with the comparative history of France and England.[6] Why, then, America?

To this question, at least, there is an answer provided by Tocqueville himself, well after his return, in a letter of January 1835 to his friend Kergorlay, written just after the publication of the first volume of *Democracy in America*.[7] Tocqueville begins by stating that, since the march toward equality is inevitable, the central problem of the age is to determine whether equality is compatible with freedom; he adds:

> Thus it is not without having given the matter much thought that I resolved to write the book that I am now publishing. I am not at all blind to the awkwardness of my position, which will not elicit anyone's heartfelt sympathy. Some will find that basically I have no love for democracy and that I criticize it severely, others will think that I am recklessly encouraging its development. The best thing for me would be if no one read my book; and perhaps I shall be so lucky. I know all this, but here is my reply: it is now nearly ten years that I have been reflecting on some of the matters I shall tell you about later on.

My only reason for going to America was to clarify this point. The prison system was a pretext: I used it as a passport to gain admittance everywhere in the United States. In this country, where I came across countless unexpected objects, I gleaned several insights into the questions I had so often asked myself.

"It is now nearly ten years. . . ." Tocqueville wrote these words in 1835, and he was born in 1805: he was therefore about twenty years old when he conceived the question that was to lead him to America and, more generally, to inform his entire intellectual and political life. This is, it seems to me, a very rare instance in intellectual history—a system that crystallized so early, in the mind of a young man brought up, moreover, in a confined environment and hardly trained in any subject other than law. One is naturally reminded of Sainte-Beuve's remark: "He began to think before he had learned anything."[8] Repeating the idea in a different form, one could say that Tocqueville is an extreme example of an intellectual who never "learned" anything outside of a conceptual framework that he had developed beforehand. Apart from the time and energy saved, this gave him exceptional narrowness and exceptional depth: Tocqueville recorded nothing haphazardly, for the simple pleasure of knowledge. The visit to America, like the history of France or England, was an element in the systematic experimentation carried out by this deductive mind. It remains to be explained why Tocqueville proceeded in this manner, and one must therefore retrace the antecedents of his "thinking."

I would argue that if his "system" was constituted so early, it was because *even in its explicit aspect* it rested on a base that was not intellectual, but purely existential. Tocqueville belonged to the world defeated by the French Revolution—an event from which he deduced, as all his generation did, the feeling of the irreversible march of history. But, as he was given to abstraction, he gave the well-known romantic notion of "fate" the form of a concept, drawn directly from the experience of his milieu. This concept was the victory of the democratic principle over the aristocratic principle. Tocqueville's entire work can be regarded as an endless reflection on the nobility.

This reflection was his point of departure, both existentially and intellectually—a meditation begun in adolescence and focused on himself, his family, his life, the historical significance of what his parents had lived through and what he himself was living, or reliving, through the failure of the Restoration and the events of 1830. For his father, Hervé de Tocqueville, saved from the guillotine by 9 Thermidor, the same questions had been an ever-present preoccupation. In 1847, he even published a historical study of the causes of the Revolution, under an antiquated title that testified the generation to which he belonged.[9] A disciple of Montesquieu, the old count centered his analysis on the worsening relations between absolute monarchy and nobility and on Louis XV's incapacity to adapt the regime to the aristocracy's demands for liberalization:

> Richelieu and Louis XIV imposed absolute authority to the detriment of public liberties because the nation was weary of the strife that had bloodied earlier reigns. Louis XV misjudged the spirit of his age. Words of freedom were repeated everywhere: they echoed under the vaulted ceilings of the courts of justice and were uttered even by courtiers. The weak hand of a discredited monarch could hardly sustain the edifice built by Louis the Great. The Revolution had already made its appearance in the upper class; it was gradually to descend to the lower class.[10]

Thus, Hervé de Tocqueville, in order to understand what he had lived through, invoked the "spirit of the age," embodied by the nobility and misjudged by the monarchy. From his cradle, Alexis encountered, as an integral feature of his milieu, this questioning about the great historical drama experienced and conceived as inevitable and yet as being linked to two specific agents: the nobility and the king of France.

This questioning had lost neither vigor nor relevance. Since 1815, the restored monarchy had actively fostered it by pressing the fight against the "spirit of the age" in the name of the restored alliance between the king and his nobility. This increasingly aristocratic monarchy led to the *journées* of July 1830: the French Revolution continued. And it is no coincidence that this date crystallized Alexis de Tocqueville's deep choices by revealing the manner in which he invested his inheritance in new issues and new reflections. The affair of the oath to the new king—an act made compulsory by the law of 31 August 1830—turned Tocqueville into something of an outcast from his milieu. His closest friend, Louis de Kergorlay, left the army and was later involved in the adventure of the duchesse de Berry. Tocqueville, instead, took the oath, without joy ("it is an unpleasant moment," he observed in a letter),[11] but also without any real pang of conscience. He merely regretted that his gesture might be interpreted as having been dictated by self-interest, whereas in fact it was a token of resignation. And the decision to visit America (even if this long absence may have been calculated to efface the memory of the somewhat awkward position in which the affair of the oath had placed Tocqueville with respect to his milieu) reveals the same indifference, but on a theoretical level. For Tocqueville's decision was connected with an already constructed intellectual system, which gave a powerful new impetus to his father's query, stripping it of the conventions of tradition and nobiliary rhetoric.

In this system—about whose development we know next to nothing, since Tocqueville was already Tocqueville at the age of twenty—it mattered little whether the reigning dynasty was legitimate; indeed, it mattered little whether there was a dynasty at all. The central question did not concern the relations between nobility and monarchy; it concerned the compatibility between nobility and democracy. Out of the three diverse elements that his milieu used to explain historical misfortune—monarchy, nobility, spirit of the age—Tocqueville built a very simple, two-dimensional system. He kept nobility as one pole: it was the necessary starting point, the primordial social experience, the taproot of his theory. As a type of government, of society, or of culture, the "aristocracy" was a model for the nobility. At the other pole, the heir to a defeated principle placed the victorious principle of democracy, at once a government by the people, an egalitarian society, and, to borrow his father's vocabulary, the "spirit of the age."

This intellectual process did involve a certain degree of fatalism, an acquiescence in the inevitable that corresponded to the historical experience of Tocqueville's milieu: it was the march toward an ever more complete democracy that defined the direction of the trend revealed by the French Revolution. But Tocqueville was not searching for the causes of this trend, at least not at the time. Unlike Marx, for example, who thought that one could demonstrate the march of history and that the end of capitalism could be deduced from the economic laws that governed it, Tocqueville posited as an axiom, or a self-evident truth, that mankind was moving in great strides toward the age of democracy. This conclusion was not the outcome of a systematic inquiry; it was merely the abstract expression—in keeping with the nature of Tocqueville's genius—of the actual experience of Tocqueville and his milieu. Nor was it a new idea (although Tocqueville played a considerable part in spreading it); one finds it in many authors of the period, and even in his own milieu (witness his relative Chateaubriand). But Tocqueville, having established it as a starting point, was the only one who sought to develop the idea and explore all of its aspects. For him, the idea was to be understood at various levels—cultural social, and political—but only the cultural and social levels defined that which was inevitable. While the societies of his day seemed to him to be drawn by a sort of fate toward an increasingly widespread belief in equality, and toward a greater equality of conditions, the political forms that could accompany this evolution continued to depend on human choice. Thus, the problem that came to dominate his entire intellectual life was not so much that of the causes of equality as that of its consequences on political civilization. Once again, this approach and this formulation of the problem placed him at the opposite pole from Marx. Marx was interested in the laws of economic structure and the relationship between economics and society, from which he tended to "deduce" political phenomena. Tocqueville explored the connections between the principle that governed societies and the type of political system that could issue from it, but he never regarded those connections as inevitable.

Thus, Tocqueville constantly combined two types of analysis and two types of beliefs. In his reasoning, he juxtaposed a logic of typology—based on the opposition between aristocracy and democracy—and a logic of evolution, based on the inevitable triumph of democracy. As for his general world view, he compensated for his rational acceptance of democracy by fighting for the values that were inseparable from the aristocratic world, freedom foremost. His entire life, from an early age, revolved around this problem—a blend of theory and experience—or around this theory of family experience, which constantly combined facts with values, conceptual richness and exhaustive documentation with political convictions.

If the visit to America was already implicit in this exploration, it was because America provided the young, systematically minded aristocrat with an existential and conceptual laboratory. A homeland founded on the negation of the nobility (a country, therefore, where Tocqueville himself could not have existed), America offered the example of a chemically pure experiment in democracy. Tocqueville used this discovery—truly a brilliant one in its simplicity and boldness—to verify and elaborate on an idea. He must have had a premonition, when he set sail, of the great secret that he later shared with Comte Molé on his return from his second visit to England in 1835, in a letter that belatedly answers the question of 1831, Why America?

> One would have to display considerable philosophical presumption to imagine that one could judge England in six months. One year has always seemed to me too short a time in which to appreciate the United States properly, and it is infinitely easier to gain clear ideas and accurate notions about the American Union that about Great Britain. In America, all laws issue so to speak from a single idea. All of society, as it were, is founded on a single fact; everything flows from one principle. One could compare America to a great forest with a myriad of straight roads built through it, all of them leading to the same point. One need only find the crossroads and everything will become visible in a single glance.[12]

Thus, America was the ideal site for analyzing *in vivo* the democratic principle at work, that is, the risks it involved and the advantages it offered to freedom. As for the European nations, they stood midway between aristocracy and democracy; they were torn by the conflict between two principles and two worlds and often prey to the extreme form of democracy represented by revolution. The American example did not constitute Europe's future—which was necessarily different—but it gave

Europe some basis for conceiving its future so as to ensure the most favorable conditions and the least number of obstacles to freedom. Tocqueville was prepared to resign himself to the end of the nobility, provided the aristocratic legacy of freedom were capable of surviving the democratic age.

Actually, in order to understand the close connection that exists between Tocqueville's visit to America and his analysis of France, one can also look directly at *Democracy in America*, which is entirely aimed at a comparison between America and Europe. The most explicit text on this point is the end of chapter 9 of part 2 of volume 1. Tocqueville begins by examining the importance of laws and mores in preserving American democracy, as opposed to what he calls the "material causes," that is, the specific features of the New World and the advantages it offers to man in his relation to geographical space. Tocqueville is confronted with a classic problem—perhaps the central problem—of social sciences: how to isolate the role and influence of a variable or of a limited set of variables on a complex process. That he was well aware of the difficulty is proved by his attempt to find a point of comparison in a country situated outside the American continent, and therefore deprived of the geographical advantages inseparable from America, yet possessing comparable laws and mores. However, he cannot find any such country. He draws the conclusion that, in the absence of objects of comparison, "we . . . can only hazard opinions."[13]

This is a typical passage in that it illustrates Tocqueville's fundamental mode of reasoning and demonstration: the comparative method. Having found one or more ideas as explanatory hypotheses for a phenomenon he was attempting to elucidate, Tocqueville tested them on various "grounds." When he could not find relevant grounds for the problem at hand, he "hazarded opinions"—that is, to his mind, indemonstrable and, at best, plausible propositions. And America represents one of the poles of the intellectual two-way journey that forms the fabric of his entire book.

But, as always in the human sciences, there were no terms capable of being compared rigorously. Not only was Europe deprived of the "physical advantages" enjoyed by the Anglo-Americans but its historical traits made it radically different from the New World. Tocqueville cites Europe's large population, its big cities, its armies, and its "complicated politics." These legacies would be enough to prevent a transfer of the laws of American democracy to Europe, since these laws would clash with other mores, other ideas, and other religious beliefs. For Tocqueville, who never clearly distinguished between facts and values, the United States did not constitute for Europe either a conceptually comparable experience or a model to be followed. For "one can imagine a democratic nation organized in a different way from the American people."[14]

Yet what confers a universal value to his analysis of American democracy is the existence of a problem common to the American people and to European peoples; this common problem stems from the fact that men are not different on the two continents and that they experience in America and Europe the same characteristic passions of the democratic social state: impatience with their condition, anxiety over promotion, yearning for superior status. From this *state of mind*, Americans have derived the very nature of their society—its driving force—but they have channeled it through law, religion, institutions, and mores. The European peoples, gripped as they are by identical social passions, are faced with the same institutional problem, in the broadest sense: how can these passions be organized into laws and mores?

This problem is all the more difficult to resolve as the European peoples are less "democratic" than "revolutionary." Tocqueville, refining his analysis, makes this point in the second volume of his book (part 3, chapter 21); he thereby introduces an essential distinction that runs through the entire second volume and serves to explain American consensus and political stability. The democratic social state is shown to be unpropitious to revolution, owing to the tight-knit fabric of conservative microinterests that it is constantly creating and maintaining. On the contrary, it is inequality that leads to revolution; it was to destroy the aristocratic social state and the ideology of inequality that the French carried out their revolution. But the passions and state of mind that have characterized the French since the Revolution have not been conducive to institutional stability. "In America, there exist democratic ideas and passions; in Europe, we still have revolutionary ones."[15]

But even if the European problem is harder to solve than the American one, the fact remains that only a comparison can enable one to define the elements of the European problem: "The great problem of our time is the organization and establishment of democracy in Christian lands. The American have certainly not solved this problem, but they have furnished useful lessons to those who wish to solve it."[16] The pages that follow this statement provide the key to Tocqueville's intentions. His discussion of the situation in Europe anticipates some of the analyses presented in *L'Ancien Régime et la Révolution* twenty-five years later. For Tocqueville, what was taking place or had taken place in the Old World was the creation of historical conditions exceptionally favorable to the establishment of a truly absolute central authority: therein lay the peril that had to be seen in order to be exorcised. For although the old monarchies were regarded as absolute, they were not so in practice. Political institutions (especially corporate bodies and local communities), intellectual and moral traditions (especially the "family" tie between the king and his subjects and the aristocratic values of independence and honor), and religion had prevented these monarchies from becoming absolute.

But these institutions, these traditions, and even religion itself had disappeared or were withering away, to be replaced by a society in which classes were less and less differentiated, individuals increasingly alike and isolated from one another, and public opinion ever more malleable and indistinct.

> [N]owadays, when monarchic honor [writes Tocqueville, in a tone reminiscent of Montesquieu] has almost lost its sway without being replaced by virtue, and there is nothing left which raises a man above himself, who can say where the exigencies of authority and the yielding of weakness will stop?[17]

In other words, the nations of Europe had acquired a democratic social state and a democratic state of mind without possessing the corresponding institutions or even, in their absence, political and religious traditions capable of counteracting democracy. This explained why their history was characterized by the silence of passive and demoralized peoples in the face of strong and organized governments—a prelude to a situation comparable to the end of the Roman Republic.

> For my part, when I consider the state already reached by several European nations and that toward which all are tending, I am led to believe that there will soon be no room except for either democratic freedom or the tyranny of the Caesars.
>
> Is this not worth thinking about? If men must, in fact, come to choose between all being free or all slaves, all having equal rights or all being deprived of them, if the rulers of societies are reduced to this alternative, either gradually to raise the crowd up to their own level or to let all citizens fall below the level of humanity, would not that be enough to overcome many doubts, to reassure many consciences, and to prepare each man readily to make great sacrifices?
>
> Should we not, then, consider the gradual development of democratic institutions and mores not as the best but as the only means remaining to us in order to remain free? And, without loving democratic government, would one not, then, be disposed to adopt it as the readiest and most honorable remedy against the present ills of society?[18]

This is to my mind a crucial passage, because it links the visit to America not only to Tocqueville's fundamental intention, to the goal of his life, but also to the internal structure of his thought. Tocqueville—in the facet of his analysis that he does not make explicit—is a fatalist. He believes in the inevitable, namely, in the march of societies toward "democracy." This process is common to the Old and the New World, but it appears in its pristine purity only in the American experience. However, the American people have adopted mores and laws suited to this social and cultural state, while the European peoples have inherited centralized states that are in contradiction with the development of democratic political institutions or democratic national mores. In the first case, history has subordinated the state to society. In the second, it has handed society over to the state.

But the second process is not inevitable. This is the second facet of Tocqueville's thought, the facet that gives his books an almost militant character. His aim is to encourage the evolution of the laws and mores of the old European nations—and above all of France—in harmony with the material and spiritual inroads of democracy. Such an evolution is indispensable in order to avoid the dictatorship of a single individual in control of the state. For an aristocrat like Tocqueville, there was a price to pay, feelings and interests had to be sacrificed, but he gave his prior consent to this in view of the stakes involved:

> The will of a democracy is changeable, its agents rough, its laws imperfect. I grant that. But if it is true that there will soon be nothing intermediate between the sway of democracy and the yoke of a single man, should we not rather steer toward the former than voluntarily submit to the latter? And if we must finally reach a state of complete equality, is it not better to let ourselves be leveled down by freedom rather than by a despot?[19]

Thus, Tocqueville went to the United States in search, not of a model, but of a principle to study and a question to illustrate and resolve: In what conditions does democracy, if it is a state of society, become what it *must* also be if it is not to lead to dictatorship—a state of government?

Tocqueville's system, which he developed very early, is essentially built around a few simple oppositions of which he makes sophisticated use through a constant dialectic between the cultural, the social, and the political spheres. On the social and cultural level, there are two historically conceivable states: the aristocratic state and the democratic one. The first is inseparable, on the political level, from local government, while the second leads to centralized government. But here a second, purely political choice presents itself, for not all centralized governments are necessarily oppressive. They can either be tyrannical or respect their citizens' freedom. On a first level, Tocqueville's reasoning is constructed on the opposition between aristocracy and democracy. On a second level, it revolves around the alternative between democratic Caesarism and democratic freedom, that is, around the analysis of the conditions for compatibility betweeen democracy and freedom. This explains why—as has often been said[20]—Tocqueville is constantly shifting from the social to the political meaning of the term *democracy*, and vice versa, according to which one of these two conceptual levels he is exploring.

Socially and culturally, American provides him with an example of pure democracy and of a government derived from this pure democracy. In both respects, America is an anti-Europe, with no aristocratic inheritance, no legacy of absolutism, and no revolutionary passions. Instead, it has a tradition of local community freedom. Because of all these features, *mutatis mutandis*, America is a crucial topic for Europeans to reflect upon.

Democracy in America was published in two stages. The first volume, mainly devoted to an analytical description of American institutions, appeared in 1835. The second, which studies in more abstract fashion the influence of democracy on national mores and habits, using America as an example, was published in 1840. The commentary on the most intelligent journey of the nineteenth century demanded of Tocqueville nearly ten years of additional study and of intense intellectual work. The major seminal ideas, particularly those of the first volume (the more specifically "American" of the two), were already contained in his travel notes[21]—a proof that the traveler arrived with his "system" in mind. But, if he took his time to write, it was not only because of a fondness for stylistic elegance; it was to "lay out" his object of study—a preparation that involved reading widely, in particular in the constitutional, political, and legal fields.[22] Furthermore, and above all, Tocqueville wanted to "think through" what he had "learned," to refine his conceptual scheme with the help of American material, and to work out the "lessons" it contained for European peoples. Tocqueville was a thinker who worked over the same ideas indefinitely and always uncovered new facets of them. The second volume of *Democracy in America* is the best example of this type of intellectual patience.

In addition to its simplifying virtues, America gave him, as a bonus, even though he was hardly interested in the question, the secret of its origins. In the New World, democracy was not shrouded in the mists of time or in the designs of Providence; it was brought by immigrants—New England Puritans or Pennsylvania Quakers—as a founding religious principle for the new homeland. Thus, American democracy had a cultural matrix, a logical evolution embedded in the history of its origins—a history that for once was clear and known. Better still, America offered on its very territory the antithesis of this history: the South, inhabited by a subaristocracy of planters who lacked genuine power over the free population, because they ruled slaves. On the one hand, one found the spirit of religion and the spirit of freedom indissolubly linked; on the other, a civilization founded on slavery, a principle destructive of the social state.

But Tocqueville did not dwell on the genealogy of American society; he put far less emphasis on this aspect of reality than did, for example, his contemporary Michel Chevalier in his *Lettres sur l'Amérique du Nord.*[23] Here again, Tocqueville was less interested, at the time, in the historical question than in understanding the present and making a prognosis about the future. The center of his analysis is the "social state" of the Anglo-Americans, not their history. The social state "is commonly the result of circumstances, sometimes of laws, but most often of a combination of the two. But once it has come into being, it may itself be considered as the prime cause of most of the laws, customs, and ideas which control the nation's behavior; it modifies even those things which it does not cause."[24] Tocqueville thus avoids a scholastic debate about prime causes. He methodically holds fast to his analytical system. He does not move from the celebrated crossroads in the forest, from which he is supposed to see all the paths.

This aspect is discussed in the chapter on the "social state of the Anglo-Americans" (volume 1, part 1, chapter 3), a state characterized by an extreme form of democracy, a tradition of origins, the uprising for independence, and a series of laws, particularly the law providing for equal sharing of inheritance. Equality, the dominant feature of democracy, does not mean that fortunes are equal or that Americans wish that they were; on the contrary, it simply means that fortunes are not rooted in a system of family inheritance and that money circulates very rapidly. One could even say that "democracy" is legitimized by innate talent alone, with no consideration for preexisting hierarchy. That is why democracy has attained a sort of absolute level in an area where society does not yet exist but where the social passions of the inhabitants are nevertheless intensified by familiarity, or impatience, with an earlier social tie: this area is the frontier of European colonization. But the reign of equality does not manifest itself only through the mobility of fortune and the distribution of wealth. It also creates uniformity in educational levels and even in mental endowments. For equality provides a basic instruction to all without creating a privileged class characterized by the leisure or taste for devoting itself exclusively to intellectual pursuits.

This social situation—absolutely unique in history—can have one of two incompatible political consequences: freedom or servitude, the sovereignty of the people or that of a master. We thus reach the second level of Tocqueville's conceptualization, a level clearly deduced from the first (since he is dealing explicitly with the "political consequences of the social state") but not determined by it, since this time a choice is offered: the Anglo-Americans have been able to construct political democracy on the basis of social democracy.

By understanding how and why they were able to do so, one can examine the series of connections that bridge the gap between the two levels of analysis. Tocqueville does not—at least immediately—spell out these connections, since he goes from the chapter on the "social state" to the famous and very detailed description of the American political system. But the connections can be found in chapter 9 of part 2 of volume 1 and also in Tocqueville's travel notes, which testify to the fact that the elements of his explanation were already in place by 1831. For Tocqueville, what has preserved American political democracy, after historical circumstances gave it birth, is not only a fidelity to origins but something resembling a state of mind, so widespread and so deeply rooted that one can call it "national mores." It is this factor that is responsible, day after day, for maintaining society's independence and its preeminence over politics.

First, religion plays an admirable regulatory role in two ways: by what it prescribes and what it forbids. While Catholicism, according to Tocqueville, encourages equality and obedience (except when Catholicism is separated from the state, in which case it acquires new characteristics), Protestantism, especially in its sectarian and pluralist form, encourages equality and independence. American religion is made of a set of republican varieties of Christianity. But religion also sets limits on what can be known to—and transformed by—man; hence, American boldness is tempered by a sort of collective moderation. By preventing citizens from "imagining certain things," religion acts as an obstacle, in other words (in words that Tocqueville does not use), to the revolutionary spirit, which is the negation of democracy in the name of democracy. Tocqueville wondered about this paradox all his life without ever fully mastering its breathtaking implications; but, in America, religious consensus had destroyed its attractiveness.

Another key factor in the independence of American society was its high level of culture. Here Tocqueville parts company with Montesquieu: the mainspring of republics is not virtue but instruction, by which Tocqueville means the democratization of knowledge, particularly in political matters. Speculating on the "thousand reasons that make republican freedom tolerable in the United States," he wrote in his travel notebooks:

> There is one major reason that towers over all the others and, after one has enumerated all of them, carries the day. The American people taken as a whole are not only the most enlightened in the world but—and I consider this a far more important advantage—the people with the most advanced education in practical politics. It is this truth, in which I strongly believe, that arouses in me the only hope I have for the future happiness of Europe.[25]

Despite their lack of refinement, the vulgarity of their manners, and their obsession with money, the American people were, for the French aristocrat, the most *civilized* on earth. Tocqueville thus measured the worth of the human investment that America represented—with eighteen centuries of European history behind it. America was a nation of town dwellers out to conquer nature, bypassing the unending curse of the peasant condition in Europe. The pioneer was the unlikely breed between the height of civilization and the height of savagery—the quintessence of history and the quintessence of nature. Tocqueville's travel notebooks contain some unforgettably beautiful passages on this theme,[26] but he used only a small portion of them in his book.

It is this high degree of civilization that supplied the Union—setting aside the South, undermined from within by slavery—with one of the basic ingredients in democratic mores: uniformity. Tocqueville, in his notes, admits to being surprised by this feature of American life. Accustomed as he was to observing differences of "several centuries" between the provinces—or parts of provinces—of European nations, he expected to find an all the greater disparity within the New World as it was still being colonized and ought to have presented, according to the locality, "an image of society at every age . . . from the wealthy urban patrician to the desert savage."[27] But Tocqueville observed the opposite. As the Americans who were settling on the "frontier" came not directly from Europe but from the oldest settled territories, they had already been exposed to the spirit of equality and subjected to the uniformization of tastes and mores. "You will find the same man you left behind in the streets of New York in the almost inaccessible wilderness: same clothing, same attitude, same language, same habits, same pleasures."[28] Tocqueville did not believe, as Michel Chevalier did,[29] that the frontier constituted a third America, after that of Puritan businessmen and that of slaveholding planters. The Saint-Simonian's criteria were economic, while Tocqueville's were moral and cultural.

Actually, in analyzing the West and the American spirit in general (for the West merely reveals its quintessence), he borrows—albeit with some modifications—a concept dating from the previous century: "civilization." Like the eighteenth-century philosophers, Tocqueville uses it to refer to a set of cultural features that make societies both more regulated and more active; but, unlike Voltaire, he does not regard it as the upper ridge of a succession of cycles or, like Condorcet, as the terminus of a linear progress. He wrests the concept from history—an undefinable vector, another name for Providence—and incorporates it into his own intellectual system. For Tocqueville, "civilization" is the particular form of social activity that democracy, in its free state, makes available to all citizens. By the same token, this definition allows him to relativize the field of his analysis and to confine the benefits of civilization to the European stock of mankind. Hence the well-known passage on the genocide of the Indians, a passage that I cannot resist quoting at length, not because its tone corresponds to present-day attitudes, but because it gives a good illustration of the exceptional virtues of the interpretative system analyzed here:

> The Indian races melt away in the presence of European civilization like snows in sunshine. Their efforts to resist their fate only accelerate their destruction at the hand of time. Every ten years or so, the Indian tribes that have been pushed back into the western deserts realize that they have gained nothing by retreating and that the white race is advancing even faster than they are withdrawing. Irritated by the very feeling of their helplessness, or incensed by some new affront, they assemble and swoop down on the areas they used to inhabit, which are now dotted with European settlements, rustic pioneer cabins here, the first villages there. They scout the country, burn down settlements, kill herds, and take a few scalps. Civilization retreats, but it retreats like the flow of the rising sea. The United States sides with the last of its settlers and declares war on these wretched tribes. A regular army is sent out to fight them; not only is American territory reconquered, but the whites, driving the Indians in front of them, destroy their villages, seize their herds, and establish the outermost limit of their possessions one hundred leagues beyond the previous boundary. Deprived of this newly adopted homeland by what educated and enlightened Europe has felt like calling the *right* of war, the Indians resume their westward march, until they stop in a new wilderness, where the sound of the white man's hatchet will soon be heard again. In the area they have just plundered, now safe from invasion, new villages rise and will soon turn into teeming cities (at least so their inhabitants believe). Marching ahead of the vast European family, of which he is, as it were, the vanguard, the pioneer takes over in turn the forests recently inhabited by the savages. There he builds his rustic cabin, and waits for the next war to open the way toward new deserts.[30]

Thus, "democracy" is not the end of history or one of its universal phases, or even less the reconciliation of humanity with itself. It is a concept that enables Tocqueville to imagine a state of society and mores specific to Europe, and more particularly specific to the extension of Britain in the New World represented by the American Republic. Indeed, in America the historical experience of democracy has been so radical in the social and cultural spheres that the entire realm of politics has been suffused and taken over by democracy to the point of being completely subordinated to it. For one of Tocqueville's strongest impressions during his visit was that of the virtual absence of "politics" from American society. He speaks in his notes of the "absence of government,"[31] an asset that man can find "only at the two extremes of civilization," either in the savage state, when he is alone in the face of his needs, or, after the formation of society, when the individuals that compose it are sufficiently enlightened and sufficiently independent of their passions (or law-abiding, which amounts to the same) to do without government. In a later passage,[32] he distinguishes two clearly separate "social states": "In the first, the people are sufficiently enlightened and they find themselves in sufficiently favorable circumstances for them to be able to govern themselves. Here society acts upon itself. In the second, a power external to society acts upon it, forcing it to march along a given path." America, of course, fits the first description—that of a self-administered society. It offers the example not only of what could be called "pure democracy," but also, up to a point, of "pure society," with politics excluded.

Naturally, my analysis goes too far, since a great portion of the first volume of *Democracy in America* is devoted to a description of the American political system. But it does serve to emphasize Tocqueville's intellectual approval of political democracy, despite what he regards as its "excesses." Political democracy, which provides for the freedom and responsibility of citizens through administrative decentralization (which Tocqueville is careful to distinguish, as we know, from governmental decentralization), basically embodies the advantages of an aristocratic political system while increasing the number of its beneficiaries. Consequently, the problem, on both the administrative and the governmental levels, is to compare the advantages and drawbacks of the two systems, one in the hands of society as a whole, the other controlled by a hereditary elite. This fascinating and justly famous part of the book is of little import here, in that it is informed throughout, explicitly and implicitly, by the conceptual opposition described above. What makes these chapters interesting is the exceptional thoroughness with which Tocqueville explores this contrast from every angle, using American institutions as the basic example; but he does not modify the central structure of the dichotomy.

However, there is one chapter in the first volume of *Democracy in America*—the last chapter—in which he is compelled to abandon his conceptual "core." In the extraordinary chapter 10 of part 2, he specifically leaves American "democracy" aside in order to examine the future of what he calls the "three races" that inhabit the United States, namely, the Anglo-Americans, the Indians, and the Negroes. Hence, Tocqueville feels obliged, for once, to discard his analytical system, which has no relevance to the two marginalized "races"—Indians and Negroes—the two peoples who by definition are not "democratic"; and, as their existence is not without consequence on the future of the Union, this future itself is not entirely contained in the prognosis concerning democracy. Curiously enough, and almost regretfully, Tocqueville adds to the list of subjects left aside by his type of analysis "the commercial activity prevailing in the Union" and its importance for the future, as if his task were to enumerate, even in an intellectually chaotic fashion, the questions he has not treated and to say why: "These topics are like tangents to my subject, being American, not democratic, and my main business has been to describe democracy. So at first I had to leave them on one side, but now at the end I must return to them."[33]

With regard to the Indians, we have already seen from Tocqueville's travel notebooks that, in analyzing their society, he resorts to a modified version of the concept of "civilization" inherited from the eighteenth century. He uses it to describe not so much the historical "backwardness" of this savage world as its insulation from the civilized world, namely, from American democracy. Once again, he proceeds from the "social state" of the Indians—a world of nomads, tribes, warriors, and hunters—to their mores and beliefs, which remind him, *mutatis mutandis*, of those of the ancient Germans according to Tacitus. Thus, his vision of history, far from being restricted to a belief in mankind's inevitable evolution, links up with his typological analysis. Tocqueville does not believe that Indian societies, by coming into contact—even conflictually—with Anglo-American "civilization," will gradually be raised to its level. On the contrary, he thinks that their nomadic social state, consolidated by their system or mores and beliefs, isolates them thoroughly and permanently. Either the Indians react by waging war, in which case they are defeated and driven westward, or they consent to become "civilized," in which case they enter an alien world where they are irremediably inferior, exploited, and doomed. Both recourse to war and submission to laws will seal their fate. Tocqueville's sociological genius guards him against the humanist illusion concerning the benefits brought by European civilization to other continents.

As for the Negroes, their fate cannot be sealed as dramatically, for it is tied to that of the whites. But it poses a twofold problem for the Union, and here, too, Tocqueville's outlook is not optimistic. The conjunction of an institution as anachronistic as slavery in a century of equality with its confinement to a particular race among the population—the Negroes—seems to Tocqueville to entail catastrophic consequences for the activity of white society in areas where slavery exists, as well as an inevitable struggle for its abolition, particularly in places where slavery does not exist. But this struggle, which is rooted in the self-interest of the whites, not of the Negroes, does not imply the disappearance of race prejudice; on the contrary, the emancipation of the Negroes would not be followed by interbreeding—vehemently refused by the Anglo-American settlers—or by equality, impossible to achieve between two peoples alien to each other. It is more than likely that the abolition of slavery would be offset by the intensification of color prejudice, of what today we would call racism. Thus, even if slavery were abolished by the masters, and not through Negro violence, the Union's cohesion would be seriously threatened.

In these brilliant pages on Indians and Negroes, Tocqueville sets aside his concept of "democracy," since it would be incapable of explaining the two societies he is discussing. Nevertheless, his analysis here is linked to his general intellectual system by the priority he assigns to the notion of "social state" and to its defining principle. For Tocqueville, Indians and Negroes are not so much races distinct from the Anglo-Americans as social groups organized according to principles incompatible with the democracy prevailing in the Union. But they are incompatible in different ways. Indians form a distinctive and introverted society whose "savage" rules, beliefs, and mores are less an expression of humanity in its primal state—as it was thought in the eighteenth century—than features of a nonagricultural and nonsedentary mode of social organization. As slaves, Negroes form a nonsociety, since servitude is by definition a relationship based exclusively on power and not a "social" tie. But the principle of slavery compromises the existence of the free society that has established it. Having introduced and maintained slavery, this society is, therefore, undermined from within by slavery itself. The Indians can and will be destroyed by the law, as they are a society situated outside it. The Negroes, on the other hand, owe their presence to an institution of American democracy that is contradictory with that democracy but a deliberate product of it. They are at the same time indispensable and impossible to assimilate, necessary and destructive of the basic social compact. Egalitarian America has incorporated an unavowable and noxious principle into its life; and if this paradox puts its very existence at stake, it is because it is even more destructive of white democratic society than of the black slave population.

This pessimistic diagnosis of the black problem is accompanied, as we know, by some doubts about the survival of the American federal system. But Tocqueville's pessimism in no way diminishes his admiration for the "spirit" in which the British settled in America, the social state to which it led, and the usages and ideas engendered by this social state. It has often been said that Tocqueville the aristocrat had "resigned himself" to democracy. *Democracy in America* does not seem to me to justify such an expression, no doubt more appropriate to describe his judgment on the European situation. In actual fact, Tocqueville is a critical admirer of American democracy, and one could quote many passages from his book to show that on the whole, and despite its shortcomings, he prefers it to the aristocratic system, both as a social state and as a form of government. On these two counts, America showed him the power a society could exercise over itself. It is precisely this lesson—this example—that he had gone to America to seek.

Five years later, in 1840, Tocqueville published the second volume of *Democracy in America*. He could assume that his readers were familiar with the American political system, since it was the main topic of the 1835 volume. Tocqueville's problem now was to explore in greater depth the question that he had already touched on and outlined in the first volume without discussing it systematically: the influence of the democratic social state on the American spirit and, more generally, on the spirit of the peoples among whom it prevails. Tocqueville does not want to treat this "democratic social state"—that is, equality—as the sole cause of the characteristics of American society or "of everything that is happening now."[34] He is well aware that the opposite is true and that one must take into account a host of circumstances independent of equality. However, it is this trait, common to the Old and the New World, that enables him to compare America and Europe. Moreover, this trait is his subject, the starting point for his examination of society and history, because he regards it as the most likely key to an understanding of the present state of the world. The most surprising aspect of Tocqueville's intellectual obsession with the concept of equality is the very *obviousness* of this concept's capacity to explain the present state of societies and their future as well. As for its capacity to explain the present, the least one can say is that the societies of Tocqueville's time—and particularly his own society, that of France under the July Monarchy—did not exhibit equality. Furthermore, his own existence, in its outer aspects, was entirely governed by the spirit of conformity to the values of his family environment and by the strictest observance of the principles of social hierarchy:[35] one need only glance at his correspondence to see this. Even after the July Revolution, France under Louis Philippe was a country in which men like Tocqueville, the descendants of the old aristocracy, continued to exercise, without having to seek it, an almost natural ideological and tangible authority. What, then, is the source of Tocqueville's intellectual conviction, which his very existence contradicted daily?

The origins of his belief lie less in the present state of society than in its history—that is, in his own past. It is probably difficult to imagine today what the thunderburst of the French Revolution represented for a family such as his—the mass of recollections and dramatic stories that filled his childhood, the horrified fascination that he must have felt at a very early age. By the end of his adolescence, he had succeeded in transforming this family experience into an intellectual problem. His genius lies in the precocious appropriation of his inheritance on another level and in another manner. It is from a tale of misfortune, handed down by family tradition, that he constructed both the idea of equality and the idea of inevitability.

These two ideas are inseparable precisely because they are rooted in the same existential soil: in the feeling that the French Revolution is part of the course of history—in other words, that it is not over—and that, having manifested itself by such a radical hostility toward the nobility and even toward all notion of social superiority, it can be defined only by the passion for equality. Little does it matter that this equality was not "realized" in postrevolutionary societies. If it is true that Tocqueville conceptualized only his own experience (and this is probably what distinguishes him from most great philosophical thinkers, trained primarily in the abstract study of doctrines and ideas; it is also what explains his obstinate investigation of a single idea, which one can properly speak of, as one says of a woman, as the idea of his life), this experience told him, in effect, that the French Revolution continued—through the Empire, the Restoration, and 1830—and that equality remained at the heart of political debates and events. Actually, this conviction was Tocqueville's way of appropriating the celebrated melancholy of the romantic generation, of which he was also a son. But at the same time this feeling is a concept.

Hence its constant ambiguity, situated on two distinct levels. The use of the word *democracy* as an approximate substitute for *equality*, but in an even larger sense, leads Tocqueville to use the word in different semantic ways—ways that, in particular, do not distinguish between the social sphere and the political sphere. But the ambiguity also exists—and perhaps at a deeper, because more hidden, level—in the specific use of *democracy* to designate an egalitarian social state (in fact, this is the most frequent use). What does our author mean by a society or a social state characterized by equality? It is not easy to answer this question.

The simplest answer is a commonsensical one: a society in which equality reigns is a society in which class barriers between individuals have disappeared. Sometimes Tocqueville does give such a definition, for example when he writes, "When a people has lived for centuries under a system of castes and classes, it can only reach a democratic state of society through a long series of more or less painful transformations."[36] A little later, in a note to chapter 26 of part 3 of volume 2, there is an even more explicit statement, since the words *that is* introduce a definition: "When a people has a democratic state of society, that is to say, when there are no longer any castes or classes in its community . . ."[37] These quotations are wholly consistent, as they equate social classes and castes, at least with respect to their character, which is contradictory to democracy and makes the classless society the condition for equality. This type of definition, both maximalist (equality as a real social state) and naïve (equality corresponding to the way in which social actors conceive it), occurs elsewhere: for example, in the comparison Tocqueville makes between aristocratic marriage and democratic marriage.[38] The first is a socially programmed union, offering, in any event, little freedom of choice; it is a union of properties rather than of people. The second, in contrast, results from a free choice; it is based on the spouses' feelings and the similarity of their tastes (also, in this respect, it makes greater demands on marital fidelity). One can see from this example how, in order to comply with a mode of reasoning that proceeds by opposition, Tocqueville can be led to confuse what he calls the democratic social state with this social state's self-image and the image of itself that it wants to project. In an age when bourgeois marriage as a union of wealth was one of the favorite themes of novelistic literature, Tocqueville, because of the requirements of his conceptual system, was oddly and temporarily blind to the obvious reality of class marriage, a practice masked by the apparent freedom of individual sentiment.

His blindness was both odd and temporary, for he was obviously well aware—as he wrote elsewhere—that "there has not yet been a society in which conditions were so equal that there was neither rich nor poor, and consequently neither masters nor servants." How does the democratic social state change this situation? "Democracy in no way prevents the existence of these two classes, but it changes their attitudes and modifies their relations."[39] This passage is crucial for understanding what he most often meant by *democracy*—not a real social state, but the egalitarian perception of social relationships, which are usually hierarchical (at least judging by human history), by the actors in these relationships. This egalitarian perception in turn modifies the nature of the relationship, even when it has remained totally grounded in inequality. An example of this is the master-servant relationship: it exists in the democratic society of the United States but does not constitute, as in aristocratic societies, a principle of the social order. Hence, in America, this relationship does not create a separate, subject people whose mores and mentality are handed down from father to son. Instead, it is the outcome of a freely consented contract, by means of which the interested party negotiates its provisional subservience and the limits of this subservience. "Equality [of conditions]," says Tocqueville, "makes new men of servant and of master and establishes new connections between them."[40] Thus, "equality of conditions," one of his favorite expressions to characterize democracy, does not mean that master and servant are truly equal but that *they can be*; in other words, the relationship of temporary subordination does not constitute a "state" that provides a complete definition of both parties, since the relationship can, for example be reversed as a consequence of their individual careers. As the servant can become a master, and wants to become one, he is no different from the master. Furthermore, outside the sphere of the revocable contract that ties him to his master, the servant is a citizen enjoying the same rights as his master. "Equality of conditions" must not, therefore, be understood in the material sense of the expression but as a constituent principle of the democratic social order, in contrast to the aristocratic world—as a norm and not an empirical observation.

Tocqueville is aware that this norm is a sort of unattainable and endlessly elusive objective, never a reality: hence the perpetual instability of democratic individuals and societies. As it is impossible for a people to achieve perfect equality and as there will always be dominant positions coveted by ambitious individuals, the presence of an egalitarian rule in social life, by opening all careers in principle to all men, sharpens their desires and struggles. This explains why Tocqueville shifts so often from equality as a dominant social state (that is, as a norm) to equality as a passion (that is, as both a feeling and an ideology). One could almost say that the democratic social state is characterized more by the passions it engenders than by their fulfillment, since actual equality of conditions is never achieved but always yearned for. "When inequality is the general rule in society, the greatest inequalities attract no attention. When everything is more or less level, the slightest variation is noticed. Hence the more equal men are, the more insatiable will be their longing for equality."[41]

In other words, this genuine equality—an avowed but elusive aim, a reference to a norm but also an object of desire—is subdivided into a host of partial attempts to establish social differences. Tocqueville understood that the belief in equality as a value does not eliminate what he calls "private individual pride," that is, the passion for distinguishing oneself from others. On the contrary, the belief in equality intensifies this passion, while modifying and increasing its scope. The tendency to "distinguish" oneself is all the more legitimate as classes are less defined by custom or law, as is the case in aristocracies. In addition, democracy increases the number of signs of differentiation because, by making conditions equal, and even more by making citizens uniform, it gives added value to the slightest advantage; and, by increasing social mobility, it replaces traditional hierarchies with recent and temporary privileges, conspicuously displayed by their beneficiaries while they enjoy them. There is in *Democracy in America* (particularly in chapters 14 and 16 of part 3 of volume 2) an outline of a theory of how equality breeds symbolic inequality and how this process gives rise to the restlessness and envy that are the sentiments characteristic of democracies.

Nevertheless, Tocqueville believes that this inherent instability is compensated by certain factors enabling the system to function in harmony. First, there is religion, which he regards as a key element of the social consensus and as a protection for "democratic" citizens against the inordinate pretense to know everything and thus to change everything. But there is also a built-in corrective, hidden within the very desire for equality and the passion for social promotion: in a democratic state, where careers are relatively slow and where individuals have become used to making a daily effort to climb up the social ladder step by step, there is a tendency for desires to become commensurate with means, and ambitions with chances. Tocqueville was the first to discover this basic law of modern societies, according to which men internalize by their desire only a probable future, in the statistical sense of the term. They look forward only to what can happen to them, thus avoiding both exaggerated ambitions and insurmountable disappointments.

Moreover, it is the absence of these correctives for equality that characterizes an intermediate social state between aristocracy and democracy: the state of revolution. It is an intermediate state in the chronological sense, since revolution marks the transition from aristocracy to democracy, but also in the sociological sense, since revolution suddenly creates the ingredients of democracy without, however, enabling it to function: it introduces the notion of a break while unwittingly embodying a tradition. "Revolutionary" individuals inherit the immoderation of aristocratic ambitions; their feeling of creating a totally new world is part of this immoderation, and the emergence of new men and new laws prevents desires from becoming adjusted to chances. Thus, revolution is characterized more by the explosion of egalitarianism than by that of equality; it thrives on a vast discrepancy between what individuals want and what society can offer them. It creates in turn a tradition that outlives the exceptional years and explains postrevolutionary instability: "The passions roused by revolution by no means vanish at its close. A sense of instability is perpetuated amid order. The hope of easy success lives on after the strange turns of fortune which gave it birth."[42]

Thus, for Tocqueville, "democracy" in France is not the "normal" form of this social state: it is its revolutionary form. This fundamental distinction runs through the entire second volume of *Democracy in America* and constitutes the leading strand of the comparison whose elements the traveler had come to seek. In the United States, he found a pure democracy, that is, one that resembled his ideal type—a democracy since its inception, which had been generated from a religious matrix that extolled its values and which, therefore, had never had to struggle against an earlier aristocratic state. The concept of revolution, which Tocqueville constructs entirely on the basis of the French experience, thus strikes him as alien to American history (except as a potential civil war between the southern aristocracy and Yankee democracy). More important, he regards it as incompatible with the functioning of democracy, in that equality constitutes a far more homogeneous and resistant social fabric than aristocratic society. Tocqueville devotes a chapter[43] to a discussion of why the democratic social state, because of the social and cultural uniformity it induces and because of the mesh of conservative microinterests in which it involves citizens, is a poor breeding ground for revolution; on the contrary, it is the destruction of aristocratic inequality that provides a pretext and an objective for revolution, as the European example demonstrates.

Thus, the idea of democracy, in all the aspects that Tocqueville never ceases to examine, does indeed merge, in most cases, with the idea of equality; but it also takes on the ambiguities and various connotations of the latter. There is just one aspect of equality that does not interest Tocqueville: that of its objective reality. He is satisfied with the belief that real social conditions have already begun to level off and are continuing to do so gradually. But he never tries to be more specific about this assumption, much less to measure it: it is an existentially, not a statistically, obvious fact. When he discusses this aspect of the question, he speaks as a descendant of a great family of the *ancien régime*: he has in mind the leveling of the material conditions of the nobility and the middle class (exactly like Guizot, who agrees with his analysis but takes the middle class as a starting point).

But Tocqueville's greatest and most abiding interest is both the role of equality as a norm of social life and the mental mechanism of which the emergence of this norm is both the consequence and the cause: the passion for equality. With regard to the first aspect, democracy never ceases to carry within itself, as a consubstantial and inseparable element, a threat to its own future, a prospect for the sake of which democracy must allow itself to be continually challenged. Equality is a value that cannot be realized by any social state (just as democracy, in the commonest sense of the term—government of the people by itself—is an ideal type of power whose conditions cannot be met by any modern community); and it is in the inevitable gap between values and facts, between a society and its norm, that equality as a social passion takes root. This is one of the features of Tocquevillian democracy. Aristocratic societies do not suffer from such a discrepancy, since they are not in conflict with their own values of subordination and hierarchy. If these societies happen to be overturned, it is in the name of an inverse legitimacy, that of equality, which appropriates for its own purposes a set of passions that are similar in nature and directed toward the same goal. But an egalitarian society, once established, cannot abide by its own values without being in constant contradiction with its real state; and the passions that it has intensified by its victory or by its mere existence pose a challenge to it in its everyday functioning.[44] That is why democracy, while it has the advantage over other states of society of mobilizing its citizens through their egalitarian passions, also poses a problem unknown to aristocracies: the problem of its daily viability.

In any event, this is a difficult problem to solve. It becomes dramatic when the passion for equality takes precedence over all others, and particularly over men's fondness for freedom. It is this hierarchy of preference that constitutes the chief danger for democracies. If the two passions were of equal strength and were equally widespread, they would combine their effects, and each citizen would actually enjoy an equal right to participate in government. However, experience suggests that equality and the passion for equality can exist in civil society and yet be absent from political society; such is the case in a system based on property franchise. One can also find equality and the passion for equality in a political society without freedom; such is the case with despotism.

The relation between the passion for equality and the other passions in democratic life thus emerges as one of the essential elements of democratic society. Basically, Tocqueville believes that the passion for equality is the overriding and distinctive passion among democratic peoples and that the fundamental problem it raises is precisely how it can be kept within limits compatible with freedom. Why is the passion for equality stronger than all other political feelings? The first chapter of the second part of volume 2 offers a series of reasons: prevailing conformity, rootedness in the deep-seated habits of the social state, and, above all, the fact that the passion for equality is consonant with the logic of democracy, since it can be shared by all, whereas the benefits of freedom can be perceived by only a very few. Conversely, the excesses of freedom (anarchy, for example) are obvious to all, whereas those of equality are imperceptible and can be discerned by only a few. Finally, Tocqueville does not forget the French example, since it is his lifelong concern. In France the passion for equality is all the stronger for its being considerably older than freedom and for having been fostered by the leveling policies of absolute monarchs. The tradition of freedom is fragile, intermittent, and limited; the tradition of equality is a constitutive element of the nation.

This is not the case in America, which Tocqueville sees as a democracy where the passion for equality is kept in check both by religious consensus, which places man's ultimate destiny in the hands of the divinity, and by political institutions, which give precedence, and even power, to society over the state: the celebrated chapter on associations[45] shows that the latter play in democratic society a role comparable to that of the aristocracy in aristocratic society, in that they each constitute a corporate body expressing a social initiative independent of the state. Consequently, Tocqueville's analysis does not simply consist in studying the passion for equality—even if this is a crucial phenomenon—but also aims at understanding how, in the case of America, democracy has spun a web of feelings, ideas, and mores that have given society its distinctive features and its particular way of life. Thus, the intellectual architecture of the 1840 volume becomes clearer. Tocqueville is not out to reconstruct the history of American democracy, its origins, or its causes; instead, he regards democracy as the central element in American history, as the key to its interpretation, both because of its normative function in social life and because of its existence as a complex of passions and individual desires. In the second volume, Tocqueville is interested not in causes but in consequences—in how democracy tends to produce what we could call a "public spirit" *sui generis*, that is, a set of ideas and mores that, in turn, help to strengthen the system.

To be frank, the second volume is so brilliant and dense that it is quite impossible to look at its analyses in detail here. The reader must be left with the enjoyable yet arduous task of discovering the depth and complexity that lie underneath the apparent clarity of style. Nowhere else does Tocqueville's conceptual genius stand out more vividly than in this text, which deals with the central concern of his life at its highest level of abstraction and intellectual ambition.[46] By studying in succession the "intellectual movement," the "sentiments," and the "mores" of the American people, Tocqueville grapples with the most important question in the social sciences, the question we have been asking ourselves ever since: What is the connection between the production of ideas—of mental images—and the other levels of social life? This is the question that the young Marx was also trying to solve, at almost the same time, by positing a connection between ideas and the social state in general. But Marx characterizes this social state only by objective and, so to speak, material elements—the productive forces and the production relationships that they engender. Tocqueville, instead, focuses directly on social phenomena without prior examination of economic factors, which are absent from his type of analysis; and the social phenomena he examines are in reality cultural.

When Tocqueville analyzes equality in its objective sense, he is actually discussing only the leveling of conditions, a process whose terminus cannot be predicted, since its goal is elusive. Equality is not a state but a history that gives a meaning to individual behavior and to the notions that govern this behavior. Equality exists more by virtue of the significance it confers on social relations than by virtue of the changes it has brought about in these relations. As a source of legitimacy, it imparts to all of society—including people's perceptions of society—the movement of conflictual autonomy that characterizes American democracy. One does not find in Tocqueville's work the gap—which Marx was unable to fill—between the production of material life and the production of ideas. As Tocqueville's chief analytical tool is not so much equality as notions about equality, both as social norms and as the focus of individual passions, he has no trouble descending from that level to the production of ideas and of moral and intellectual traditions.

This "descent" does not necessarily imply a single or constant central link between social states and ideas. Indeed, this link is even less exclusive in more "intellectual" fields. On the subject of literature, for example, Tocqueville warns the reader against a determinism based on a social state—democratic or aristocratic:

> I should say more than I mean if I asserted that a nation's literature is always subordinated to its social state and political constitution. I know that, apart from these, there are other causes that give literature certain characteristics, but those do seem the most important to me.
> There are always numerous connections between the social and political condition of a people and the inspiration of its writers. He who knows the one is never completely ignorant of the other.[47]

Thus, whatever precautions Tocqueville takes in order to temper its systemic character, the nature of his thought is deductive: from "democracy" stem the intellectual traits, the mental habits, and the mores of the Americans. This proposition is partly tautological, since the definition of democracy includes equality as a norm and as a passion. But Tocqueville manages to compose variations of almost infinite subtlety and richness on this proposition, in that his aim is to rework his central definition unceasingly by examining its correlates.

Thus, it is not of the greatest importance, in my view, that the plan of the admirable second volume has only the appearances of rigor; that the distinction between "ideas," "sentiments," and "mores" is often debatable; that even within each of the parts, especially the third, the arrangement of topics is not very logical. What does matter is the extraordinary congruence between America as an object of study and the definition of democracy that Tocqueville uses in order to explore it. By virtue of their origins, at once recent and homogeneous, their social state, and their political institutions, the Americans fulfill the requirements for a laboratory experiment in democracy. The assertion that every aspect of their life is a consequence of democracy is a convenient expository device for saying that every feature of America can be understood by reference to a social consensus on equality. The association of new men for the purpose of exploiting a virgin territory—an association with no other historical foundation than this common belief—provided Tocqueville with a field of study providentially suited to his conceptual genius, which was both profound and simple.

Profound and simple: a comparison with Marx[48] will perhaps enable us to add a final word of explanation concerning these predicates.

Marx's concepts, in every period of his intellectual development, are never simple. They are reworkings of concepts inherited from German philosophy or borrowed from English political economy; they owe nothing to Marx's subjective experience and almost everything to his reflection on the reflections of others. In contrast, Tocqueville's system is founded not on an intellectual construct but on a self-evident empirical notion transposed to the abstract level, where it is defined as the irreversible progress of equality. This notion becomes the centerpiece of Tocqueville's analysis, which aims at deducing its consequences.

Marx delves behind the equality proclaimed by the French Revolution, a value that has become the source of social legitimacy in the West. He unmasks and denounces actual inequality, the contradiction between facts and values. He writes a genealogy of the cause of this contradiction, a cause that he locates on the economic level and in the social relations arising from the production of wealth. Equality becomes no more than an ideological lie, or a higher goal that cannot be achieved without the destruction of capitalism. This dichotomy destroys all the features of Tocquevillian equality, that is, equality as a social norm and as a passion. Marx is interested in the workings of economic life and in the connections between economics and society. Tocqueville explores the relation between the social principle and human behavior: by bringing his analysis to bear on the motives of the individual and collective action of his contemporaries, Tocqueville has no need to reduce the political sphere to another order of reality that is supposed to underlie and determine it. He thus breaks with the obsessive search for the foundations of society so characteristic of the eighteenth century and of Marx, who in this respect is the heir to that century. Tocqueville deliberately focuses on what lies "downstream": he regards the founding principle as a sort of historical datum that is both evident and impossible to reduce to a causal demonstration; what counts is to deduce its consequences on social life. For Marx, freedom lies in the abolition of surplus value; for Tocqueville, in the intelligent handling of the belief in equality.

In this sense, Marx's thought is infinitely more complex; it approaches politics only through a series of mediations (in which, as it turns out, Marx gets lost). But, in another sense, Tocqueville's "simplicity" goes deeper. Despite appearances, Marx's entire system is directed toward the realization of the promises of equality. In denouncing inequality through the analysis of capitalist social relations, he rediscovers equality in the guise of the historical necessity of socialism but never ceases to regard it as the basic value of the social compact. He criticizes the capitalist version of equality only the better to demonstrate that it must act *once more* as a founding principle for history, through the new departure represented by revolution. Tocqueville, on the contrary, does not internalize equality as a value: he is an aristocrat. But he does observe the *fact* that equality has become the legitimating principle of modern societies, and he tries to measure this phenomenon. By using a method that is both spatially and temporally comparative, he confers a relative value to equality as a legitimating principle and a new belief that must be compared to older principles and beliefs in order for its immense impact to be appreciated. Tocqueville is thus the first to view modernity in an anthropological perspective.

Paradoxically, the "simpler" his thought and the less bookish his theory, the more the two—thought and theory—are directly fed by a contemporaneous psychological experience and the more they enable experience to be dissociated from its conceptualization. Tocqueville went from the aristocratic world to the democratic world, and it is this very passage that constitutes the thread—and the anguish—of his life. With a foot in each world, he regards as a self-evident truth that equality is only one of the modes of social life. It is out of his archaic existential position that he constructs his modern conceptual inquiry.

Marx's thought, on the contrary, aims at a totally scientific investigation into the most hidden sources of inequality, which it unmasks under the misleading disguise of a free contract between equal individuals. But the more it tries to be scientific, independent of contemporary experience, and intent on discovering reality under the mask of ideology, the more it "adheres" unknowingly to equality as a choice, forbidding the slightest deviation and without conveying the slightest doubt as to the moral necessity of equality as a social principle. Marx's thought dresses up the quintessentially modern value of equality in the language of science. No doubt it is this juxtaposition of prophecy and analysis that explains the great posthumous destiny of a weighty treatise on political economy.

Marx remains inside the system of belief in equality; Tocqueville subjects it to a comparative analysis. This surely provides the fullest and most satisfactory explanation of why their works had such a different impact or, rather, why one enjoyed universal glory and the other a somewhat muted success. But this contrast may also explain Tocqueville's superiority over Marx in the realm of predictive accuracy: it would not be difficult to show that the French aristocrat's forecast of the contemporary world (I am referring to what we call today the "developed" European world, since the two authors did not study any other) is infinitely closer to our present experience than the forecast of the German socialist. The predictive value of Tocqueville's work remains extraordinary, even in its detail, and the famous pages (not very original for their time) on the imperial future of America and Russia are in this respect less extraordinary than a host of observations on the ideology that still informs our existence. Moreover, the disparity in the predictive accuracy of Tocqueville and Marx is all the more striking as it seems to be inversely proportional to the veracity of their empirical points of departure. The social equality with which Tocqueville seems obsessed does not appear to the historian to be a characteristic feature of European societies of the first half of the nineteenth century. In contrast, the misery of the working classes, which forms the backdrop to the theory of capitalist exploitation, is indisputable.

But, in constructing the doctrine derived from this situation, Marx focuses on an economic mechanism that explains practically nothing about the great events of the nineteenth and twentieth centuries. Not only does it ultimately reduce the political sphere to the economic sphere, but it "freezes" the evolutionary process by equating it with the development of an "objective" contradiction in production relations. This scientistic view of the future as the extinction of surplus value through the proletarian revolution turned out to be less prophetic than the study of the connection between equality and the administrative state. The reason for this is not only that a subjective feeling of evolution—provided it is developed in an abstract mode—can turn out to be more accurate than the pretense of a scientific knowledge of history. It is, above all, that by analyzing equality not as a situation, but as a principle, a complex of passions, and an open-ended political dynamic, Tocqueville has a double advantage over Marx. First, his analysis is wholly compatible with an age of expectation ushered in by the French Revolution, an expectation whose outlines he can discern in the United States; second, he tries to understand, not the causes, but the consequences of this phenomenon. In so doing, he made a prediction that proved to be correct, namely, that the world of equality and the forms of behavior it engendered were durable and irreversible phenomena that would decisively affect the future. To that extent, Tocqueville was already analyzing the world in which we are still living.

11

Today's America: A Metamorphosis of the Idea of Equality

For any traveler in modern America, the most glaring phenomenon is the urban crisis. It has hit hardest in the oldest industrialized areas of the United States—the Northeast and the Great Lakes—the areas that are the most traditional symbols of America's success. These chosen lands of democracy, affluence, and individual promotion have become the sites of collective revolt and hopeless poverty. Yesterday, they embodied the nation's promise; today, the frailty of basic values and principles: equal opportunity, individual success, free enterprise, and liberty.

It all began when the blacks, driven from the South by farm mechanization, migrated to the North, where they were attracted by industrial wages. This movement dates from just after the First World War, but it assumed massive proportions only during and after the Second World War. The great American cities had grown in the nineteenth century, thanks to European immigrants, who contributed to their expansion, their construction, and their rising prosperity. By the mid-twentieth century, these cities were in the hands of the only peasants in American history: the blacks who had lived in the old plantation economy.

The blacks have indeed settled in the inner cities. For a European accustomed to the gloomy housing complexes of working-class suburbs and the concentration of wealth in the inner cities, it is extraordinary to observe the reverse phenomenon in the United States: the poor, that is, the blacks, in the heart of the city, surrounded by a vast middle-class area within a radius of twenty, thirty, or fifty kilometers. What is extraordinary is not that blacks and whites cannot live together. After all, the urban history of Europe also involves the separation of rich neighborhoods and poor neighborhoods and even, more recently, the ethnic

First published in *Le Nouvel Observateur*, 24 January 1977.

197

segregation of North Africans, Pakistanis, or Turks. It is the specific features of segregation in America that are intriguing: its inverse geographical distribution relative to the European pattern and its extraordinarily rapid rate of increase.

The first of these features is often attributed to economic reasons, such as the availability of low-interest building loans for new "suburbanites" anxious to become homeowners or the flight of businesses from midtown districts in order to escape excessively high municipal taxes. But these factors accompany and accelerate this phenomenon, rather than inducing it. I suspect that, behind the white exodus and the abandonment of the inner city to the poor, there lies a cultural choice consonant with the historical origins of the nation: the detached wood-and-brick house versus the skyscraper; a small parcel of nature versus the pollution and corruption of the big city; the homogeneous community, the "nice neighborhood," clustered around its churches and supermarket, versus the faceless, atomized individuals of the metropolis.

The heart of America has always been made of small and medium-sized towns—barely distinguishable from what we Europeans call "the countryside"—with their wooden houses so widely scattered that they have no real geographical or architectural center; yet these towns are the home of living communities that act as guardians of a domesticated pioneer tradition in which lawns have replaced forests and the Sunday-morning lawn mower the first settlers' axes. For the past twenty years, the American middle class of the big cities has been rediscovering and rebuilding its traditional habitat. In a country so close, in many respects, to eighteenth-century philosophy, ecology is more an ideology than a fashion, and one would not have to delve very far to find a lingering notion that rural life predisposes to virtue and that the metropolis is the mother of all vices.

The case of the blacks provides a counterexample of this. For, if the white exodus toward the wealthy green suburbs has been so massive, it is also because the increasingly rapid urbanization of blacks has upset all the traditional equilibriums of the environment, starting with the most fundamental of all: the family. The mechanisms and causes of this process are still not fully understood, but its effects are clear: a pauperization of vast numbers of blacks in the inner cities, the precariousness of family units, a standard of living too low to provide durable funding for adequate municipal services, the rapid growth of crime (especially juvenile delinquency). The combined effect of these mutually aggravating phenomena has been the creation of sinister ghettos situated in the heart of the big cities and more or less "self-managed" by gangs whose chief victims are the blacks themselves.

Even during the period of great prosperity and full employment of the 1960s, many black mothers with dependent children managed to survive only with the help of a weekly municipal welfare check. Today, with unemployment particularly high among young blacks, the welfare system has become both more necessary and more costly. As a poor palliative for an unsuccessful urbanization and an economy in a state of semicrisis, it helps to perpetuate an evil it was supposed to cure. It makes taxpayers unhappy while demoralizing its beneficiaries. It ruins municipal finances without preventing urban blight.

New York's bankruptcy has become the best-known example, but New York is not alone. Gary, Newark, Cleveland, and Detroit, for instance, also face the same deadlines for the same reasons. The example of New York will mark a milestone, for better or for worse.

The problem, in economic terms, is simple. In a system of decentralized municipal management, as in the United States, the accounts of a city like New York must obey the same rules as the accounts of any company: receipts must balance expenditures. But, on the receipts side, the production of wealth, which provides the basis of local tax assessment, has steadily declined. Only twenty years ago, New York was still a great industrial metropolis, with innumerable small and medium-sized firms producing consumer goods (beer and clothing, for example). The big city created jobs and managed fairly successfully to absorb an immigration that brought its population up to eight million inhabitants.

Today, industry is leaving New York: none of the advantages the city used to offer still exist. The transportation system is deplorable, the railroads are in a state of ruin, and trucks are bogged down in traffic jams; today, relatively cheap labor can be found everywhere; production costs in the inner cities are constantly rising owing to traffic problems, the increasing cost of energy, and industrial disputes.

When a municipality tries to make up for these drawbacks by offering tax breaks to new industries, it comes into conflict with the old industries, who see no justification for this unequal treatment, and with ecological activists, who accuse city hall of favoring business at the expense of the people's interests. The deterioration of urban living conditions even threatens to reduce the volume of tertiary activities in the near future. Nor can it encourage the development of tourism, already hit by the world economic depression. Hence a structural employment crisis (worsened by the cyclical recession since 1975), a shrinking of the tax base, and an impoverishment of New York.

Simultaneously, the city has to increase its spending considerably, not only to meet the rising cost of municipal services, but to finance welfare for the poor. Municipal services are far more wide-ranging than in a centralized country such as France; in addition to public order, sanitation, and firefighting, they include the school system, from grade school to university, and the hospital system. Thus, they entail considerable expenditure on wages, including pensions—an all the more formidable obligation as the latest mayors of New York, who were unable to grant the wage increases regularly demanded by municipal employees, have guaranteed in exchange an increase in pensions, thus handing over the problem to their successors.

But to this "normal" expenditure were added the rising costs of welfare during the 1960s and especially under the Lindsay administration, owing to the influx of an uprooted and impoverished black population. These costs involved municipal support of families without resources (particularly the countless families where the father had disappeared without a trace) and a minimum of reimbursement for medical expenses. This huge program spawned a new municipal bureaucracy, poorly suited to the complex tasks of registration and selection; it also gave rise to widespread fraud among eligible (and less than eligible) claimants.

In short, everything conspires to plunge the New York administration into a deepening chasm of debt: decreasing tax revenues, enormous operating expenses, and an urban welfare state that feeds, or helps to feed, several million people. As things now stand, all the elements of the problem are tending to make it worse. Economic difficulties are increasing the population of welfare beneficiaries while reducing tax revenues even further. The municipal authorities are cutting expenditures, laying off policemen, and consequently reducing police duties. In certain neighborhoods, they are even closing down schools and laying off sanitation teams. But the deterioration of all these city services, which further weakens the mechanisms for maintaining social order, leads to even greater delinquency, which in turn stimulates the middle-class exodus and thus the impoverishment of the city.

There are some areas of New York, in the Bronx, for example, that now resemble the blocks of a bombed city. The smashed windows and broken-down doors testify to the desolation of what was once a living neighborhood. Even in Manhattan, when one walks south from 38th or 36th Street to the Village, the gradual "desertification" of the city is patent. There are several hundred thousand abandoned dwellings in New York, while in the suburbs there has been a speculative real-estate boom for the past ten or fifteen years. New York's financial bankruptcy can be plainly read in the urban landscape as one of the great social and political crises that America has experienced.

One cannot accuse the United States of not being honest about its crises. This reformist country is a violent country. What it is displaying so forcefully, what it is paying the price for so visibly, is still the black problem. The old curse of the American dream, which civil-rights militants thought they had exorcised in the 1960s, has now returned in American history, in a new, unexpected, and diabolically *reversed* form. It is now a problem for the North, not an element of the civilization of the South; a threat to the very fabric of Yankee America, not the expression of the immemorial ties of hatred and connivance that had produced the old plantation world.

Southerners have lived, as it were, on familiar terms with their crime against equality; they are aware of its extent and historical roots; they know the value of time and that it will take long to make amends. In contrast, the American civil-rights generation—the young students who went down south in the sixties to spread the good word—believed in regeneration through ideas. This generation overturned, reinstated, and revitalized the lessons of the great founding principles; it at last extended to the blacks, who had been excluded from the original promise, the blessings of Enlightenment philosophy. Thus, it created both a movement toward progress and an illusion. The movement toward progress was represented by the Johnson legislation, the legal ban on racial discrimination, the massive registration of black voters, the forced promotion of an entire people in American public opinion. The illusion was that this moral pedagogy would be enough to change the fate of the blacks—even as they were being uprooted on a vast scale and their living conditions were radically modified. The power of ideas not only came up against the inertia of history; it also encountered market forces.

At this point, some misunderstandings must be avoided. There is no lack of "radical" intellectuals on the American far Left to say that the moral puritanism of the young, the antiracist campaign, and the Johnson laws in no way changed the real situation of blacks, that all this is a new ruse of the whites' good conscience. I disagree. Political maximalism always leads to the belief that if not everything is transformed, then nothing is. That is the mirror image of the idealist illusion. In this particular case, the maximalist position fails to take into account the tremendous change wrought in American public opinion, an undertaking unparalleled in the contemporary world: the blacks have been integrated into the nation's egalitarian ideology. This is not to say that racism as ideology or that every form of racial discrimination (in hiring, for example) has disappeared; but there is a huge difference between a society in which these phenomena are tolerated or even encouraged by a public consensus and a society in which they are condemned and campaigned against at the explicit insistence of the authorities, the media, and the law.

This difference is all the greater because American society is more flexible, more receptive to the lessons of the media, and also more used to espousing and extolling the democratic consensus. Nowhere else in the world can one find a more *integrative* social machinery. It owes this capacity to its adaptability, its malleability, its traditions, and its founding creed—to its qualities and defects, to its combination of conformism and innovation. And, in the 1960s, Americans decided to integrate the black minority and to pay the ideological, political, and moral price at once. This is hardly an insignificant change.

The fact remains that at the same moment, and for reasons of another nature, the black population changed civilizations and posed novel problems. The two phenomena were not unconnected: it was by becoming a problem for the North that the black minority escaped from the old southern segregationism and succeeded in forcing the mental barrier that excluded it from the Yankee egalitarian creed. This vast migration, this massive urbanization, many of whose features belong to the sphere of social pathology, has also provided an opportunity for collective emancipation. Since the late nineteenth century, Yankee America has been the refuge of poor immigrants in search of a happier identity. Southern blacks—along with Puerto Ricans and Jamaicans in New York and Chicanos in the West—represent the massive final wave of these poor immigrants. This time they have come from within the country, but from its defeated and accursed part; they thus bring with them a special challenge, which reaches down to the roots of the nation. Will the America that was the image of paradise and the land of real opportunity for so many poor Europeans be—can it be?—a belated providence for its blacks?

This problem is infinitely more difficult than that of giving a new future to the Greeks, the Jews, the Irish, or the Sicilians. For the blacks never chose America: it was forced on them. Even when they "went up" in droves to the North and its big cities, their expectations played a far lesser role than the crude mechanism of market laws: farm mechanization in the South versus demand for labor in the North. Blacks are both considerably more alien to America than the Greeks or the Irish, and much closer to it. They are totally foreign to the white Anglo-Saxon Protestant cultural model of meritocracy based on work, and yet they are totally involved in its history, of which they represent the tragic side. They are just as impossible to assimilate as to forget.

The sort of obstinacy with which every branch of officialdom in the United States, echoed by the press and television, preaches antiracism and equality is a sign of this psychological obsession, as well as of the traditional faith in the reassertion of great integrationist ideals. But the ghettoization of the blacks, delinquency, urban decay, and the dramatic conflicts over school integration indicate that, with respect to the black question, other forces are at work than those that enabled a pluralist nation, from its very inception, to find a consensus. This crisis also indicates that other solutions are required and that the assertion of equality is only a preliminary step. In other words, it will not be enough to resort to tradition.

One of these solutions, dating back to the 1930s, has been precisely the recourse to social legislation, culminating in today's welfare system. This solution involves the transfer of revenue from the federal level to states and municipalities, with the aim of guaranteeing a minimum standard of living to the poorest strata of the population. Initially, at the time of the New Deal, this system was designed to protect the poor against the economic crisis. Both the Kennedy legislation and Johnson's ambitious programs—through their impact on housing, employment, education, and hospitals—were basically aimed at hastening the urban integration of the black minority. However, they did not release local, that is, municipal, authorities from the obligation of paying most of the bill.

We have seen that this system is expensive and has missed its objectives. At the federal or state level, it is limited by American taxpayers' hostility to big spending, that is, to the increase in public expenditure and thus in taxes. At the municipal level, the system is supported by its beneficiaries, mainly blacks, and by the municipal workers for whom it provides jobs. These groups represent the bulk of the Democratic clientele in the big cities. But, as it has not benefited from massive federal aid—an unlikely prospect—the system is worn out, debt-ridden, and bankrupt. It was just efficient enough to accelerate a vast black immigration but not efficient enough to integrate it.

The price paid by American society to try to solve "its" black question is therefore twofold: on the one hand, the existence of a very large "ghettoized" and subsidized urban population; on the other, a phenomenal "social-democratization" of big-city government. The second of these new features was originally designed to obviate the first; but now they are inseparable and complementary, as if the benefit of a Swedish-style welfare system were granted—on a paradoxical yet permanent basis, in the name of equality, and within a society founded on principles contradictory to that policy—to an ethnic minority.

This development is worth pondering over, for it probably marks an important date in the history of the United States. First, the state—or at least a certain number of political institutions—has taken charge of society. Although Washington still confines its intervention to short-term social programs, the fact remains that the survival of the various municipal welfare systems will depend, and already depends, on federal help. However, the intervention of political forces in the social sphere, the systematic redistribution of revenues by democratically elected institutions, and the ensuing inflation of bureaucracy are all features of American society that run counter to its tradition, according to which free social initiative offers the best solutions for poverty and inequality.

The conviction that each individual could find in the new nation the success and wealth corresponding to this merit has been consubstantial with the United States. It made it possible to conceive of poverty as a purely individual and temporary condition, to be alleviated by the charity of the rich and by the philanthropy of private foundations, religious associations, or local communities. The state had no jurisdictional powers over society: the hatred of "bureaucracy" is still one of the basic traits of American political consciousness, as both Carter's and Reagan's successful campaigns have plainly shown. A testimony to another age, this attitude has survived the extraordinary growth of federal government over the past thirty years and also what Alain Touraine calls the "social-democratization" of the big cities.

But, by making its way in such an adverse human environment and by running counter to such lively historical traditions, the urban welfare state of Yankee America has transformed the old doctrine of equal opportunity and of the connection between success and merit. If the United States has belatedly implemented—along with a legislative ban on racial discrimination—a massive welfare program for the very poor, that is, for the population of non-European origin, it is because the introduction of the blacks into the so-called Yankee melting pot has revealed the falsehood, or rather the limits, of the equal-opportunity principle. If this principle does not in fact lead to a statistical distribution of success and employment among blacks comparable to that of the rest of the population, it is because a certain number of elements, *at the level of the ethnic group*, are working against equality.

What is important is not that this sociological fact has been established; it was established long ago. What matters is that this fact has been integrated into the American egalitarian ideology and that it has led so quickly to a new consensus aimed at guaranteeing equal opportunity, not for individuals, but for groups. This is an ambitious project that, in many respects, goes against the ideas on which America was founded: antidiscrimination laws and their jurisprudence, for example, challenge the freedom of employers and landlords. In a deeper sense, these measures lead to the notion of preferential treatment of individuals belonging to an oppressed minority—that is, to the notion of reverse discrimination, which is expected to have a corrective effect.

In this respect, American society is still what it was for Tocqueville a century and a half ago: a laboratory for the idea of equality. The secret of this experimental longevity is that, even after two hundred years, America has not given to injustice the traditional consent based on the argument that "there is nothing new under the sun." For America has steadfastly continued to regard itself as the embodiment of a set of values and as a complex of statistically measurable performances—beliefs one could describe as a religion and a sociology of equality. Consequently, it has now come to grips with the truly awesome idea of *real* equality.

This idea was imposed by the blacks as well as by the young students of the 1960s, at a time when equality began to be conceived at the collective level as the establishment of equal employment opportunities for the various ethnic groups. This change introduced a tremendous dynamic in such a diverse society and a new stake in social conflicts over housing, employment, school integration and so on. I am not suggesting that Americans woke up one fine morning as antiracists determined, as one says, to "make amends." Many of them, as in any society, did not like, or simply did not go along with, the new desegregationist policy. This group included even democrats, even members of traditionally liberal minorities: one of the factors—but not the only one—in the latent hostility between blacks and Jews in the United States is the attachment of Jews to the meritocratic, individualistic model and their distrust of the notion that advantages should be guaranteed or offered on the basis of ethnic ties. I am not suggesting, therefore, that everything has been solved but, quite to the contrary, that everything has been "destabilized" by the definition of new rules for the game of equality. One can qualify these rules as asymptotic, utopian, unattained, unattainable, or whatever other adjective one cares to use; nevertheless, in a certain sense, they have changed everything.

This is the price that has been paid not for integrating blacks but for admitting the possibility of their integration, which remains American society's major problem. On the one hand, there is the urban welfare state; on the other, an extension of egalitarian legitimacy to groups: in short, the end of liberal individualism. None of the mechanisms of the ideal America outlined by these choices is functioning properly. Welfare costs too much for an enfeebled economy, and it perpetuates urban decay as well as, no doubt, demoralization among blacks. The policy of non-discrimination favors the promotion of a black bourgeoisie more than it changes the lot of the poor. Finally, the general orientation of these measures has aroused hostile reactions in Reaganite heartland America.

Yet, even though reality still lags far behind ideas and even though reforms, as always, are tremendously costly in financial and psychological terms in relation to their actual impact, it seems to me that the dynamic of the new American consensus is irreversible. It has been fueled less by government (since it has survived the eight years of domestic immobility under Nixon and Ford) than by society itself and by the numerous local associations and institutions that society continues to control and organize. However much American society may seem, on the surface, to have returned to the conservative consensus of the 1950s, after the turmoil of the 1960s, I believe that the opposite is true—that the demands for greater democracy voiced in the 1960s have been assimilated into the body social and that they serve as a model for the new reformist consensus.

Let us take, for example, the women's movement, which is infinitely more powerful than in Europe. It follows the black model so closely that American women are demanding, among other things, equal access to all jobs as members of a minority group. This is an absurd demand, if one examines it literally; it acquires force and significance only in the context of the new American democratic consensus, arising in response to black nationalism. Feminism has been able to rush into the breach opened by ethnic demands because public opinion is less sensitive to the absurdity of this analogy than it is familiarized with the notion that a certain number of *collective* inequalities have to be set right. By shifting from the free competition of individual merit to a determination to introduce social equality at the group level, the dominant ideology, so crucial to the survival of this segmented society, provides the famous melting pot with an almost infinite range of objectives and standards—as infinite as there are imaginable social groups and as long as inequality will persist among them.

Thus, America continues to live in conformity with its original message, while adapting it to the circumstances of the second half of the twentieth century, that is, to the uprooting and reintegration of the blacks.

PART FOUR

ASPECTS OF MODERN JEWISH HISTORY

To the Reader

I have assembled in the last part of this book four studies on modern Jewish history, three of which have been published in a different form by *Le Nouvel Observateur* (the fourth, "Israel, Zionism, and the Diaspora," is here published for the first time).

The first of these studies is devoted to the Jewish problem in modern French history; the second is a presentation for the French public of the work of the Israeli historian Gershom Scholem; the third deals with the relations between the French Left and Israel. The third essay is the only one to have appeared more or less in its present form in *Le Nouvel Observateur* (15 May 1978). The first two have been somewhat revised and rewritten.

References to the original articles are given in the notes. I should like to take the opportunity of thanking my friend Jean Daniel for having published them in the first place and for allowing me to use them in this book.

12

Jews and French Democracy: Some Recent Books

The history of French Jews has been affected by the repercussions of its characteristic feature: the willingness to submit to Jacobin assimilation. The reason why this history has been so unobtrusive is that it was also almost pointless. Since the French Revolution, the Jews were a part of French history. Even if the Right denied them this title to joint ownership of the French patrimony, the Jews had chosen to receive at least precarious tenure rights to it from the liberals. What was the use, then, of dwelling on the factors that made them a distinctive category of citizens?

In this respect, the increase over the past few years in the number of works on the history of the French Jewish community from 1789 to today is the sign of a major change, many of the reasons for which are obvious. First, the impact of the war, which has taken several forms: the Vichy persecutions, the existence of an officially anti-Semitic French government, and the massacre of Jewish refugees from Germany and eastern Europe have reactivated the residue of bad conscience inseparable from any successful assimilation. And then there was Israel, the unlikely and tragic victory of the destitute Jews scorned by the French consistories, the survivors par excellence of the Holocaust, the outcasts of Europe promoted to the central role in Jewish history, the proletarians of the community who had become its national flag.

I am writing as if this were an exclusively Jewish history. Of course, it is also our history, that of the gentile French, and it is not a particularly glorious one. But it derives its true weight and universal value from the way the Jews experienced it, suffered from it, acted on it, and interpreted it. The French Left has been all too prone to deal only with the outer

First published in *Le Nouvel Observateur*, 5 April 1976, 17 September 1979, and 28 April 1981.

aspect of the Jewish question, even with the best possible intentions (which was not always the case), even when trying to reduce it to anti-Semitism, and especially when treating it as a capitalist diversion. Now that the Jews have gained a national history, that of the French Jews—which seemed frozen, withdrawn, and dependent—is stirring again. For a fairly long time, the history of French Jews has fluctuated according to the variations of our "thermometer": is it not time we looked at theirs?

First, I should like to take this opportunity to pay tribute to a series of books that are an honor to postwar French publishing. The "Diaspora" series, edited by Roger Errera, is precisely an expression of the renewed interest in Jewish history in France. It has brought to the attention of the French public a first-rate collection of authors and books, such as Gershom Scholem's admirable *Messianisme juif* (*The Messianic Idea in Judaism*). On a less fundamental but no less valuable level, this series also aims at providing a survey of modern French Judaism.

Patrick Girard's book concerns the oldest period, 1789 to 1860.[1] While it does not contain any new information on the history of French Jews between these two dates, it gives an excellent summary of their progress from revolutionary emancipation to gradual integration into French society. The tremendous impulse of liberal universalism marked the contribution of the Revolution to the Jewish question. By granting full citizenship first to the Sephardic Jews of Bordeaux and of the Comtat Venaissin (1790), then to the Jews of Alsace (1791), the Revolution brought these old ghetto communities back into the mainstream of history. The Revolution offered them the historical model of French "regeneration"; and the consequent substitution of a politically oriented form of messianism for traditional values became a key factor in the fragmentation of the old Jewish communities. No Jew had an *ancien régime* to mourn. All Jews responded to both the most modern idea and the oldest idea introduced by the new regime: the rights of the citizen and the right to participate in a just undertaking.

Yet this "assimilation" was to take half a century, owing to the persistence of traditional French attitudes, first in the form of popular anti-Semitism during the Terror, then in the policy of the Empire. Napoleon reversed the Revolution's perspective on the Jews. Whereas revolutionary emancipation had consisted in replacing their religious status by a political status, Napoleon, in convening the Great Sanhedrin—that is, the notables of the Jewish community—in 1807, made their French citizenship conditional on a religious pact with the Christians.

What the revolutionaries had regarded as the cause of the moral decay of the Jews became for the emperor the guarantee of their good conduct. This renewed focus on religious identity explains the confiscation of some of the benefits acquired by the Jews through the Revolution. In particular, it explains the "infamous decree" of 1808, which reestablished the juridical inferiority of Jews before the courts, with the exception of the

Jews of Paris and Bordeaux (but, at the time, the Alsatian Jews, against whom the decree was directed, were by far the largest community).

The decree did not survive the fall of the Empire for very long. The July Monarchy definitively granted the Jews equal status in law and recognition of their denominational rights, by creating a budget for the Jewish religious establishment. French Jews, now legally assimilated, entered a relatively happy phase of their history as a dynamic community of bourgeois, of shopkeepers and artisans dominated by eminently successful bankers and professionals. This community was increasingly urban, Parisian, and—in short—bourgeois in character, cemented by a secularized complex of traditional religious beliefs, by a strong minority feeling, and by a deep attachment to France's liberal image.

Was it an "assimilated" community? Patrick Girard's whole book is centered on this basic question. In his view, assimilation is a dynamic process "in which individuals belonging to a community with a distinctive way of life attempted to formulate a doctrine combining a very old religious heritage with the values of the surrounding society, values intended to justify the preservation of an identity reduced to its denominational aspect." This somewhat weighty vocabulary, nonetheless useful for its relative precision, expresses a positive judgment on the cultural crossbreeding arising from the encounter between the Jewish tradition and Western liberalism.

The author feels no idealized regret for the old, closed community. He does not project on these mid-nineteenth-century French Jews the catastrophes of the twentieth century. Surprisingly, for such a young man (he was born in 1950), he does not detest the "middle-of-the-road" Judaism of moderate and prudent notables, who preserved traditional practices in the privacy of family life while adapting themselves to the modern world in their professional and public life. He admires them for having handled so skillfully the intercommunity tensions between the orthodox, who rallied round *L'Univers israélite*, and the liberals, who published the *Archives israélites*.

In both camps, French Jews had become *israélites*. This was their way of saying that they were no longer Jews like those of the eastern European ghettos but that they nevertheless remained Jews in their attachment to a past and a religion. These "assimilated" communities, products of the encounter between Judaism and the French Revolution, were not national communities, but neither did they mark the end of Judaism. They represent a phase of its history that was "just as Jewish and collective as other [phases]."

This analysis echoes—without ever saying so explicitly—a fundamental debate in Jewish historiography and particularly a book in the same series, published in 1973; the book of a Canadian professor, Michael Marrus, devoted to French Jews during the Dreyfus affair.[2] The two authors, while following each other chronologically, do not have the same opinion on the nineteenth-century "assimilation" of French Jews; nor, it is true, do they use the same analytical tools.

For Michael Marrus, assimilation is "the mechanism by which individuals of Jewish origin would assume a basically French identity." The period studied is obviously an ideal terrain for a definition of this type. As the period was characterized by an extraordinary flare-up of nationalism, it enables one to measure the extraordinary acceptance of this nationalism by French Jews, even during the Dreyfus affair, in the name of their patriotism. By a series of fascinating portraits and texts, the book shows that, among the factors at work in this internalization of the opponent's values, there was more than the pressure of the surrounding society, more than the desire not to add fuel to the flames. One could almost say that there was anti-Semitism, particularly toward immigrant Jews, symbols of a repressed Judaism. In fin-de-siècle France as described by Michael Marrus, assimilation was the guiding thread of a Jewish anti-Semitism. One could also find some grounds for this accusation in the book by David H. Weinberg,[3] which shows to what extent, in a later period, between the wars, the French Jews of the Sixteenth Arrondissement and the Polish Jews of the Marais constituted in every sense two watertight, if not antagonistic, societies.

Is one to conclude that the successful assimilation of the nineteenth century led, thirty or forty years later, to an impasse? Of course there is some truth to this statement, as evidenced, for example, by the explosion in the decade from 1880 to 1890 of a massive and organized anti-Semitism unknown during the July Monarchy or the Second Empire. But the gap between the analyses of Girard and Marrus is not only due to the periods they examine. I am inclined to believe that, on the contrary, these periods have been chosen because of the two authors' conceptual and political divergences regarding assimilation. Patrick Girard has written a liberal history of French Jews; Michael Marrus is searching that history for the hidden sources of a national history. The first admires French Jews for their extraordinary adaptation to modern civilization; the second celebrates only one fraternal voice in the Dreyfus affair, that of Bernard Lazare, the first Jewish nationalist born in the French community.

Thus, Jewish history is drawn toward the dilemmas of the present.[4] If the case of French Jewry takes on in this respect an exemplary value, it is because it marks the invention of the Diaspora Jew—no longer the exiled Jew, cut off from his land, yet still hoping to return to it at the end of time, but the Jew of the Diaspora, comfortably settled in a foreign land, a new metamorphosis of collective Jewish destiny. Do these "privileged Jews,"[5] to borrow the title of an article by Hannah Arendt—who inspired Michael Marrus—represent the end of Judaism or just one of its varieties?

Perhaps it is more useful to examine the question by starting from the past rather than from the future assigned to that past as a hypothetical outcome. Annie Kriegel, in an article in *L'Arche*,[6] reminds us that it was the French Revolution that invented the two responses to the Jewish question: the individual solution and the national solution. Naturally, it preferred the first, because revolutionary thinking could not imagine a better path to the "regeneration" of the Jews than individual success within the model nation, namely, France. But, at the same time, the Revolution spawned the notion that the emancipation of the Jews—like that of any oppressed people—could assume a collective or national form. The right of peoples to self-determination flows from the Declaration of the Rights of Man. The conquest of legal equality and individual liberty by the French Jews, by exposing them to the values of the surrounding society, certainly secularized them but also contributed to their fondness for democratic, national, and socialist ideas. These ideas also played a part in the Jewish national awakening at the end of the nineteenth century.

The ambiguity of Jewish "assimilation" stems perhaps from the ambiguity of the idea of Zionism itself. Unlike nineteenth-century "national" movements, Zionism stands at the crossroads of a secular notion (national emancipation, the nation-state) and a religious notion (the return to Jerusalem). "Assimilation" weakens the second while promoting the first. For that matter, one would have to examine closely what "assimilation" abandoned or preserved of the spiritual tradition by "privatizing" and secularizing it. This analysis is somewhat lacking in the books I have discussed. In the unstable mixture of community and individualism, of national and religious ingredients, out of which the destiny of the Jewish people was built in the nineteenth and twentieth centuries, nothing is as simple as the peculiar hatred that accompanied the Jews through time.

The Vichy regime is the most tragic illustration of that hatred in modern French history. Although it is true that it was established only in the wake of the German victory of 1940, it represents a very distinctively French type of regime, in many respects independent from its Nazi protectors. This is the paradox once again explained by the American historian Robert Paxton, in a new work devoted this time not to the general history of Vichy but to its policy toward the Jews.[7] No doubt this explains why he enlisted the help of Michael Marrus, an expert, as we have just seen, on "modern" French anti-Semitism.

France's defeat brought to power a set of groups and individuals who were not directly appointed by the Germans (even though, without them, they would have stood no chance of coming to power) but owed their success to their determination to revenge themselves on the Republic. Their action was informed, not by foreign ideas, but by a national tradition. Hitler's victory provided them, not with the substance of their policy, but with an opportunity for implementing it. The Jewish question provides a virtually perfect example of this nationalist exploitation of

France's defeat. The proof of this is that no clear connection exists—either before or during the war, in Vichy or in Paris—between ideological sympathy with Nazi Germany and the intensity of anti-Semitism: Doriot was a fascist and not very prone to Jew hating; Xavier Vallat, an anti-German of long standing, was an anti-Semitic minister in the Vichy government; Céline, a Nazilike anti-Semite, was hostile to Vichy. The politics and ideology of the first two years of Vichy were, in fact, characterized less by racism, in the biological and Nazi sense, than by considerations or pretexts related to the cultural cohesion of the national community.

One of the reasons for this is that, during the 1920s and 1930s, France took in many foreigners, more than any other country in the world, the United States included. The first wave of immigrants came in search of work; they were followed by a stream of political refugees. France displayed first a self-interested hospitality, then an increasing reluctance, owing to the economic depression and the political situation. The "foreigner" became the scapegoat for the international complications that an appeasement-minded France saw as portents of war. And the Jew became the prime embodiment of this "foreigner," since he represented one of the most prominent issues of the coming war. After France lost the war, he thus remained one of the most obvious "culprits." Not only a part of the Left but also a part of French Jewry were prisoners of this insane belief. One need only read what a man as intelligent and refined as Emmanuel Berl wrote in 1938 and 1939 to appreciate to what extent the tragedy of the period was unfolding in a veil of deep mystery.

Furthermore, Paxton and Marrus cite the two statutory orders of the spring and autumn of 1938, which reinforced control measures against aliens—in particular by extending the obligation to maintain an assigned residence—and prescribed the establishment of "special centers" for those aliens (Spanish Republicans in particular) who were deemed to be a threat to public order. Thus, Vichy was to inherit concentration camps dating from the Daladier period; it was to use them systematically against foreign Jews even before Germany adopted the procedure. One of the most dishonorable episodes of this story was the internment of several thousand German Jews who were fleeing the occupied zone in the summer of 1940 and were made so desperate by their internment that some turned to the Nazis for protection against France! The fact is that, until late 1941, Hitler's policy aimed less at exterminating the Jews than at chasing them out of Germany. In putting them—women and children included—behind barbed wire at Gurs and elsewhere, in frighteningly overcrowded and unsanitary conditions, Vichy was somewhat ahead of the German timetable. Unknowingly, but without, however, being able to rule out the hypothesis, the Vichy regime carefully laid the groundwork for the tragic outcome.

In actual fact, the French anti-Semites did not advocate forced emigration. Very few Jews managed to leave the occupied zone between 1940 and 1942. Apart from internment, a fate reserved for foreigners, the aim was to set up a special status, an idea borrowed from the monarchic tradition and from the Action Française. A second-class citizenship within the bounds of the law was to be defined for French Jews. This was the purpose of the decree of 18 October 1940, drafted by the minister of justice of the first Laval government, Raphaël Alibert, former member of the Conseil d'Etat and a faithful disciple of Maurras. But this decree, which barred Jews from the civil service, was reinforced on 14 June 1941 by a new statute, extending the ban to the professions and to business; this was the work of the *commissaire général aux questions juives* under the Darlan government, Xavier Vallat. And what a highly typical figure Vallat was: a right-thinking member of parliament under the Third Republic, a former teacher in the Catholic school system who had become a professional war veteran after the First World War, a Catholic monarchist who had made the rounds of all the right-wing parties; not a fascist, even less a germanophile, but simply a symbol of a milieu and a culture that had finally taken its revenge on democracy. Professing an anti-Semitism "in the national interest" for which he was actually attacked by Parisian "collaborators," Xavier Vallat was the perfect embodiment of something worse than Vichy's submissiveness: its duplicity. On every level, he pushed anti-Semitic policy further than the Germans were asking, but in the name of his convictions against theirs. He cloaked the unequal bargaining with the victor, which was both Vichy's principle and its excuse, with the domestic flag of French nationalism. Thus, he was able to stake out an original position for himself in the process whereby Vichy outrivaled the Nazis in their own policies.

But the most surprising feature in Paxton and Marrus's merciless description is not the existence of anti-Semitic ministers or doctrines at Vichy, nor the relative passivity of public opinion, dazed by a defeat as sweeping as that of June 1940. After all, this type of policy, this brand of minister, and this spineless acquiescence of public opinion can ultimately be explained by the Nazi victory and the state of French politics. What is more surprising, and frightening, is the absence of any reaction on the part of the civil servants who enacted all these measures, prosecutions, and confiscations. The Conseil d'Etat examined the statutes concerning Jews as if they were ordinary laws. Law professors demonstrated their validity and novelty. The prefects enforced them. The police carried out orders. Never, nowhere, did an official resign or even protest! The entire French administrative machinery obeyed the new ministers as if they derived their authority from the people in the normal way.

All these officials had served republican France. Their behavior cannot easily be accounted for either by invoking their prewar attitudes (as in the case of Alibert or Vallat) or by the all too easy recourse to the oldest exorcistic myth of Catholic France (as in the case of the average Frenchman). This sinister history nevertheless seems to demonstrate two things: first, that what one can call the French elites of the period were much more imbued with deep and lively anti-Semitic feelings than one would be led to believe by the number of far-right deputies in the 1928, 1932, and 1936 parliaments; second, that the incantatory recourse to the Jewish plot or poison was perhaps more vital to bourgeois France than to grass-roots France, in that the defeat provided the first with a twofold revenge for the Dreyfus affair and for the Léon Blum government, while the second was not asking for that much. Consequently, this recourse was more a technique for conquering power and public opinion than an active ideological and emotional act of communion. Of the two classical poles of anti-Semitism, Vichy embodied manipulation far more than preaching. This feature, it seems to me, gives it a distinctive—and, moreover, particularly vile—character in the annals of this inexhaustible passion.

The next period is better known and tragically simple. In late 1941 and early 1942, when Hitler decided to exterminate the Jews and inaugurated the policy of deportation to the East, a policy extended to France in June, Vichy's "independence" in anti-Semitic matters came to an end. Darquier de Pellepoix, the racketeering hoodlum, replaced Xavier Vallat, the Catholic member of parliament. A card-index census of the Jewish population was patiently put together by French civil servants and police between 1940 and 1942. It became the matrix for the deportation of Jews, which began with the massive roundup of the Velodrome d'Hiver (indoor sports stadium) on 16 and 17 July 1942, carried out by 9,000 French policemen. In its camps, Vichy held in reserve thousands of other foreign Jews, whom Laval gradually handed over, on request. By the end of 1944, slightly more than 75,000 Jews (out of 300,000) had been deported from France to the concentration camps located on former Polish territory. Some 2,500 returned.

Thus, from the autumn of 1942 on, the mechanism of wholesale deportation continued on its lethal course, with the help of the censuses, identity checks, and internments carried out by the French authorities. In February 1943, in the southern zone, a series of arrests of foreign Jews second in magnitude only to the July and August 1942 roundups was carried out exclusively by the French police. Yet, as the liberation approached, this task was assumed by the German police, with the help, it is true, of the Milice. This is probably one of the reasons why the deportation figures for 1943 and 1944 are lower than those for 1942, when all the resources of the French police were at the Germans' disposal. Some 33,500 Jews were deported in 1943 and 1944 as against 42,500 in 1942 alone.

Unfortunately the relative decline in these sinister figures does not mean that the Vichy government had finally taken a stand against German policy. Paxton and Marrus cite only two examples of genuine opposition. The first dates from the spring of 1942, when Vichy refused to extend the obligation to wear the yellow star to the Jews of the still-unoccupied zone; the second dates from the summer of 1943, when Pétain resisted pressures to "denaturalize" recently naturalized Jews (by virtue of a law of 1937) and to add to the categories of "deportable" Jews. But neither of these refusals led Vichy to protest against the deportation of Jews or to withdraw its consent and support for the measures that brought it into effect. The deportation of foreign Jews, or of French Jews arrested for having violated the legal restrictions imposed on them, ceased only with the liberation of the country.

Finally, what can one say about the balance sheet? A classic argument in favor of the thesis that Vichy was a "shield" is that three-quarters of the Jewish community living in France in 1939 survived; moreover, it is known that the overwhelming majority of the 75,000 Jews deported from France to the camps where they were exterminated was composed of foreign Jews. And this dismal distinction, borrowed from Vichy, still serves as its posthumous justification. In reality, the argument would have a demonstrative value—within its own anti-Semitic logic—only if it could be accompanied by proofs showing that the Vichy government actively protected French Jews from deportation after having persecuted them by its laws. But these proofs do not exist, and no one has ever been able to produce any. Furthermore, Paxton and Marrus show that there is no link between the number of surviving Jews and the various policies of occupied or satellite countries. The tragically essential factor in the extermination of the Jews, and in its magnitude in each European state, was the means implemented by the Nazis for that purpose.

Thus, one cannot give Vichy policy the credit for what was actually due to circumstance. If three-quarters of the French Jewish community succeeded in escaping deportation and genocide, it was owing to a shortage of manpower in the German police operating in France and to the possibilities for shelter both in the Italian occupation zone and in rural France. Public opinion in these areas became increasingly sensitive to the Jewish plight as the prospect of Nazi defeat became clearer and the Service du Travail Obligatoire simultaneously deported greater numbers of workers to Germany. But none of this is attributable to a determination or to a policy—even at a clandestine level—of the Laval government. As far as Vichy's action proper is concerned, the historian can only document its original and autonomous contribution to Nazi anti-Semitism, particularly between 1940 and 1942, and its objective contribution to extermination, through its own concentration camps, its police, and the assistance it provided the Germans in their roundups, particularly in connection with the foreign Jews who took refuge in France between the wars.

The evidence marshaled by Paxton and Marrus thus leads the reader less to a condemnation of France in general—which would not make much sense—than to a harsh verdict on the section of its governing class that found in France's defeat an opportunity for taking a long-awaited revenge on the Republic. That people do not behave heroically in misfortune is not a new phenomenon, nor one peculiar to France in 1940. But that a certain part of the Right should have availed itself of the national debacle to take its revenge for 1789 and the Dreyfus affair is instead characteristic of our history. Not that the process was determined solely by indigenous factors, since, on the contrary, it took the Nazi victory to make such revenge possible. But this episode does belong to our history in that its protagonists represented the repressed forces, the camp of those who had been defeated a century and a half earlier, or at least since the birth of the Third Republic. Vichy France revealed the obverse side of democracy inseparable from our history, and inseparable, too, perhaps from democracy itself. In this respect, the work of Paxton and Marrus does more than explain the facts and establish responsibilities; it also teaches a moral lesson.

Since the war and the inglorious disappearance of the Vichy regime, my generation especially remembers having lived through a period haunted by the return from the camps—a return that also meant the discovery of the camps. But the taboo that consequently weighed on anti-Semitism also led to a somewhat furtive burial of the Jewish question. A spontaneous conspiracy of silence, as it were, was hatched to exorcise this specter. Gentiles tried not to think of it, and Jews carried a secret too heavy and too peculiar to talk about.

But this uneasy equilibrium between a guilty conscience and the willingness to efface was upset ten or fifteen years ago. The generation that reached twenty at the end of the 1960s—Jews and Gentiles alike—rediscovered the Jewish problem. To understand how and why this occurred, one can start with the family photograph taken in 1979 by two journalists, Harris and Sédouy.[8] From this collection of interviews conducted by them in all the milieus of French Jewry, only a single common feature emerges: anxiety. No doubt this is an age-old trait, but, in the midst of the apparently reassuring uniformity of our prosperous society, it is more alive, more entrenched, and more varied than ever. And what if France were to become once again a country where Jews could not live? This question is always latent in the answers given in the interviews; it is even implicitly voiced by French Jews who have "always" been assimilated.

This patent erosion of the democratic certainties of assimilation can be clearly explained by certain structural reasons. French Jewry (600,000 to 700,000 French Jews) is a population replenished by a recent influx of North African immigrants, whose arrival has modified the balances within the community. The assimilated bourgeoisie is less predominant among the North African Jews, and the assimilationist creed is not necessarily accompanied by the abandonment of religious practices and traditional ways of life. Consequently, the face of French Jewry has changed and become more visibly Jewish. This greater capacity to assume the particular Jewish heritage (even in its secularized form, that is, as a set of habits more social than cultural in nature) poses novel problems for all French intellectual traditions, both left-wing and right-wing. To understand this, one can listen to Rabbi Guedj expressing regret—in the unlikely setting of Sarcelles—for the secular environment of Constantine and answering the question "Is it possible to live in a country without espousing its dominant philosophy and its way of life?" in the following words: "Tell me, please, what is the dominant philosophy in France today? I cannot go along with those who think like that. That's how Nazism started. . . ."

The thoroughgoing renewal of French Jewry was marked by two major and equally destabilizing events (if one takes assimilation as a reference point): the Holocaust and the birth of the state of Israel. The first exterminated nearly all the eastern European Jews who had recently immigrated into France. The role of the Vichy authorities also struck a deep blow at the belief of assimilated Jews in the safety of their own destiny. It showed them that even in France, a hundred and fifty years after the Revolution, their future was not settled forever.

On top of that, after the war, came the birth of Israel and, twenty years later, the Six Day War, which seems to have played a crucial role in crystallizing the attitude of French Jews toward the new state. French Jewry, no longer so assured of being able to stake everything on democratic assimilation, could at least refer to a new image and at most count on the help of a new homeland. Through innumerable channels, Zionism transformed the Jewish consciousness in the Diaspora by confronting it, on the strength of Zionism's own historical success, with a series of ultimatum-questions that, in accordance with the nature of Zionism, led from the religious sphere to the national sphere. At the same time, the international dimension of Israel's existence led the Diaspora communities to establish forms of solidarity that are probably in turn transforming anti-Semitism into a worldwide phenomenon, in an unprecedented form and on an unprecedented scale.

Hence the new tremors in Franco-Jewish identity that one can discern in the interviews assembled by Harris and Sédouy. Thirty-five years after the war, one can measure the impact of a twofold evolution: on the gentile side, the ban on anti-Semitism imposed when death-camp survivors returned is gradually weakening, not because it has disappeared from living memory, but because the young generations do not have that memory; and, on the Jewish side, the community is much more willing today than before or just after the war to assert and accept its distinctiveness, as regards its special ties with Israel, its traditional way of life, its culture, or its religion. Even the intellectual climate in which we have been living for the past several years has contributed to this evolution by extolling ethnic minorities, criticizing the Jacobin state's passion for leveling, and somewhat naïvely rediscovering the religious experience behind the illusions of Western nationalism. Thus, fashion confers its transient appeal on the age-old problem of Jewish identity. The Jewish people, miraculously adapted to "modernity," have never ceased, however, to be simultaneously rooted in archaism.

Thus, French Jews have rediscovered that their prospects are always uncertain: on the religious level, on the national level, and on the level of individual destinies. They have consequently reinvented one of the classic accusations leveled at them by anti-Semitism: that of being a mobile and universal people, present everywhere and nowhere. But it is to their credit that they accept this role and do not shun it. For they know that the history of the last half century has made them, as it has made European Judaism, the prime symbols of modern tragedies. The Holocaust has tragically deprived them of their happy belief in assimilation, and the calamities of communism have ruled out a recourse to revolutionary messianism. Apart from seeking refuge in archaism and traditional solidarity, the only choices left in "modernity" are difficult, uncertain, or disheartening.

One should read, for instance, in Harris and Sédouy, the reasons given by Maurice Kriegel for his departure to Israel. A former French leftist of 1968, a descendant of an Alsatian Jewish family deeply assimilated "on the Left" through Jacobin patriotism and socialism, this young history professor at the University of Haifa sternly criticizes his adopted homeland. For example, he detests its all too often anti-intellectual and parochial reactions; but his choice was dictated by exactly the same reasons that led his ancestors, in the nineteenth and twentieth centuries, to choose the France of the Revolution: so that his children's happiness (or, for that matter, their misfortunes) should no longer be "specifically Jewish" but determined by other factors—by so-called normal factors. What led his ancestors to Paris led him to Haifa.

By the hazards of publishing, the appearance of this self-portrait of French Jews coincided with that of a short book by Alfred Fabre-Luce titled *Pour en finir avec l'antisémitisme*.[9] Let us be thankful for this coincidence, which enables us to compare Jewish anxieties about the way of the world and the voice of a French intellectual whose ambition is to soothe them. In this particular case, the parallel offers a nearly perfect example of lines that never meet. To soothe, one would have to lend an ear. But what does Fabre-Luce hear? Next to nothing.

And yet he has an intuition of the basic phenomenon—of the fact that the assimilationist creed is in a state of crisis and that the two phases of this crisis were the experience of the Second World War and Zionism.

But this notion, which should mark the starting point of any discussion of the topic, is where Fabre-Luce leaves off. Taking up the idea of assimilation precisely where the Jewish community has left it, he turns it into a sort of no-man's-land protected from Christian anti-Semitism and Jewish proselytism. Assimilation becomes an abstract, unreal zone where passions are extinct and anxiety has vanished because only the author's limpid ideas prevail. In the typically French realm of blind intelligence, Alfred Fabre-Luce finds a refuge from the historical density of a problem that he finds more shocking than intriguing.

His idea is to propose to French Jews a sort of pact that would define a minimal consensus, which both parties would endeavor to maintain: the gentile French would act to prevent the rebirth of anti-Semitism as a way of drawing attention away from national difficulties, and French Jews would abide by a sort of code of good conduct, characterized by the abandonment of cultural proselytism and Zionist militancy. In this curious deal, two concrete clauses could serve as guarantees: the search for a common position of the French on the Middle East and the establishment of a "good" version of the history of Vichy.

The mind boggles at these chapter headings. The first belongs to the realm of wishful thinking—an idea that is unworkable in practice and, moreover, not very interesting in the abstract. But the second is more revealing of Fabre-Luce's polemical obstinacy: he wants to rewrite the history of Vichy.

Indeed, the bulk of his short book is devoted to an analysis of Vichy, a crucial period in the relationship of Jews with France, especially if one focuses exclusively on assimilation. For Fabre-Luce, there is a Jewish version of the history of Vichy, characterized by an emphasis on the purely French responsibility for the persecutions. Curiously, the protagonist in this enterprise is the American professor Robert Paxton (a Gentile, and rather of the southern aristocratic sort). I shall not dwell on this curious assertion, since Fabre-Luce knows that, naturally, one finds Gentiles in every Jewish lobby. But what I find bizarre, and even somewhat disturbing, in this type of historiographical analysis, is the suspicion that there exists a Jewish determination to produce and circulate a history of Vichy that is contrary to the truth and serves the interests of an avenging minority.

I have no objection—far from it—to discussing the editing of *Le Chagrin et la Pitié* or certain excessively systematic allegations made by Paxton. But what seems less admissible to me is to pin the same yellow star on Ophüls, Paxton, Stanley Hoffmann, and Léon Poliakov, whom Fabre-Luce regards as a lobby of historians and film makers entrusted with the task of "presenting to the French the history of their war years through a Jewish prism." Indiscriminate amalgamations seldom proceed from a form of thinking that is not somewhat crude. In this instance, the notion of a Jewish plot is being reintroduced into the interpretation of our modern history, turning the victim into a culprit. Instead of "putting an end to anti-Semitism," this argument feeds and even expresses it.

Consequently, such an approach fails to deal with the problem it raises. Let us for a moment give Fabre-Luce the benefit of the doubt and accept his hypothesis of "Pétain the shield." Even if that were true, one aspect of the history of French-Jewish relations would still require explanation: why a defeated people resorted to a familiar demon to exorcise its defeat, under the authority of a national glory. The enactment of the statute of 1940 concerning the Jews was an act of French politics; the statute was drafted and implemented in the name of a national tradition by men who were not forced to do so by any foreign pressures. And if the generation of assimilated Jews, even of those who supported Pétain for a few months between June and the autumn, saw his gesture as a break by the French with the tradition of 1789, it was because Vichy proclaimed it to be just that. Politics in a democratic age is a simple art, in which ambiguity is never long-lived. In this case, the ambiguity ceased within three months.

Alfred Fabre-Luce does not feel this wound, which is still unhealed and cannot be healed by any comparative quantification of the history of Jewish suffering in Europe. More generally, his treatment of the Jewish problem reveals a deliberate insensitivity to the somewhat overwhelming nature of the question. This is both strange and typical. It is strange on the part of a knowledgeable and discerning mind, but typical of the way the much-vaunted French intelligence grapples with a question whose historical and psychological implications are almost infinite. Finally, one must take into account prevailing currents of thought: at present, in late 1979, Paris is under the sway of an arrogant variety of "liberal" thought that seems to me contradictory to the spirit of liberalism. The impassioned attempt to "normalize" the Jewish problem and the collective existence of French Jews (or Jews in France) is a good example of this arrogance— shallow thoughts on a vast question. The fact is that the Jewish problem cannot be "normalized." One must live with it, such as it is, in the present day. Everyone's freedom depends on this acceptance, because it is one of the criteria of democracy.

Gershom Scholem and Jewish History

Gershom Scholem, born in Berlin in 1897 and settled in Palestine since 1923, belongs neither to the Jewry of eastern Europe that supplied troops to Zionism after the First World War nor to the community of German Jews who fled their country after Hitler came to power. He has had no direct experience of the Polish or Belorussian ghettos, nor of their traditionalist rabbis, who unwittingly fostered the growth of Zionism as an angry modernist movement. On the contrary, it is from within this modernity—that is, the assimilation into German culture—that he became aware at a very early stage, even before the First World War, of the irreducible specificity of Judaism. The Zionism he espoused as a young man was thus—as was Theodore Herzl's Zionism, for that matter—a resurgence, a rediscovery of sources. It was not a revolution, even less a revolt, but a history.

In this respect, the long interview in one of his books,[1] in which the old historian talks about himself, is immensely fascinating. Scholem was born into a small dynasty of Berlin printers that went back four generations. For the Scholems, the Friday-evening family dinner represented the last, infinitesimal vestige of old religious observance. The father, and his milieu, believed in assimilation, in the German identity, in German patriotism. This petty Jewish bourgeoisie, whose outlook and social life remained strictly Jewish, lived its cultural life on a borrowed tradition. Scholem perceived this rift by his adolescence, at the age of fourteen or fifteen; his reaction was more one of unease or revolt than of analysis. He wanted to be a Jew, not a German. "So you want to return to the ghetto?" asked his father. "But it is you who are living in a ghetto, even though you think you are not," answered the son.

First published in *Le Nouvel Observateur*, 19 February 1979.

As if to round out the story and give the example of family the pedagogic simplicity of an ancient tragedy, Gershom Scholem had three brothers. Two of them sided with his father, and one of these two was even more German—in fact, an outspoken German nationalist. The fourth brother, in contrast, soon joined the Social-Democratic party, became a Communist member of parliament after the war, was expelled from the party as a Trotskyite in 1927, and died at Buchenwald at the hands of the Nazis precisely for having been a Communist member of parliament. Thus, the Scholem children entered the twentieth century each under his own flag: assimilation, revolution, and Zionism. Of the three options for solving the famous "Jewish question" that accompanied their childhood, the third seemed at the time the most outlandish and the most shaky; it alone was to withstand the century.

Moreover, Gershom Scholem's books continually explore this variety of Zionism, for it represents not just a youthful awakening but the central question of a lifetime. It was less a political commitment than a moral choice. The young Scholem was motivated not by the desire to build a Jewish state but by the refusal of the duplicity inherent in the daily existence of the Jewish bourgeoisie in Germany. Basically, it is the very same feeling that led one of his brothers—as if by chance, the only one with whom he had close ties—toward revolution and socialism. Admittedly, it is hard to explain what drove one brother to Marxism and Leninism, the other to study with a professor of Hebrew and to take Talmud courses: such are the mysteries of individual existence. But if one accepts the idea that their contradictory choices had a common origin, one cannot help observing that the choice of the future historian was better suited to the problem at hand than that of the future Communist deputy of the Reichstag. The first wanted to identify the elements and sources of the problem, while the second sought to eliminate its very terms and thus began by negating them.

In this respect, the Zionism of the young Gershom Scholem, because it was a postassimilation Zionism, a return and not just a breach or a vision of the future, was inseparable from the central paradox of the entire movement—from the chemical process that produced national ideas from religious ideas, modernity from archaism. In the Zionist movement to which its youth rallied at the turn of the century despite their rabbis' hostility, the ghetto Jewry of eastern Europe saw only its new, secular, modern, socialist, and nationalist aspects—Zionism as a break with the past. In contrast, because he was the rebel child of a historical Jewish experience rooted in the cult of modernity and in the repression of tradition, Scholem knew in advance that the Jewish national movement conveyed, took hold of, and revitalized an age-old cultural heritage through the agency of modern political categories. What the Jews have in common—and what provides the least unsatisfactory explanation for their extraordinary survival and their national ambition to return to

Zion—is a religious anthropology. Gershom Scholem's entire work is contained within the historical exploration of this proposition.

Naturally, this meant that the historian had to define his relationship with his native cultural soil, Germany. Scholem discusses this subject at length in several of the studies collected in *Fidélité et Utopie*: he sees no cross-fertilization between Jewish culture and German culture. The assimilated Jewish bourgeoisie gradually gave up its own tradition, but the Germans never recognized the Jewish tradition. Modern Jewish historiography, founded by Leopold Zunz in the nineteenth century, never obtained a university chair, and the discipline was never granted academic or social legitimacy. Nor can one find in nineteenth-century German literature the equivalent of the well-known passages of *Notre jeunesse* in which Charles Péguy hails Bernard Lazare as a descendant of the prophets of Israel—even as French Jews, out of prudence or ignorance, remained silent about one of their most daring sons. Replying in 1962 to a young German writer's question on the Jewish-German dialogue, "whose core is indestructible," Scholem denied that such a dialogue ever existed: "The unbounded exhilaration of Jewish enthusiasm never aroused a corresponding note that had the slightest connection with a creative response to the Jews, that is, a response that would have been made to them on the basis of what they could contribute as Jews, and not on what they had to abandon as Jews." For Scholem, the Nazi genocide did not, as it were, accidentally interrupt an exchange or even the beginnings of an exchange. Rather, it was a tragic sign of its absence. It crowned the violence wrought on Jewish minds by annihilating their bodies.

Yet it so happens that there was one exception to Gershom Scholem's militant demonstration: himself. The great German historiographical tradition of the nineteenth century, when grafted onto the study of the Jewish tradition, produced at the very end, just before the catastrophe, a practitioner of a history of Judaism emancipated from its overbearing tutors. In reaction against most of his predecessors and their tendency to "flatten," to secularize, the Jewish tradition in order to make it acceptable to the assimilated bourgeoisie of the nineteenth century, Scholem has devoted most of his work and his life to studying the aspect of this tradition that may seem the most alien to modern rationalism: the Judeo-Spanish Cabala mystique between the thirteenth and sixteenth centuries, and especially the extraordinary offspring of the cabalistic teachings of Isaac Luria, the wise man of Safed in Galilee—the Sabbatian movement of the mid-seventeenth century. The entire Jewish world, from Yemen to Morocco, from Poland to Holland, went wild over the pseudo-Messiah Sabbatai Zevi, who ended his life with an inglorious conversion to Islam. In his scholarly way, Scholem dissects this episode to show the infinite plasticity of the religious phenomenon at work, from its adjustment to the expectations contained in the messianic scenario down to its later ramifications, leading to the philosophy of the Enlightenment. This extraordinarily learned thousand-page book displays the intellectual eccentricity characteristic of Scholem's talent. The young man who scandalized his milieu of good German bourgeois by learning Hebrew has become the historian unearthing before the Israeli rabbinical establishment the awesome treasures of Judaism.

Indeed, if, by devoting his life and intellectual powers to the endless reconstruction of the expressions of the Law and the promises it contains, Scholem sought to *épater le bourgeois*—the twentieth-century bourgeois, in whatever guise—then, he has succeeded only too well! His historical work does not fit easily into any of the intellectual traditions prevailing in Europe. Moreover, what are known as "Jewish studies" are concentrated today in the United States and Israel alone. But, while my lack of competence in the field prevents me from giving a specialist's introduction to his work (on this point, I can only recommend the admirable *Jewish Messianism*, published in French a few years ago),[2] one can probably examine in some depth here what makes his work so closely connected to the world in which we live.

Unlike his immediate predecessors, Buber or Rosenzweig (whom he constantly uses as reference points in defining his own position), Scholem does not study Jewish mysticism from the inside, as a closed and timeless universe. He is neither a theologian nor even, strictly speaking, a believer, but purely and totally a historian. He manifests toward Judaism not only a filial affection but an admiration such as romantic historiography displayed toward the inexhaustible wealth of cultural or national phenomena. The underlying feature of his entire work is basically the simple and baffling question that we all ask ourselves as contemporaries of the genocide and of the birth of the state of Israel: After centuries of misfortune, culminating in the absolute tragedy, how is it that Judaism still exists? Scholem retraces, strand by strand, the thread of this survival, through its cultural—that is, religious—forms, and the endless variants of the notions of God, the Law, and the Messiah devised by the Jewish people in its exile throughout Europe.

An old people, endowed with an age-old culture, ceaselessly reworking its heritage in order to construct a distinctive identity in every circumstance—such are the Jews, according to Scholem. Theirs is the history of a faith more than of a developing society. But if one treats Judaism as a religious culture, while excluding from its definition both rabbinical orthodoxy and modern criteria of national identity, where does one put Zionism and the state of Israel? Scholem relegates them to the profane, that is, the political level. A man who left Berlin for Jerusalem in 1923 cannot be suspected of underestimating their importance. Zionism, in his view, represents the advent of the Jewish people in political history, the assumption by a Jewish state of its historical duties. But this order of realities does not encompass the spiritual and religious

sphere. Zionism fulfills no promises; it realizes no messianic expectations. It marks a renewal in Jewish history, but precisely at the historical
level, not at the eschatological level.

If Scholem watches so zealously over the dividing line between the
religious and the profane, between the spiritual and what he calls "the
historical," it is primarily because he is a religious man, with a religious
view of the continuity of Judaism. For this old opponent of the rabbis, the
human adventure has no meaning other than that conferred on it from the
outside by revelation. But if he puts such emphasis on the hidden meaning of Israel—a meaning that remains to be discovered—it is because he
knows the dangers that threaten a "historicized" Jewish people: the
dangers of being a nation like the others, of contributing acts of injustice
to history, of rebuilding the Bronx in Palestine, of turning the descendants of the Hasidim and the Cabalists into "modern" petty bourgeois. At
the close of his life, the old historian recognizes in the Jewish state itself
the specter of the demon he fought in his father's house in Berlin at
fifteen: Jews in danger of being dispossessed of their past.

In the words of R. P. Blackmur, quoted by Leon Wieseltier in an
article devoted precisely to Gershom Scholem: "Beholden to his fathers,
the Jew is still in search of a son."[3]

14

Israel and the French Left:
The Misunderstanding

As long as Israel was only the reflection of Jewish destiny, that is, of Jewish suffering, it was not hard for the Left to love Israel. Indeed, the Left saw the new state as the embodiment of its traditional conception of the Jewish problem as the sign of capitalist injustice, of the Jews as the exemplary victims of a system, and of Jewish distinctness as the obverse of persecution. The Second World War and the Holocaust brought this feeling to a peak—a feeling theorized by Sartre: what "coagulated" the Jewish problem was the anti-Semitic hatred displayed by Christian Europe; the men and women who in those years were settling in their new homeland could not be colonizers, since they were wanderers, survivors of the tragedy in the camps. Even this dignity was not enough to preserve them from suffering, since they were being rejected from shore to shore by their new persecutors: the British. In fact, the French Left had not yet learned to hate colonizers, whom it was often fond of regarding as the overseas exporters of its own values. It felt far more guilty about the plight of the Jews than about Arab or Vietnamese suffering.

This democratic universalism, so popular and yet so sectarian in the immediate aftermath of the war, was dealt a heavy blow by the decolonization wars. Once again, the force and legitimacy of nationalism became manifest, in their simplest and yet most conceptually elusive aspects. A new Left began to define itself with reference to this struggle, which was helping to put an end to Jacobin Europocentrism. The new Left gradually exerted its pressure on the two great traditional parties by waging intellectual guerrilla warfare on the outskirts of the Communist party and by provoking a definitive split within the Section Française de

First published in *Le Nouvel Observateur*, 15 May 1978.

l'Internationale Ouvrière (SFIO) through the creation of the Parti Socialiste Unifié in 1959.

Israel was not only left out of this anticolonialist movement; it was also a logical scapegoat for it, as evidenced by the Suez crisis, when Ben Gurion's troops came to the aid of the paratroopers sent by Guy Mollet and Eden against Nasser's Egypt. The short war of 1956—which, with hindsight, still seems to me the major error in Israeli foreign policy— nevertheless established, with a sort of miraculous malevolence, the new image of the Jewish people for the outside world. It was a political image, in which the Jew became the ally, the accomplice, of the old colonial powers; but also a moral image, which destroyed the stereotype of humiliation and created the victorious Jew.

This intellectual and emotional turning point was not always easily accepted by the French Left, which, as we have seen, needed the presence of calamity in order to conceive the Jewish identity—or, if not calamity, at least the threat of calamity. This is the secret of the explosion of sympathy, and even affection, for Israel in French public opinion on the eve of the Six Day War: the Jewish state was threatened with annihilation, and the words of Shukairy conjured up the ghost of Hitler. But the fact remains that from Suez onward, Israel's image was *also* that of a soldiering people, strong and victorious. But, just as in the nineteenth century the French Left had had the greatest difficulty in evoking the rich or simply "successful" Jew without sinking into anti-Semitism or an outright denial of the problem, so it had no intellectual tools for conceiving Israel without evoking the tragedies of European history and the French Left's own share of guilt in them.

On the contrary, the intellectual tools developed by the French Left in the course of its struggles may well be an obstacle to its understanding, no longer the Jewish destiny, but the Israeli destiny. Once oblivious to colonial realities, it has now made anticolonialism a dominant element of its ideology. Once obsessed with Jacobin narcissism, it has made anti-imperialism the key interpretative concept in a now-global history. Through this prism, Zionism appeared to be moving against the historical current: it was an "objectively" colonial movement at a time of worldwide decolonization, an "objectively" imperialist force at a time when the struggle against imperialism was a watchword the world over. The passengers of the *Exodus* had once again become colonizers, admittedly unwilling ones, but colonizers all the same. And the suburban Chicago Jew who paid an annual contribution to his second homeland unknowingly revived one of the oldest images of anti-Semitism, that of all-powerful international financiers fighting against the freedom of peoples.

Naturally, in order to discourage this type of analysis, I am more or less caricaturizing it. But my reason for doing so is that I do not think it derives its strength from any conceptual rigor. Rather, it seems to me to be a rearrangement of old elements drawn from French political culture—most of which, incidentally, are common to both Right and Left. First, there is a latent anti-Semitism, which is never as widespread as when it is directed against the "successful" Jew: in the new configuration, the victorious Israeli takes the place of the Jewish plutocrat in the nineteenth-century right-wing or left-wing imagination. An even stronger ingredient is the hostility toward the United States, one of the greatest passions of the French Left since the end of the war: Israel became a substitute object for this hostility, enabling France to reap an easy benefit as interpreter of the Third World. Thus, the Jewish state took on the function traditionally assigned to the Jews in our political life, by serving after a fashion as a witness to French national greatness. The best expression of this amalgam of ideas and feelings can be found, in my view, in what has been called "left-wing Gaullism," located precisely at the confluence of Right and Left; but it would not be hard to find other traces of it in the Communist party, the PSU, and on the left of the Socialist party.

For the Left still bases its vision and understanding of Israel on the impulse that led it unanimously, thirty years ago, to hail the birth of the new state as an act of reparation. It never tried to develop a doctrine corresponding to that feeling, as if the latter were simply a powerful sense of guilt, irreducible to rationality. In truth, the Left has never had very much to say about the two elements that would need to be analyzed and confronted in order to attempt to interpret the history of Israel: the national phenomenon and the religious phenomenon. In all its versions, Marxism ignores these phenomena, or, rather, it conjures them away instead of explaining them. The nearly irresistible reaction of the French Left to national phenomena is to give them a universal dimension, by means of which they can be inscribed in the great book of world history (as phenomena pointing in the right "direction"). Thus, the slightest tribal conflict is dignified with the status of democratic universalism, and every Chadian maquis becomes the successor to the Spanish Republicans. But Israel is precisely excluded from this universalist vision in that it is the product of a latter-day national European movement, impossible to fit into the dialectical process of colonial liberation, and even (if one wants to cling at all cost to this frame of reference, which is more than sufficient to bias the analysis) contradictory to that process.

As for the religious aspect of Israel as a historical phenomenon, it quite obviously contributes to the Left's incomprehension, since, in the European tradition, national emancipation and secularization of the state have always gone together. But there is more. When the debate over Israel has been freed of the unsavory variety of metaphysics that sometimes encumbers it, the fact remains that the (re)creation of the Jewish state in the mid-twentieth century, in biblical Palestine, is not an easy event to understand if one clings to a materialist interpretation of history. The circumstantial factors—above all the Holocaust—are easy enough to perceive, but they do not provide an exhaustive explanation of the phenomenon, which is inseparable from Jewish messianism. In this field, Gershom Scholem is a better guide than Marx, but the Left is in no way prepared by its culture for a reading of that great work! When the Left is secular, it is Marxist. When it is not secular, it is Catholic. In both cases, its approach to Jewish history is conditioned by intellectual traditions that negate that history.

That is why the Left, ever since Israel donned the features of a strong and victorious country, has never stopped oscillating between its emotionally charged memories and the notion that Israel is "a country like any other." When the Jewish state is threatened, the specter of final extermination looms up again. After an Israeli victory, café strategists take out their maps and start talking about "rightful boundaries." Neither of these attitudes contributes one iota to a better understanding of the problem: neither that of identification with guilt nor that of "rational" diplomatic arbitration. The first attitude will eventually fade away, except from Israel's memory; moreover, it is incomprehensible to the Arab world. The second presupposes that the Israeli-Arab conflict is in a sense "normal," whereas it lies precisely outside the norms of international politics, since its roots are exceptionally deep and complex.

In truth, there is no conceptual or emotional shortcut to a full understanding of a country that embodies mankind's oldest written memory as well as the miracle and tragedies of modern Europe—a country that is the offspring of religion, nationalism, and socialism. Thirty years after the birth of the state of Israel, nothing is yet clear in its history except to the simpleminded. There is still only one way of approaching Jewish history without avoiding its singular destiny: it is to confront its specific features, which alone can shed light on its universal import.

15

Israel, Zionism, and the Diaspora

The fascinating feature of the history of Zionism is that it reveals better than any other episode the radically unpredictable character of twentieth-century European history.[1] Let us imagine for one moment that an opinion poll could have been carried out at the turn of the century—when the notion of Zionism was just emerging—on the following question: During the next fifty years, which of these two events seems to you most likely to occur: the advent of socialism in Germany (or France, or England) or that of a Jewish state in Palestine? Public opinion, and particularly among educated people, would have overwhelmingly chosen the first hypothesis. By indulging in this exercise in imagination, public opinion would have based its erroneous prediction on an optimistic vision of the relationship among democracy, socialism, and nation in the Europe of the future. Zionism, instead, invented another future by placing itself on the fringe of this triangular system, or, if one prefers, on its obverse side: it took as its starting point the situation of the Jews in Europe, but, in order to understand and "resolve" this situation, it adopted the three key elements of European political civilization. The Zionist movement advocated a break in the name of an identity, a separation from the very environment that had shaped it. And it is through this contradiction that Zionism provides the observer not only with the secrets of its success but with the best vantage point for analyzing its current problems.

Zionism was born at the confluence of two currents, of two visions of European Jewry, whose combined effect was to anathematize the way of

Published in *Le Nouvel Observateur*, 27 February 1982, to coincide with the appearance of *L'Atelier de l'histoire*. The documentation for this essay has been drawn primarily from Joseph Heller, *The Zionist Idea* (New York: Schocken Books, 1949), and Arthur Hertzberg, *The Zionist Idea: A Historical Analysis and Reader* (New York: Doubleday, 1959).

life to be abandoned. The first vision was that of Herzl, for Zionism was born in western Europe, specifically in Austria, where the Jewish community had made brilliant progress in the nineteenth century but where anti-Semitism, too, had flared up violently. Lueger, the leader of the Christian Social party—the man whose anti-Semitic diatribes fed the young Hitler—was elected mayor of Vienna in 1897. The fact is that Jewish assimilation had apparently provoked a rejective reaction in the body social. Through Theodore Herzl, the Zionist dream emerged in this society at the crossroads of democratic progress and resistance to that progress. Like many memorable ideas or great events, it was predicated on a revolution made of expectations, a revolution thwarted by the counterrevolutionary force of reality.

Thus, the starting point of Zionism was both the success and the failure of assimilation. The success, since Herzl belonged to a completely secularized milieu that was cut off from the Jewish tradition. He was the perfect representative of the intelligentsia integrated into German culture since the Enlightenment—a milieu whose fundamental belief was that democracy was the necessary and sufficient condition for emancipation. But, at the same time, Herzl witnessed the failure of this central creed, since the development of a new anti-Semitism within democratic culture, in Austria, Germany, and France, proved to him that his youthful convictions were mistaken. Thus, "assimilated" Jews were the first to understand that democracy did not solve the Jewish problem, as all of enlightened Europe had believed since the French Revolution. And it was a "modern" anti-Semitism, born of democracy, that triggered Zionism. By founding a national state and a homogeneous Jewish society, Zionism aimed at enabling modern Judaism to lead a collective existence modeled on European nations and yet in opposition to them, or at least to the ideology of individual Jewish assimilation that they professed.

It is probable that Austro-German Jewry was the only branch of European Jewry whose intellectual sensibility at the time made it a suitable breeding ground for the Zionist idea: it was sufficiently integrated into modern culture (unlike the traditionalist eastern European ghettos) to adopt the idea of nationality and yet close enough to its origins (unlike the French-style *embourgeoisé* varieties of Jewry) to preserve a connection, if not with a religious belief, at least with the idea of a separate culture. But, as evidenced by the episode of Herzl's temporary endorsement of the West African compromise as a substitute for Jerusalem,[2] that connection is easier to define in negative terms, as a consequence of anti-Semitic rejection, than in positive terms, as a taking into account of the cultural heritage.

Unlike that of Herzl, the second vision of the European Jew that contributed *a contrario* to the birth of Zionism was not informed by the need to put an end to anti-Semitism or by the impossibility of assimilation. It was centered not on the external aspect of the Jewish problem,

but on its internal one—on the cultural, and consequently national, identity of the Jews. In this respect, it was more radically opposed to the Diaspora than the first vision, since it did not reject the exile, the *galuth*, on empirical grounds relating to anti-Semitism and the impossibility of assimilation: it rejected it for reasons having to do with the very essence of Judaism. This vision did not originate in a factual observation of the failure of assimilation. On the contrary, it regarded assimilation as a natural and inescapable consequence of the existence of Jews as individuals in the democratic states of Europe; hence, assimilation would eventually put an end to anti-Semitism by depriving it of sustenance. The only way to avoid the democratic elimination of the Jewish problem (that is, the elimination of the Jews themselves), and thus the only way to keep Judaism alive, was to create the conditions in which Jews could exist as a nation.

This argument, the most systematic expression of which can be found in the articles published by Jacob Klatzkin on the eve of the First World War,[3] treated the modern anti-Semitism of European states as in some sense a rational phenomenon. Such anti-Semitism was the obverse side of nation building, the will to reject whatever was alien to national culture, and consequently the decisive proof that Judaism continued to exist as a potentially national tradition, since it was perceived as such by the European nations. The enemy, for Klatzkin, was not the anti-Semite; it was the assimilating liberal. The Jewish national identity was to be salvaged in the name of the same values that led the anti-Semite to an exclusive worship of his own nation—that is, because the Jews formed a distinctive people with an identity of its own.

Thus, of the two visions of the Diaspora Jew the negation of which led to Zionism, one originated in the anti-Semitic rejection that followed assimilation—a rejection regarded as insurmountable; the other, on the contrary, stemmed from the propositions that a Jewish nationhood existed in a positive sense—on a par with European nationalities that emerged in the modern age, particularly in the nineteenth century—and that this nationhood had to be saved from the perils of assimilation. These analyses of the Jewish problem at the turn of the twentieth century were, therefore, contradictory. But both of them, in their opposite ways, sought to resolve the central paradox of Zionism: how to abandon Europe and its culture while at the same time holding on to them. Herzl's brand of Zionism regarded contemporary anti-Semitism as a pathological aspect of modernity, a nationalist deviation of the national idea, an unexpected but indestructible product of democratic ideology. On the contrary, Klatzkin's brand of Zionism regarded it as the natural offshoot of European nationhood—as consecutive to, and not incompatible with, the existence of modern democratic states. The two approaches were probably rooted in different perceptions of the Jewish experience at the time: the first was totally emancipated from tradition and patterned

negatively on the modern nationhood of European states; the second was closer to tradition and defined in positive terms by a cultural specificity that had to be saved because it was threatened. But these two experiences, these two analyses, ultimately led to the same conclusion: the need for a Jewish state. For they shared at least the same opinion about the "abnormality" of Jewish life in the Diaspora and the need to put an end to this predicament.

Naturally, the picture is not as simple as this point-by-point opposition between the two types of Zionist ideology would suggest. For example, one could discern in the "spiritual" Zionism of Ahad Haam the desire to find a definition based neither on external factors—on the existence of anti-Semitism—nor on a purely national view, but rather on the Jewish cultural heritage, in the widest sense of the word. To this extent, although he shared with Klatzkin the idea that the situation of the Diaspora was no longer conducive to the advancement of Jewish culture, Ahad Haam had an infinitely more positive opinion of Diaspora Judaism in general. He felt it essential for the Jewish renaissance in Palestine to maintain a constant dialogue with what would consequently have become a peripheral form of Judaism but would have remained an indispensable element of Jewish national history.

Yet one of the factors that gradually brought cohesion to the Jewish population in Palestine, even more forcefully than the condemnation or analysis of modern anti-Semitism, was precisely the radical rejection of the situation of the Diaspora Jew. Anti-Semitism was in everyone's memories, but the sort of intellectual quasi acceptance of it in advance eliminated all justification for the survival of the Diaspora from the moment Judaism existed in Palestine. One need only consider the ideology and practice of the Zionist movement in the early twentieth century, at the time when the outlines of Israel were emerging, to understand the extent to which the Zionist "Western" saga, in a blend of Russian populism and Marxist social democracy, manufactured images of the Jewish future that were tantamount to final condemnations of the Jewish past. The return to Zion represents a new version of Judaism, based on European ideas and on a rejection of the ghettos and the Diaspora.

From the outset, the success of the Zionist project was due to the extraordinary activity and determination of a few individuals: Weizmann was a new Cavour, and Jabotinsky a reincarnation of both Mazzini and Garibaldi. The first, a visionary but adroit diplomat, abided by the official plan for a national home and kept a watchful eye on the international scene; the second, a flamboyant, romantic man in a hurry, sought a historical shortcut to the state of Israel. Between the two there existed the same secret connection as between the Haganah, the Jewish settlers' self-defense army, and the Irgun, which preached and practiced terrorist tactics—a violent conflict but a fundamental agreement on what all parties regarded as the Jewish revolution.

The same situation prevailed somewhat earlier in the "working-class" Zionism that, in combination with the Jewish tradition, constituted the most important—and, incidentally, the most touching—cultural ingredient of the future state. The great pre-1914 *aliyah* (several tens of thousands of Lithuanians, Poles, Ukrainians, and Russians) was an immigration of qualified labor. It brought together—as the American adventure in the seventeenth century had done—a body of dynamic and faithful individuals. These latter-day pioneers were militants who had often had to overcome the hostility of their rabbis—staunch believers in the age-old curse—and of their comrades, locked into the internationalist dogma of the labor movement. They brought to Palestine the peasant myth of Russian culture and the interminable discussions of the European working-class Left—Tolstoy and Marx united in the fraternal atmosphere of absolute new beginnings. On this new "frontier" of Europe, they planted the flag of a new agrarian and military Rome. On this infertile soil, these impoverished settlers invented an unpolished and egalitarian civilization. They had left the urban ghetto; they founded the rural antighetto. The Jew had been landless; now he was to be a farmer. He had been a usurer; now he would scorn money. He had been disarmed; now he would be a soldier. He had been humiliated; now he would be a victor. One could go on indefinitely contrasting these two images point by point. By defining itself as both a radical break with the past and a return to origins, Zionism unites the two cardinal but divergent notions contained in the modern idea of revolution in seventeenth-century England and late eighteenth-century America and France. In so doing, it categorically condemns—in a manner not unsimilar to that of the anti-Semites—the existence of Jews in exile, cut off both from their origins and from their future.

The Nazi extermination engraved these features of the Zionist revolution in tragedy. It gave them the force of an earthquake. The reasons why the extermination has constituted, since the inception of the state, one of the foundations of Israel's national consciousness go far beyond the material fact that it drove toward what was not yet the Jewish state the survivors of the genocide. In the Jewish historical consciousness, but also in gentile public opinion and in the political world at state level, the vision of Jewish destiny offered by Zionism—for so long a marginal vision—has assumed since Hitler the status of a self-evident truth. Inseparable from its three preconditions—the German will to annihilate, the consent or passivity of gentile Europe, and the weakness of Jewish resistance—the genocide has become the Diaspora's truth, while the state of Israel and the law of return have become the only guarantees against its reoccurrence.

Thus, Hitler's genocide lies at the origin of Israeli society for factual reasons, since so many Israelis are its survivors, but even more so because of the basic truth that the state of Israel was born of the conjunction between the irrepressible violence of anti-Semitism and Zionism's preventive response to it. The massive *aliyah* of European Jews beginning in the 1920s and 1930s only served to drive home the original message of the founders about the impossibility of being European *and* Jewish and the need to leave Europe in search of a Jewish nation in order to live as Europeans. In the light of the genocide, acceptance of the Diaspora became tantamount to a warrant for crime; condemnation of the Diaspora, on the contrary, turned out to be justified by the stark tragedy of history.

Everything, therefore, has conspired to turn the Israelis into a people set against its past sufferings. The contemporary experience has cut Jewish history into two parts, the interminable exile representing its negative half, the Zionist revolution representing its renaissance. But the words *exile* and *renaissance* imply a political world wholly informed by the search for a "past" that is supposed to give them a meaning. We are confronted here with the exceptional character—by the standards of European history—of the constitution of the Israeli nation, despite the fact that it was built with two classic elements of the European repertoire: the idea of revolution and the idea of nationhood. The reason for this peculiarity is that the revolution of the Jewish people, carried out in the name of a secular ideal, with the aim—similar to that of the French Revolution—of rebuilding society on the basis of principles originating in society itself, was at the same time a means of reuniting the Jews with an archaic history and a religious promise. Jewish nationhood, reinvented not on the basis of a collective presence but on that of a scattered people, found its symbolic cohesion and the shared treasure-trove of its memories only in the oldest of old books, the Hebrew Bible. Thus, the two great mooring points for the pedagogy of nationhood and for the national consensus are the two extremes of Jewish history, the most ancient and the most recent: the Bible and Zionism. What lies in between—that is, nearly all of the Jewish past—is the object of a collective semicensorship, inherent in the very nature of Israeli national feeling. To put it differently, the central figure of Israel is Ben Gurion, not Ahad Haam.

However, it seems to me that these characteristic traits of Israeli national consciousness, which can be explained both by the history of Zionism and by that of twentieth-century Europe, have contributed to the present predicament of Israeli society—at least to the share of its predicament for which it is alone responsible. The European obsession in reverse that constitutes the basis of the Zionist movement has long made it blind to the Arab problem. But, at the other end of the Jewish revolution, the biblical point of reference has not made the problem easier to solve, ever since the "problem" of the 1920s took on the inevitable dimensions of a question of life or death. The idea of election and of a promised land, clashing with that of Palestine as a holy land of Islam, has again turned this patch of barren land, whose inhabitants once eked out an existence in the shadow of the Turkish pashas, into the stake of a battle between two messianic movements. More generally, as far as Israel is concerned, the emphasis on biblical origins turned religion into a cofounder of the state, inseparable from public authority. Religion has made Israeli society a hostage to a conservative rabbinate, despite the deliberately modernist aims of that society's founders.

But it is probably the relationship between Israel and the Diaspora that provides the best insight into the Israelis' curious relation to the Jewish past. It is true that the converse analysis is no less interesting and that the attitude of Diaspora Jews toward Israel is composed of varying degrees of love and hatred, from which a guilty conscience is never absent. The very existence of Israel has transformed the general condition of Diaspora Jews owing to the way they are perceived by Gentiles; yet these Diaspora Jews have remained in the Diaspora. At the other end, Israel's vision of the Diaspora is most often centered either on the early-twentieth-century eastern European ghettos or on the Nazi tragedy—that is, on the negation of the new Jewish farmer and soldier. Occasionally, one can even discern a certain anti-intellectualism in this spontaneous reconstruction of the past as a foil. Furthermore, as in the early days of Zionism, the unfortunate and endangered Diaspora is only an instrument or a source of recruitment: its fate is to become assimilated or to enlist. While awaiting the inevitable outcome, Israel contributes to the process by propagating a vision of the Diaspora's natural submission to Israel as its potential state. Having normalized the Jewish destiny within its borders, Israel expects the same to happen to Judaism as a whole. Because it has altered the image of Judaism the world over, Israel assumes that it has unified Judaism from every point of view and thus no longer feels the need to be aware of its diversity. Hence, geographical space confronts Israel with the same enigmas and the same impasses as historical time, and for the same reasons: the Jewish nation, whatever the intentions or beliefs of Zionism, is not "like the others."

Indeed, a modification of this vision could well be the first step toward the general reappraisal of Zionism that everyone in Israel regards as a necessity. To begin with, a very simple observation: aside from its extraordinary historical achievement, Zionism has not realized its chief objective, which was to bring all of the Jewish people together in Palestine. Immigration has virtually ceased, and Israel's population growth is now solely dependent on its domestic birthrate. The annual migratory balance is actually negative: this is a sign of the relatively high emigration rate, but the phenomenon is hard to evaluate since the Israelis who leave their country present their departure as a temporary absence. Emigration apparently involves both the poorest social strata and the professions (doctors, lawyers, and engineers): in both cases, the American dream remains the natural pole of attraction. This phenomenon, which is quite "normal"—and, moreover, easy to understand in a country where wages are relatively low, taxes very high, and military service interminable—has become, no less understandably, the object of anxious concern in a country founded on the law of return. Apart from its statistical impact, emigration is a vivid sign of the psychological limits of the Zionist idea.

In fact, these limits have never ceased to exert a constraining effect, since, from the very outset, at the turn of the century, emigration to America was infinitely greater than the *aliyah* to Jerusalem; but these constraints had been masked both by the spectacular triumph of the creation of the state of Israel and by the massive immigration tragically engendered by Hitler's genocide. Today, more than thirty years after the birth of Israel, no Zionist leader can seriously base a policy on the assumption that Israel will absorb the entire Diaspora. The Diaspora Jews, if they were supposed to have come, would already be there. Russian Jews will perhaps continue to emigrate to Israel, since the Israeli visa is the only one that allows them to leave the Soviet Union. However, these immigrants will be few and far between, and there is no guarantee, as experience has shown, that they will settle easily or definitively in Israel. Barring an unpredictable catastrophe in the United States or western Europe, Zionism does not solve the problem of the Diaspora. It is condemned to coexist with the Diaspora.

The simplest way of rethinking Zionism, on the basis of what it has accomplished and what it has become, would probably be to take into account the abandonment of a universal solution to the Jewish problem— an abandonment that is evident in the facts. Like all great historical movements, Zionism has not fulfilled all the predictions of its founders or achieved all the desired results. However, if one compares the degree to which Zionism has carried out its initial project with the degree to which other great ideas that have mobilized mankind in the twentieth century have carried out theirs, Zionism does not come out too badly: all the more reason to limit its scope and objectives according to the historical tasks imposed on it by circumstances, while preserving its fidelity to the spirit of its founders. Paradoxically, this redefinition implies both the secularization of the state and the restitution to the Jewish people of its entire past. It is by emancipating the national feeling from the historical shortcut between the Bible and the founding of Israel that one will spare it from the temptation of a debased form of messianism. In this respect, Israel's relation with the Diaspora constitutes a test.

NOTES

Introduction

1. To illustrate my argument, I have relied particularly on Richard Cobb's "Modern French History in Britain," the Raleigh Lecture on History for 1974 (London: *Proceedings of the British Academy*, 60 [published as a separate pamphlet], 1974).

Chapter 1

1. Raymond Aron, *Trois essais sur l'âge industriel* (Paris: Plon, 1966).
2. See Raymond Aron's article on Sartre's *Critique de la raison dialectique* in *Le Figaro littéraire* (19 October 1964).
3. In *Esprit* (November 1963).
4. See Edmund Leach, "Genesis as Myth," *Discovery* (May 1962); idem, "The Legitimacy of Solomon," *Archives européennes de sociologie* (1966); idem, "Claude Lévi-Strauss, Anthropologist and Philosopher," *New Left Review* (1966).

Chapter 2

1. J. Marczewski, general ed., *Histoire quantitative de l'économie française*, 10 vols. to date (Paris: ISEA, 1961–68), esp. vol. 1, *Histoire quantitative: buts et méthodes*, by J. Marczewski.
2. The expression is Pierre Vilar's.
3. Pierre Chaunu has defended and used the term in a number of studies. See esp. *Histoire quantitative ou histoire sérielle*, Cahiers Vilfredo Pareto (Geneva, 1968), and "L'Histoire sérielle: bilans et perspectives," an article published simultaneously in *Revue historique* (April–June 1970) and *Revue roumaine d'histoire*, no. 3 (1970).
4. See esp. P. Deane and W. A. Cole, *British Economic Growth, 1688–1959: Trends and Structure* (Cambridge: Cambridge University Press, 1962); David Landes, *The Unbound Prometheus* (Cambridge: Cambridge University Press, 1969); François Crouzet, "Angleterre et France au XVIIIe siècle: essai d'analyse comparée de deux croissances économiques," *Annales: économies, sociétés, civilisations* (March–April 1966).

5. Marcel Couturier, "Vers une nouvelle méthodologie mécanographique: la préparation des données," *Annales:économies, sociétés, civilisations* (July–August 1966).

6. E. Le Roy Ladurie, "Révolution française et contraception: dossiers languedociens," *Annales de démographie historique* (1966), and "Révolution française et funestes secrets," *Annales historiques de la Révolution française* (October–December 1965). See also A. Chamoux and C. Dauphin, "La Contraception avant la Révolution française: l'exemple de Châtillon-sur-Saône," *Annales: économies, sociétés, civilisations* (May–June 1969).

7. The bibliography is too vast even to be summarized.

8. E. Le Roy Ladurie, *Les Paysans de Languedoc* (Paris: SEVPEN, 1966; abridged ed., Flammarion, 1969). The account I give here is a shorter version of my article "Sur quelques problèmes posés par le développment de l'histoire quantitative," *Information sur les sciences sociales* 7 (1968): 71–82.

9. Crouzet, "Angleterre et France."

10. Pierre Vilar, *La Catalogne dans l'Espagne moderne* (Paris: SEVPEN, 1962), esp. vol. 2.

11. P. Goubert, *Beauvais et le Beauvaisis de 1600 à 1730* (Paris: SEVPEN, 1960).

12. R. Baehrel, *Une croissance: la Basse-Provence rurale, fin du XVIe seìcle–1789* (Paris: SEVPEN, 1961).

13. Denis Richet, "Croissance et blocages en France du XVe au XVIIIe siècle," *Annales: économies, sociétés, civilisations* (July–August 1968).

14. Michel Fleury, "Les Progrès de l'instruction élémentaire de Louis XIV à Napoléon III," *Population* (1957). See also Lawrence Stone, "Literacy and Education in England, 1640–1900," *Past and Present* (February 1968): 69–139; Carlo Cipolla, *Literacy and Development in the West* (Harmondsworth and Baltimore: Penguin Books, 1969).

15. Gaby and Michel Vovelle have given a brilliant demonstration of how iconographical series can be used to study religious sentiment. See their *Vision de la mort et de l'au-delà en Provence*, Cahiers des *Annales* (Paris, 1970).

Chapter 3

1. I.e., the essay "Quantitative History," reprinted above as chapter 2.

2. Norbert Elias, *Über den Prozess der Zivilisation*, vol. 1 (Basle, 1939).

Chapter 4

1. See esp. Donald R. Kelley, *Foundations of Modern Historical Scholarship* (New York: Columbia University Press, 1970); George Huppert, *The Idea of Perfect History* (Urbana: University of Illinois Press, 1970).

Chapter 5

1. The best discussion of this question is to be found in A. Momigliano, "Ancient History and the Antiquarians," *Journal of the Warburg and Courtauld Institutes* 13 (1950): 285–315.

2. B. Neveu, *Un historian à l'école de Port-Royal: Sébastien Le Nain de Tillemont, 1637–1698* (The Hague, 1966): 182–85.

3. These examples are taken from an unfortunately unpublished essay by Louis Trénard, "L'Enseignement de l'histoire en France de 1770 à 1885," delivered as a lecture in June 1968 under the aegis of the Fédération Belge des Professeurs d'Histoire. [French classes are numbered backward with respect to the American and British systems: *onzième*

is the first grade of elementary school, *sixième* the first grade of secondary school, *première* (formerly *classe de rhétorique*) and *classe de philosophie* (or *terminale*) the last two years of secondary school. Before the Revolution, *collèges* was the general term for secondary schools. After the Revolution, the secondary schools were divided into *lycées* and *collèges*, the former ranking somewhat above the latter.—TRANS.]

4. This information on the Collège de Juilly is taken from a recent and as yet unpublished dissertation by Etienne Broglin, "De l'Académie royale à l'institution: le Collège de Juilly, 1745–1828" (University of Paris, 1978).

5. The major speeches on education policy by the members of the revolutionary assemblies can be found in C. Hippeau, *L'Instruction publique en France pendant la Révolution* (1881). For more details, see J. Guillaume, ed., *Procès-verbaux du Comité d'Instruction publique de la Convention nationale*, 6 vols. (Paris: Imprimerie Nationale, 1890–1907).

Chapter 6

1. The example has been given in this field by the work of L. Febvre and H.-J. Martin, *L'Apparition du livre*, L'Evolution de l'humanité, 49 (Paris: Albin Michel, 1958).

2. R. Estivals, "La Statistique bibliographique de la France sous la monarchie au XVIIIe siècle" (unpublished dissertation, University of Paris, 1962); idem, *Le Dépôt légal sous l'Ancien Régime de 1537 à 1791* (Paris: M. Rivière, 1961).

3. The verso of the last leaf of Bibliothèque Nationale Ms. Fr. 22 001 lists the following fees: *privilège général*, 101 livres and 2 sous; *permission* for six years, 61 livres and 18 sous; *permission* for three years, 30 livres.

4. Diderot, *Lettre sur le commerce de la librairie*, reprinted as *Lettre sur la liberté de la presse*, ed. J. Proust (Paris: Editions Sociales, 1963).

5. Malesherbes, *Mémoire sur la liberté de la presse* (1788).

6. Diderot, *Lettre*.

7. The registers for printing license requests used as the basic source for this study are the following:

Privilèges et permissions du Sceau

Ms. Fr. 21 995	1723–28
Ms. Fr. 21 996	1728–38
Ms. Fr. 21 997	1738–50
Ms. Fr. 21 998	1750–60
Ms. Fr. 21 999	1760–63
Ms. Fr. 22 000	1763–68
Ms. Fr. 22 001	1768–74
Ms. Fr. 22 002	1774–84
Ms. Fr. 21 978	1784–89

Permissions tacites

Ms. Fr. 21 990	1718–46
Ms. Fr. 21 994	1750–60
Ms. Fr. 21 992	1760–63
Ms. Fr. 21 991	1763–66
Ms. Fr. 21 993	1766–72
Ms. Fr. 21 983	1772–82 (first occurrence of the title *permissions tacites)*
Ms. Fr. 21 986	1782–88
Ms. Fr. 22 003	1788–89 (This last register of requests for tacit permits has been mistakenly listed in the Bibliothèque Nationale manuscript catalog among the *privilège* registers.)

8. The itemized count of several books included in the same request for a *privilège* generally presents no problems. Prints and engravings, often submitted in very great numbers in a single request, have not been included in our census. However, bishoprics often applied for a single *privilège* for a whole series of liturgical or devotional handbooks, of which a summary list would be provided: breviaries, diurnals, missals, antiphonaries, directories, and so on. In this case alone, it has been impossible to distinguish between licenses and books. We have therefore adopted the method of counting arbitrarily as one book the set of diocesan handbooks (*usages*), which artificially reduces their number.

9. Malesherbes did write in his fifth *Mémoire sur les problèmes de la librairie* that tacit permits "have multiplied to the point of being today as common as public licenses."

10. Malesherbes makes this statement in his *Mémoire sur la liberté de la presse* of 1788. Moreover, a letter from the Parisian *libraires* (publisher-booksellers) Huart and Moreau to Montesquieu, dated 8 January 1749, cites the rumor that *L'Esprit des lois* had been granted a tacit permit. This fact cannot be verified on our registers, which are missing from late 1746 to late 1750.

11. After 1778, the "books entered via the Chambre Syndicale" no longer appear on the registers of requests, but only in the listings of tacit permits.

12. Madeleine Ventre, *L'Imprimerie et la librairie en Languedoc au dernier siècle de l'Ancien Régime, 1700–1789* (Paris and The Hague: Mouton, 1958).

13. Letter from Huart to Montesquieu, March 1749.

14. Most of which are to be found in the manuscript division of the Bibliothèque Nationale and in the Bibliothèque de l'Arsenal.

15. Forbidden books escape our census, but the book-licensing records invariably preserve the traces of the most significant among them: *Emile* and *Le Contrat social*, for example, spawned a long series of commentaries, which testify to their social impact.

16. This classification has been prepared with the help of Daniel Roche.

17. The division into five major categories is attested by the practices followed in library catalogs. See for ex. Louis Desgraves, ed., *Catalogue de la bibliothèque de Montesquieu* (Geneva: Droz, 1954); "Catalogue des bibliothèques des parlementaires parisiens," in François Bluche, *Les Magistrats du Parlement de Paris au XVIIIe siècle, 1715–1771* (Paris: Les Belles Lettres, 1960), 291; Durcy de Noinville, *Dissertation sur les bibliothèques* (Paris, 1758), Bibl. Nat. call no. Q. 3507; J.-M. Cels-Martin, *Coup d'œil éclairé d'une bibliothèque* (Paris, 1773), Bibl. Nat. call no. Q. 5346.

18. See library catalogs such as *Catalogue des livres de feu Monsieur le Maréchal de Lautrec* (Paris, 1762), Bibl. Nat. call no. Q. 8138; see also references in note 17 and esp. Cels-Martin, *Coup d'œil*. We have classified under this heading the *Histories* of the Old and New Testaments, the *Lives* of Jesus Christ, and similar works, for they all deal with biblical or sacred history as distinct from ecclesiastical history.

19. See references in note 18.

20. The division of theological works into Catholic and non-Catholic (orthodox and heterodox) was practiced in public libraries. See the "Catalogue général de la Bibliothèque du Roi" (1739–42), reprinted in *Introduction au catalogue général auteurs* of the Bibliothèque Nationale (1897). This section naturally includes sermonizing, polemical, catechistic, ascetic, and mystical theologians. See Cels-Martin, *Coup d'œil*.

21. The "liturgy" category appears in the bibliographical guides mentioned above, where it includes devotional and catechistic literature.

22. See note 17.

23. See Cels-Martin, *Coup d'œil; Catalogue Montesquieu; Catalogue de la bibliothèque Malesherbes* (1797), Bibl. Nat. call no. 8° INV. Q. 9128; *Catalogue Lautrec*.

24. See M. Camus, *Lettre sur la profession d'avocat, avec un catalogue raisonné des livres de droit qu'il est le plus utile d'acquérir et de connaître; Catalogue Malesherbes*, vol. 2; Cels-Martin, *Coup d'œil*.

25. Biographies and memoirs of famous men, literary history, history of theater, heraldry, archaeology, and so forth, have been classified under "ancillary sciences [of history]" (III.B.3). See Cels-Martin, *Coup d'œil; Catalogue Malesherbes*.

26. See *Catalogue de la Bibliothèque du Roi* (1688) s.v. *histoire ecclésiastique*; Cels-Martin, *Coup d'œil*, s.v. *histoire sacrée; Catalogue Lautrec*. In all of these works and catalogs, geographical studies are grouped together with historical works.

27. See note 17: certain authors equate this category with philosophy, by virtue of the tradition that *philosophia comprehendit artes et scientias*. For ex., Formey, *Conseils pour former une bibliothèque peu nombreuse mais choisie*. However, in the catalog of books belonging to M. Augry, a lawyer in Vendôme (Bibl. Nat. call no. Q. 3026), the entire category is included under the heading "mathematics." Pedagogical works are listed here under "ethics." Theodicy, ontology, anthropology, magic, and cabalistic literature have been classified under "metaphysics." The science of navigation is classified here, in accordance with Cels-Martin, under astronomy; alchemy under "chemistry."

28. Cels-Martin, *Coup d'œil; Catalogue Lautrec; Catalogue Malesherbes*.

29. The distinction between physical, mathematical, and natural sciences can be found in Cels-Martin, *Coup d'œil; Catalogue Lautrec; Catalogue Malesherbes*. See also the *Encyclopédie*, vol. 1, "Système figuré des connaissances humaines."

30. Includes works on government, politics, commerce, and finance. See *Catalogue Malesherbes; Encyclopédie méthodique* (1784), s.v. *art*; on political economics, see Cels-Martin, *Coup d'œil*.

31. *Catalogue de la Bibliothèque du Roi* (1688) *Catalogue Malesherbes*; Cels-Martin, *Coup d'œil*; Formey, *Conseils*; Maïeul de Chaudon, *Bibliothèque d'un homme de goût* (Paris, 1772–77), Bibl. Nat. call no. 5340–41 and Q. 5542–45; *Almanach de la librairie* (1781).

32. Music, painting, sculpture, drawing, etching, dance, architecture, art of warfare, epistolary art, decoration; see Cels-Martin, *Coup d'œil*.

33. Cels-Martin, *Coup d'œil; Encyclopédie*, vol. 1, "Système figuré"; *Catalogue Malesherbes*. Wood, silk, gems, iron, copper, clocks, wool, pyrotechnics, fire, and so on.

34. See note 17. Sports and pastimes.

35. Belles-lettres: see note 17. Essays, criticism, rhetoric, and so on, have been classified under "grammar and philology" (V.B), in accordance with Cels-Martin.

36. See note 17.

37. Formey, *Conseils*; Maïeul de Chaudon, *Bibliothèque*.

38. Formey, *Conseils*; Maïeul de Chaudon, *Bibliothèque*; Cels-Martin, *Coup d'œil; Catalogue de la Bibliothèque du Roi* (1688); *Catalogue Malesherbes; Catalogue Lautrec*.

39. The assistance of my friends and colleagues Jean-Louis Flandrin and Daniel Roche has been invaluable in helping me to identify a great number of these books.

40. As explained in note 8, collections of diocesan handbooks (*usages*) have been counted in this category as single units—an arbitrary but unavoidable choice.

41. This phenomenon is the chief explanation for the relative decrease in the number of "poetry" books between 1784 and 1788.

42. Daniel Mornet, *Les Origines intellectuelles de la Révolution française* (Paris, 1932).

43. This share is all the larger as the three samplings, for the sake of consistency and comparability, have not taken into account the "books entered via the Chambre Syndicale"—a category mentioned only between 1767 and 1778. These already printed books, sent in from the provinces and abroad, cover a wider range of genres than the manuscripts deliberately submitted for tacit permits.

44. In accordance with the criteria of the time, we have listed under "medicine," in the tacit-permits category, the abundant polemical literature of the 1780s concerning Mesmer's theory of animal magnetism. More generally, the bibliographical grid scatters among different headings (metaphysics, chemistry, medicine) a basically homogeneous occultist philosophy whose importance in the late-eighteenth century is well known.

45. We have excluded from these percentages the short popular novels published by the Bibliothèque Bleue and other specialized *libraires*.

46. Jean-Jacques Rousseau, *La Nouvelle Héloïse*, ed. Daniel Mornet (Paris, 1923), vol. 1.

47. The *Bibliothèque universelle de romans* is a good instrument for identification.

48. The manuscript registers of book licenses make it possible to reexamine certain problems in literary history, such as the one raised by Georges May—in a remarkable work (*Le dilemme du roman au XVIIIe siècle: étude sur les rapports du roman et de la critique, 1715–1761* [Paris, 1963])—concerning the ban on novels imposed by Chancelier d'Aguesseau in 1738. Citing the bibliography compiled by S. Paul Jones for the first half of the eighteenth century (*A List of French Prose Fiction*, New York, 1939), May rests his argument on the paucity of new novels published in Paris in 1738. According to May, only six novels appeared, of which one, in fact (*Essai sur la nécessité et les moyens de plaire*, by Paradis de Moncrif), is essentially a moral treatise followed, it is true, by a tale. But an examination of the registers of printing-license requests shows that between 20 February 1737—the date given by May as that of the enactment of the ban—and the end of 1738, the number of new, authorized novels was considerably greater. Admittedly, during the same period, the censors turned down some twenty novels, including both new titles and reprints.

Chapter 7

1. Comte Henri de Boulainvilliers, *Histoire de l'Ancien Gouvernement de la France* (The Hague and Amsterdam: Aux dépenses de la compagnie [des libraires], 1727).

2. Gabriel Bonnot de Mably, *De la manière d'écrire l'histoire* (Paris: A. Jombert Jeune, 1783).

3. Boulainvilliers, *Histoire*.

4. Mably, *De l'étude de l'histoire, à Monseigneur le Prince de Parme* (Maëstricht: Cavelier, 1778). Exhorting his pupil to choose a model, Mably adds, "I warn you lest it should be a prince. The lives of the greatest kings are always tainted by some sort of counterfeit and overweening ambition. Choose as your model a simple citizen of Greece or Rome."

5. Ibid.: "Observe attentively how the same laws, the same mores, the same virtues, and the same vices have always produced the same effects. Thus the fate of states is governed by fixed, immutable, and manifest principles. Discover these principles, Monseigneur, and politics will hold no more secrets for you. . . ."

6. Boulainvilliers, *Histoire*.

7. Mably, *De la Législation ou Principes des Lois*, in *Oeuvres complètes* (London, 1789). For Boulainvilliers, history provided more examples to avoid and abhor than models to imitate: see his "Lettre à Mademoiselle Cousinot sur l'Histoire et sa méthode," Angoulême library, Ms. 23.

8. On this theme, Mably often seems to copy Boulainvilliers: "This can convince us with increasing force of the indisputable fact that, of all the nations of the world, ours is distinguished by its thoughtlessness and inattentiveness; as a consequence, from one century to another, the French have always forgotten what their forefathers did." And Mably: "France is the most heedless nation, and the easiest to mislead, because it is the least attentive to an examination of the past."

9. The best account of these theories is provided by Elie Carcassonne, *Montesquieu et le problème de la Constitution française au XVIIIe siècle* (Paris: Presses Universitaires de France, 1927).

10. Mably, *Observations sur les Grecs* (Geneva: Par la Compagnie des Libraires, 1749): "Today we know what to make of this greensward, these wreaths of flowers, these concerts, this sweet leisure . . . etc."

11. Boulainvilliers, "Mémoire sur la noblesse de France," Angoulême library, Ms. 23. Boulainvilliers has a word of commiseration for the free men whom the conquest suddenly turned into slaves. But he immediately adds that, "as they defended themselves poorly, they were rightly subjected to the law of the victor."

12. Boulainvilliers, *Histoire*: "As if an undisputed possession of 700 years' standing could be thought of as such a mediocre claim! This weakness is all the more dangerous for

having bred the false and ridiculous argument of those who say that Hugh Capet handed over his land, fiefs, and real estate to his new subjects to reward them for having made him king. From this argument a most abominable conclusion has been drawn, namely, that all property belongs to the king, and that he is entitled to leave to his subjects whatever part of it he pleases."

13. In the "Dissertation abrégée sur les premiers Français et leur origine," which concludes the *Essais sur la noblesse de France* (Amsterdam, 1732), Boulainvilliers goes so far as to reassure those whom despotism has ennobled: "As for the new nobles and the *anoblis*, they have nothing to fear from our undertaking. Our views are summary, simple, and innocent. They never descend explicitly to an examination of particular cases. Such persons can therefore peacefully enjoy their metamorphosis."

14. Mably, *De la Législation*.

15. Boulainvilliers, "Mémoire pour la construction d'un nobiliaire général," Ecole Supérieure de la Guerre (Paris), Ms. 25–26: "The old nobility has no means for guaranteeing its status; some of these nobles have lost their patents and charters in the course of foreign and civil wars, and, with the exception of those families whose names remain in history, they are left with only partial evidence, which is bound to perish through an infinity of accidents." Moreover, Boulainvilliers makes his purpose quite clear: "the old nobility [must be able to] distinguish itself from the new nobility, the nobility granted by individual patent or consecutive to the ownership of certain offices. . . ."

16. Boulainvilliers, *Histoire*.

17. Boulainvilliers, *Abrégé de l'Histoire de France* (The Hague: Gesse et Néaulme, 1733): "Belles-lettres, after languishing for a long time, buried under the bad taste of earlier centuries, reemerged in this century in all their brilliance. . . ."

18. Mably, *Observations sur l'Histoire de France* (Geneva: Par la Compagnie des Libraires, 1765).

19. Mably, *De la Législation*.

20. Mably, *De l'étude de l'Histoire*: Mably cites the case of certain Swiss cantons as an example of this ingenious arrangement.

21. Mably, *Entretiens de Phocion* (Amsterdam, 1763).

22. This is the solution Mably advocates in *De la Législation*: "The nobility must have a patrimony that it cannot increase; on no account must the nobility be allowed to possess land or inheritances intended for another order of citizens. . . ."

Chapter 8

1. Emile Benveniste, "Civilisation, contribution à l'histoire du mot," in *Hommage à Lucien Febvre* (Paris, 1954).

2. *Politique des Romains dans la religion* (1716).

3. *Considérations sur les causes de la grandeur des Romains et de leur décadence* (1734).

4. *Voyage de Graz à La Haye*, ed. de La Pléiade 1: 663,669.

5. *Memoirs of My Life*, ed. Georges A. Bonnard (London, 1966), 134.

6. *The History of the Decline and Fall of the Roman Empire*, chap. 3.

7. *Esprit des lois*, 18: 2.

8. *History of Civil Society* (1767), 124,185.

9. *Recherches philosophiques sur les Américains* (1768), 1: 218.

10. *L'Esprit des usages et des coutumes*. This discussion owes a great deal to the attention that Edna Lemay has devoted to Démeunier's book in her study "Naissance de l'anthropologie sociale en France au XVIIIᵉ siècle: Jean Nicolas Démeunier et l'Esprit des usages et des coutumes" (unpublished dissertation, Paris, 1972).

11. *Histoire de l'Amérique*, passim.

12. *Histoire des Indes*, cited in Michèle Duchet, *Anthropologie et histoire au siècle des Lumières* (Paris, 1971).

Chapter 9

1. 2 vols. (1768–69).

2. Ibid., 2:176.

3. J.-P. Brissot, *Examen critique des voyages dans l'Amérique septentrionale de M. le marquis de Chastellux* (Paris, 1786).

4. Ibid., 105–6.

5. Mazzei, *Recherches historiques et politiques sur les Etats-Unis de l'Amérique septentrionale . . .* , 4 vols. (Paris, 1788).

6. Crèvecœur, *Lettres d'un cultivateur américain* (Paris, 1784). [Retranslated here from the French edition: the passages quoted do not correspond precisely to the original English text.—Trans.]

7. Ibid., "deuxième lettre."

8. Ibid.

9. This study is in progress, thanks to the able survey of parliamentary speeches of the French revolutionary period being conducted by Mme Edna Lemay, *maître-assistant* at the Ecole des Hautes Etudes en Sciences Sociales.

10. Tocqueville, *L'Ancien Régime et la Révolution* (Paris: Gallimard, 1953), vol. 2, chap. 7: 131–32.

11. Reprint of *Le Moniteur*, 1:142.

12. Letter quoted in Gilbert Chinard, *Volney et l'Amérique d'après des documents inédits* (Baltimore and Paris, 1923), 63–66.

13. Volney, *Tableau du climat et du sol des Etats-Unis* (Paris, 1883), preface. The quotations that follow are also taken from the preface.

Chapter 10

1. The fundamental work on Tocqueville's journey to the United States is still that of G. W. Pierson, *Tocqueville and Beaumont in America* (New York: Oxford University Press, 1938).

2. Tocqueville and Beaumont's plan for a fact-finding visit was set out in *Note sur le système pénitentiaire et sur la mission confiée par Monsieur le Ministre de l'Intérieur à MM. Gustave de Beaumont et Alexis de Tocqueville* (1831). Their findings were published in 1833. A second, two-volume edition appeared in 1836, with a long introduction: *Du système pénitentiaire aux Etats-Unis et de son application en France, suivi d'un appendice sur les colonies pénales et de notes statistiques*. A third edition, expanded to include Tocqueville's legislative work on the penitentiary problem, was published in 1845.

3. *Correspondance d'Alexis de Tocqueville et de Gustave de Beaumont (Œuvres complètes*, 8), 1:105–6.

4. René Rémond, *Les Etats-Unis devant l'opinion française*, 2 vols. (Paris: Armand Colin, 1962), esp. vol. 2, chap. 7.

5. André Jardin, "L'Amérique et les Américains vus par Tocqueville," *H-Histoire*, no. 4 (March 1980): 227–40.

6. See esp. Tocqueville's letter to Gustave de Beaumont of 5 October 1828 (*Correspondance Tocqueville–Beaumont*, 1: 47–71).

7. *Correspondance d'Alexis de Tocqueville et de Louis de Kergorlay (Œuvres complètes*, 13), 1:373–75.

8. Actually, Saint-Beuve attributes this statement to "a very judicious and very respectable person," adding a commentary of his own: "consequently, [Tocqueville's] thoughts were sometimes shallow." See Sainte-Beuve, *Causeries du lundi*, 3rd ed., vol. 15.

9. H. de Tocqueville, *Histoire philosophique du règne de Louis XV*, 2 vols. (Paris, 1847).

10. Ibid., 2:405.

11. *Correspondance Tocqueville–Kergorlay*, 1:214.

12. Tocqueville, *Voyages en Sicile et aux Etats-Unis (Œuvres complètes*, 5, vol. 1), letter quoted p. 26.

13. *Démocratie*, 1:418 [GL 309].

14. Ibid. [GL 309].

15. Ibid., 2:316 [GL 639].

16. Ibid., 1:420 [GL 311].

17. Ibid., 1:423 [GL 313].

18. Ibid., 1:424 [GL 314–15].

19. Ibid. [GL 315].

20. See esp. Seymour Drescher, *Dilemmas of Democracy: Tocqueville and Modernization* (Pittsburgh: University of Pittsburgh Press, 1968).

21. Tocqueville, *Voyages*.

22. See G. W. Pierson, *Tocqueville and Beaumont*.

23. Michel Chevalier, *Lettres sur l'Amérique du Nord*, 2 vols. (1836).

24. *Démocratie*, 1:107 [GL 50].

25. Tocqueville, *Voyages*, 205–6.

26. Ibid., 342–87, esp. the account of "fifteen days in the wilderness," Tocqueville and Beaumont's expedition to the outermost edge of the "frontier" near Lake Michigan.

27. Ibid., 346.

28. Ibid., 347.

29. Michel Chevalier, *Lettres*, esp. vol. 1, chap. 10, p. 149.

30. Tocqueville, *Voyages*, 155–56.

31. Ibid., 89.

32. Ibid., 258–59.

33. *Démocratie*, 1:426 [GL 316].

34. Ibid., 2:5 [GL 417].

35. Except, it is true, for his marriage, which his family regarded as a misalliance.

36. *Démocratie*, 2:311 [GL 634].

37. Ibid., 2:346 [GL 660].

38. Ibid., 2:256–61 [GL 595–600].

39. Ibid., 2:221 [GL 573].

40. Ibid., 2:225 [GL 575].

41. Ibid., 2:174 [GL 538].

42. Ibid., 2:300 [GL 628].

43. Ibid., vol. 2, pt. 3, chap. 21.

44. By discussing the question of equality chiefly in terms of the passions conveyed by egalitarian ideology and in terms of the relative frustrations engendered by equality, Tocqueville once again reveals his astonishing modernity. An increasing number of contemporary sociological studies have been devoted to this theme, focusing in particular on the concept of "reference group." For a good summary of these studies, see Philippe Bénéton, "Les Frustrations de l'égalité: contribution aux recherches sur la relativité des aspirations et la perception des inégalités," *Archives européennes de sociologie* 19 (1978).

45. *Démocratie*, vol. 2, pt. 2, chap. 5 [GL 513–17].

46. This aspect of Tocqueville's genius was repugnant to Sainte-Beuve, who, in the article in *Causeries du lundi* quoted above, criticized the abstract and systemic character of the second volume of *Démocratie*. Indeed, generally speaking, Sainte-Beuve fails to comprehend Tocqueville's thought, which he criticizes for its very nature.

47. *Démocratie*, 2:74–75 [GL 474].

48. This comparison is the object of an infinitely more systematic analysis in an article by Raymond Aron, "La Définition libérale de la liberté: Alexis de Tocqueville et Karl Marx," *Archives européennes de sociologie* 5 (1964).

Chapter 12

1. Patrick Girard, *Les Juifs de France de 1789 à 1860: de l'émancipation á l'égalité*, Diaspora series (Paris: Calmann-Lévy, 1976).
2. Michael R. Marrus, *Les Juifs de France à l'époque de l'affaire Dreyfus*, Diaspora series (Paris: Calmann-Lévy, 1972).
3. David H. Weinberg, *Les Juifs de Paris de 1933 à 1939*, Diaspora series (Paris: Calmann-Lévy, 1974).
4. On this point, see Pierre Vidal-Naquet's preface to Marrus, *Les Juifs de France*.
5. Hannah Arendt, "Privileged Jews," *Jewish Social Studies* (January 1946).
6. Annie Kriegel, "Révolution française et judaïsme," *L'Arche* (March 1975).
7. Michael R. Marrus and Robert O. Paxton, *Vichy et les Juifs*, Diaspora series (Paris: Calmann-Lévy, 1981).
8. André Harris and Alain de Sédouy, *Juifs et Français* (Paris: Grasset, 1979).
9. Alfred Fabre-Luce, *Pour en finir avec l'antisémitisme* (Paris: Juillard, 1979).

Chapter 13

1. Gershom Scholem, *Fidélité et Utopie: essais sur le judaïsme contemporain*, Diaspora series (Paris: Calmann-Lévy, 1978).
2. Gershom Scholem, *Le Messianisme juif: essais sur la spiritualité du judaïsme*, Diaspora series (Paris: Calmann-Lévy, 1974), trans. of *The Messianic Idea in Judaism and other essays on Jewish spirituality* (New York: Schocken Books, 1971).
3. *New York Review of Books* 24, no. 6 (April 1977).

INDEX